PARADISE, PIECE BY PIECE

ALSO BY **MOLLY PEACOCK**

And Live Apart

Raw Heaven

Take Heart

Original Love

co-editor *Poetry in Motion: 100 Poems from the Subways and Buses*

PARADISE,

PIECE BY PIECE

MOLLY PEACOCK

RIVERHEAD BOOKS

A MEMBER OF PENGUIN PUTNAM INC.

NEW YORK

1998

RIVERHEAD BOOKS
a member of
Penguin Putnam Inc.
200 Madison Avenue
New York, NY 10016

Copyright © 1998 by Molly Peacock

Library of Congress Cataloging-in-Publication Data

Peacock, Molly, date.
    Paradise, piece by piece / by Molly Peacock.
        p.   cm.
    ISBN 1-57322-097-3
        1. Peacock, Molly, date—Biography.   2. Poets,
    American—20th century—Biography.   I. Title.
    PS3566.E15Z472   1998
    811'.54—dc21
    [B]   97-49965   CIP

Printed in the United States of America
10 9 8 7 6 5 4 3 2 1

This book is printed on acid-free paper. ⊗

Book design by Marysarah Quinn

FOR **MIKE**

"A No uttered from deepest conviction is better and greater than a Yes merely uttered to please, or what is worse, to avoid trouble."

—MAHATMA GANDHI

PARADISE, PIECE BY PIECE

In beginning to write this book I wanted to tell the story of a decision—how I chose not to have children—and found myself telling the story of my life as a poet and teacher, and as a sister, daughter, lover, friend, and wife. This led me to face two necessities: saying the truth as I saw it, and protecting other people's lives. The central family players—my parents and sister, grandparents, cousin, and my husband, Mike—are all real. But the other characters and some events are invented or transformed. *Paradise, Piece by Piece* is a hybrid memoir, both true and truer, in the sense that fiction trues ideas against the blurred realities of life.

i.

A GIRL'S GARDEN of

REASONS

1.

When I was three, I decided not to have children.

2.

I knew that goodness had a shape, and I could draw it: a circle. *Very* goodness was a tighter circle. Its grip was so snug that there wasn't any need for skin between me and what I was being very good for.

Now, sometimes the difference between how I see my life and how others see it is this tightening of the good that needs no skin. Others see skin as the body's border, a boundary between them and the world. But as a little girl I knew it was permeable, and sometimes felt that I did not have a hide at all.

"You were so good when I was pregnant," my mother said after she reappeared from her terrible banishment. Polly had hemorrhaged and vanished to the hospital for a cesarean section and partial hysterectomy. With my premature new sister, Gail, stowed in an incubator for two months, our mother returned to me in the spring of 1950. Bandaged and in pain, Polly refused to set foot in the hospital, convinced my little sister would die if she did. And so my mother, half inert, lay in bed while I played on the floor nearby, no more than a foot or two distant, watching for Gram to bustle in from next door with our breakfasts, lunches, and dinners. Shocked by Polly's ghost-like figure, I played the role of child-near-her-womb, a little homunculesse at her feet, with crayons, cutout dolls, and picture books. "You are so good," she moaned.

But what good was skin? It only prevented me from getting closer to her. If only I could read her mind. How much better I could anticipate her groans and shift just slightly as I cut out another outfit for my paper doll. To be permitted to be near her meant I could not jump or yell, but I had no use for that. I wanted to be good! Now and then my father emerged from the local bar or from his shift work to disturb our honeymoon, but like a ripple he would quickly go—except for one day, when he brought Gail home. After two whole months of never being touched, she was weak and fretful and terrifyingly small.

"Hold her neck! Hold her neck! Don't let her head roll!" Where *was* her neck? When I shifted to look, Gail's head began to loll, and I froze again, not watching her, but the adults, arguing what to do. "She's too young to hold a tiny baby!" Gram snorted, "Ted, watch the baby!" My father fetched a pillow at his mother's orders and jammed it beneath my holding arm, heaping Gail on me, me heaped on Gram's bristly couch. Then Gram snatched the swaddled lump, and Ted, Polly, Gram, and Grandpa closed ranks around my sister—a series of backs, rumps, and legs, like the great gray ends of elephants circled around the newborn in *Dumbo*.

"You used to wear diapers," Polly reminded me, "just like your sister." We were in the front hall that linked our half of the house to Gram's next door. By the time we got to our own kitchen, I had gotten an idea: *I'll ask to wear diapers, too*, and Polly obliged me. The problem was, my new sister's diapers wouldn't fit. What could we do? Polly grabbed a striped terry cloth dish towel and two enormous safety pins and pinned the towel around me. I had no underpants on. No top, no socks, no shoes, only the towel diaper, just like a baby. The towel was saggy, with loopy legholes you could see up.

Into our part of the house descended my great-uncle and great-aunt and my father's cousins and my uncle and his fiancée to mill around the bassinet set up in the bright June kitchen with its green linoleum floor. Through the doorway, in the living room curtained heavily against the light, I sat in an overstuffed chair in a sea of beige wool rug and slumped, bicycling my legs out of the diaper-towel, eyeing the relatives, noticed by no one yet. My towel had stupid orange and yellow stripes. Not pure diaper white. Not really real. *I'm really not a baby anymore.* My father's smooth swimmer's body went upstairs to the bathroom, ignoring me as he walked past, swigging his beer, though he saw me on his way back to the kitchen and leaned his flushed face into mine to say, "You wanna be a baby too?" letting a surprisingly thin laugh escape from his dense body.

No, I did not want to be a baby anymore. Flapping out to the kitchen, I announced to all present, "I want my clothes on."

"Oh, you want your diaper off, now?" My mother smiled. And so we went upstairs to retransform me, leaving Gail in the bassinet to be admired, while I lay on the bed upstairs, attended to, united with my dark-haired Polly as she undid the safety pins.

3.

Pressed to the linoleum floor with a coloring book, I spied on my two-year-old sister from under the kitchen table. As she skidded noisily by on her new wooden wheel toy, my father came in from his job with the Niagara Mohawk electric company. Out scraped his chair from the table. In scraped his chair with him on it. When his beer bottle thudded above my head, I swiped my crayons back from his workboots and uniformed pant legs. From deep under the table roof, I peered at Polly's loafers moving back and forth at the stove. She was not wearing socks, even though it was winter, and this was Buffalo, and that kitchen floor was cold.

Blue snowlight outside; hot noisy yellow light inside. Gram's head of tight gray curls lingered in the doorway of our living room. Heat haze in the kitchen, then the spatter of floured chicken pieces as they hit the oily stomach of an iron skillet. Everybody was tired or angry. The squeal of the wooden wheels of my sister's ride-on toy distressed even me.

"Can't you make her stop? I just got home!" my father cried out.

"For Christ's sake, she's only two!" my mother said, not bothering to turn her plaid flannel back from the sizzling stove. If I looked up aslant, I could see her almost fully: black curls above a man's workshirt and old wool slacks. The light got yellower and the spattering louder, almost as loud as the wheels that ground against the linoleum and the bang of the empty beer bottle on the table.

"Don't ever have children, Molly," my grandmother declared, "unless you want to."

"That's right. Don't let nobody say you have to have kids," her son affirmed.

I often heard from my father, "Don't ever have children, Molly." My grandmother punctuated this with "unless you want to." And my mother said, "You can always do anything you want."

I'm not sure other families discussed having children with their kids as frequently as mine did, but I heard again and again in various ways from these three people that having children wrecked everything. Or this is how I interpreted "Don't ever have children, Molly." I looked at my little sister as she zoomed across the linoleum and hated her even more. I looked at my father drunk, and my mother frightened, and thought: *Their lives would be better if they didn't have kids. Their lives would be better if they didn't have her. If they didn't have us. Didn't have me. Their lives would be better . . . I'm not having any children.*

Somehow at five, I was past childbearing age.

Because I felt that perhaps I shouldn't have been born, there were many parts of me that waited decades to arrive. Even in a passing conversation about a garden, the phrase "dead in the bud" can stop me for a second with a metaphorical chill. There were many ways I struggled not to be dead in the bud. I knew quite early I was engaged in a test—later on, people would call it "survival"—but I felt I would be alone in it, as alone as each person in my family was.

Now, so many years later, at my dining room table eating a piece of gingerbread from Emily Dickinson's recipe—a woman who recommended that we look at life aslant—I have an additional interpretation of my father's exhausted, frustrated statement against having children. It gave me a *choice*. I could be a mother, or I could choose not to. In the same moment that he implied he did not want me, he set before me the option of saying no to being a parent myself. My *no* could open a door for me, one that was closed to him. My mother lectured me about how I could be anything I wanted to be. And he concurred. I took this to mean that they *couldn't* be what they wanted, so I was to make up for them.

As it turns out, my choice not to have children has defined my adult life. It's been like hacking through undergrowth while walking down a hardly used, perfectly paved way. The seeds they planted yielded a ter- rifying wilderness, but what they said also constructed a kind of brick path that gave the wilderness a vista, and defined the tumble of flora. In fact, on that path my choice not to be a mother became more of a *dis- covery* of a decision. My refusal came through love, terror, shame, en- chantment, and a kind of paradoxically fulfilled emptying. I had to make the choice from so far down in my own core that I was never wholly aware of it. It took insight to see and release it—an insight I didn't always have. For this is a decision you do not make once, but many times. I would leave the idea of not having children behind, only to face it again and again as I went on. Some people would say that calling such a process a "decision" is ambiguous. *Was it really a choice?*

If someone were to ask me why I could feel increasingly whole even though I was making a radical refusal, I would have answered that each time I said no, I felt a more complete sense of who I was. But if at any of those times someone had asked me if I felt like a complete woman, I would have hesitated before answering yes.

4.

Polly settled down with her library book, deep in a red upholstered chair with doilies on the arms to cover the cigarette burns. Gail napped next door at Grandma's, Ted worked far away, down in someone's basement reading a cobwebby meter for amps and volts. Polly wore his dark green T-shirt without a bra and a pair of baggy jeans. She pushed back her shiny black hair with its exciting streak of gray to the left of her widow's peak. The wall behind her was forest green, dark as the T-shirt. In 1952 no woman on Gunnell Avenue in Buffalo, New York, went braless, wore jeans, bought red chairs, or put them in deep green rooms—all to the point of sitting down to read a library book and pop an occasional chocolate-covered cherry into her mouth after she finished her cigarette. She'd whizzed through her housework, then stuck the dinner fixings on the counter. She was alone, alone and happy to be in her own world.

Little mouse at her side, I tried to read a letter that her mother, Grandma Ruth in the country, had sent me, but I wasn't in school yet and didn't know how. I had my pencil and my drawing pad. I was using my inner resources. Polly loved people who sat quietly using their inner resources. *But I can't read!* In exasperation I poked through the carefully constructed boundary of her concentration. "Read it to me, Mom," I whined. "Read it to me, Mom, OK?"

Her hazel eyes were trained on her book.

"Read me Gram's letter, OK?"

When I placed the letter on top of the open book, my mother turned and read it aloud. I'd never gotten one before, and I wondered what to do with it.

"Well, when you get a letter, you write back," Polly explained.

"OK," I said, picking up my pencil, making stray letter-like lines on the page. But my lines were disappointing, not like real writing.

"Why don't you draw Gram a picture?" Polly lazily said.

I always draw pictures. Babies draw pictures. "No! I want to write a letter back!"

"Oh, all right, here's the alphabet, Molly." She scrawled A through Z across the top of the paper. "Now, write DEAR GRAM." She underlined the individual letters. Of course I couldn't remember the order of "Dear Gram" out of ADEGMR, but I tried to figure out for myself how to write them, and after a fashion, I covered the page in cuneiform. It was the hardest thing I'd ever done and I was pleased. And Polly was pleased! The writing drew a smile from those straight, slightly purplish lips whose carmine lipstick had disappeared to find a better home on the filter tips of cigarette butts in a square glass ashtray, an ashtray so heavy that when my father let it fly against the wall in an argument it didn't even break. Nothing broke the pleasure of our solitude. Like two sides of an open locket, the side that reads, the side that writes, my mother and I lay inside the red and green jewelbox of the afternoon.

The mutual possession of our selves, without the diverting presence of my sister or the inflaming presence of my father, gave me the sense, reinforced by Polly over and over again, that *this* was how one ought to live. "Everybody should have their own room," she would say. "The only way for a family to survive is for each person to have their own place." My mother had never heard of Virginia Woolf. She didn't have a room of her own as an adult until she was nearly fifty years old, divorced, and with her children grown.

Next morning in the Buffalo house. Daddy home after working the graveyard shift. Breakfast. French toast. Sharp rectangular delineations of sunlight on the floor. Playing, eating, Gail and I were unaware of the escalating voices until our mother's usual growl of stubborn annoyance hiked itself to a soprano pitch, and our father's yapping descended to a lung rattling bass. The hefty Scotty dog we thought he was like and the big unflappable setter we thought she was like had reversed and become monstrous. They were not like dogs anymore, but like canine horror-saurs. He was pushing her toward the open cellar door and she was screaming, "Ted, Ted don't do it!" and he was panting the clear, individ-ual, disconnected words "I'll . . . kill . . . you." As his broad workshirted torso filled the doorway, she backed down the cellar stairs. He prodded her collarbone with his pointer finger. Then he pushed her again. "Ted, not in front of the kids!" was her signal to us and we ran, Gail tiny enough to squirm between his legs to get to her, me sliding past them on the stairs. Then Gail and I were below them, straining up against our mother's legs as he bore down on her. It was a tangle of legs and stairs, his workpants and boots pushing down against her bare calves and slip-pers, while Gail and I pushed up against her, trying to hold her up and save her, and in saving her rescue our lives. Her face as she twisted to-ward us was drained an almost painted white. She looked like a geisha girl beneath her black hair. "Ted, watch out! The kids!" she screamed, di-verting his attention. The cunning girls having brought the dragon to his senses, he blustered back up the stairs.

My mother read to escape so many things. I've often thought that I became a writer in order to have her read my words. Though it's hard to imagine a positive picture of a family if the one already drawn for you is negative, I did develop other ideas about families, because as soon as I could read I loved to learn about them. The voice of that childless author Louisa May Alcott parented me. Of course I fantasized I was an orphan. My fantasy life was composted from the emotional peelings and scraps of my parents' lives put out to rot in the backyard of literature. Perhaps my authors would come and take me away.

5.

"Here's Hazel." Polly stopped the Dodge by the pad-
dock fence. Hazel raised Morgan horses. She wore jeans permanently
creased at the thigh tops underneath her belly. She was old! Her steely
hair bobbed when she barked her laugh. She lived all on her own and
had a crowd of teenagers for hands. Astride her Morgan she ordered
them to do this and that, and they all did whatever she said, too. ("Every
kid dies to work for Hazel," Polly had said reverently in the car.) I fed her
horse a sugar cube that Polly had put in my pocket and waited while they
talked. ("We won't stay long," she had said. "Hazel doesn't have time to
dillydally.")

"That house is a wreck!" The old woman jerked her finger toward the
unpainted farmhouse. ("Well, it must have been painted once upon a
time," Polly said later.) Shutters hung half off their hinges, like a Halloween card. "All I've got time for is the barn." Hazel looked down at me.
"No time for little girls! Or men!"

"Hazel's got the life," Polly said in the car. "All on her own. No family. Doesn't need one. She's got those kids to keep her company. And her
horses." Anybody knew that animals were much better company than
humans. "Nobody to tell her what to do. That's the life."

We whizzed past the silvery oat fields. We were "home." When we
were all making the trip to La Grange to see Grandma Ruth and Grandpa

Gillie, my mother announced it in the same way: *We're going Home today.*
She always surprised us. Without apparent planning, we up and went,
Ted too, uncomplaining, out past Bethlehem Steel and the coal heaps of
Niagara Mohawk Power Company and Dunlop Rubber Tire into the
cool emptiness of field after field and house, then nothing, then house.

"But aren't we already home?" I asked one morning when she said it
again.

"Oh, Molly, you know what I mean!"

"Don't be stupid," Gail said, holding a Kleenex to her nose. She got
terrible nosebleeds. And she sneezed and sneezed around horses, just like
my mother's little sister, Roberta, so that's why Gail and Ted stayed at
Aunt Roberta's when we went to visit Hazel. Roberta also had the life.
"She gets anything she wants from him," Polly said. "From your uncle.
She won't take no for an answer. Look at her Pendleton suit!" And Aunt
Roberta had her own car. "She gets what she wants and she drives where
she wants. It's as good as being single!"

Polly lapsed into silence. Then, "She's selfish, that's what she is. Berta
and Hazel both. They're selfish to the core."

Buffalo Corners loomed up. "Hah! That's where we turned over Lizzie
Palmer's outhouse!" Polly recounted her peccadillos. "I graduated high
school when I was only sixteen. I'd learned Latin. Then I worked at the
mill and met Flo and Ann Louise. I bought my own car. Was your grandfather surprised! 'Oh, Pauline!' he said. He couldn't say a word but my
name. I made the only money that ever came into that house. Bought
your grandmother her couch and chair when I was eighteen years old.
Flo and Ann Louise and me had the Model A all packed to go to California the morning they bombed Pearl Harbor. Your grandmother cried
so hard we only went to Buffalo. Then I met your father."

The one-room schoolhouse loomed up. "There's where I tied up my
pony. He was piebald and blind." Piebald. Must be the hair was rubbed
off him. "Your Great-grandma sent me off to school on Paint every morn-

ing. He was so smart he knew the way there and the way home. And in the afternoon she sent that pony down to pick me up, and what do you know, he was right there at the schoolhouse door! When Paint died I cried and cried."

"He died!" I'd never expected so heroic a piebald horse to die.

"Then Great-grandma Molly, that's the Molly I named you after, she came out to the stream where I was reading, and she said I could have Shep, the plow horse with a star in his forehead, and then I rode Shep. He was big! And I rode him bareback. All us kids rode bareback."

"If you named me after Molly McMann, who'd you name Gail after?"

"I didn't. I didn't name her anything. Your father named her. We figured that was only fair, cause I named you."

"Oh," I said. That must be why Gail did everything with Daddy and I did everything with Polly. Gail must be just like him.

La Grange Garage appeared out of orchard land. ESSO it said, high above Route 246. There was the store full of candy bars and flour and oil cans and newspapers and old men in overalls and the garage connected to it with the guard dog. Pal, the dog, was blind. And my grandmother was nearly deaf. My grandfather had no teeth. "Gum my food," he said. Inside was the piano and all the patchwork squares and triangles and tiny octagons for the quilts my grandmother made with her friends. There were always people there, and they could sew.

"Ugh," Polly said. "All those church ladies and their piles of thread!"

Embroidery floss was everywhere, silky and variegated, strewn among the sheet music and the seed catalogs on the sideboard table. Polly couldn't sew and wouldn't bake.

"I hated it here!" she said as we turned into the parking area. The house was a little jut off the store, and the garage part for fixing cars was a big jut off the other side of the store. There were five flower beds and a vegetable garden all around the oddball building my grandfather built by himself.

"Your grandma would pack me a lunch and I'd go with Grandpa and hand him the nails while he pounded. Took him three years to build it. Didn't want to be a farmer. But I hated it. I loved Great-grandma's farm and I stayed there and went to school from there. Came here on the weekends. I was a selfish girl. I got what I wanted." Polly sighed as she pulled up the hand brake of the Dodge with the force of both her arms. "Then you have kids, and you can't be selfish."

"But Aunt Berta has Howie, and she's selfish."

"That's because she only has one kid. When you have two you can't be selfish." Polly was wrenching open the stuck door of the Dodge and my grandmother was coming down the cement steps with a pie for some lady who was just leaving with her quilt trailing. "I hope you get to be selfish all your life, Molsie," my mother said.

Polly went into the garage with Grandpa Gillie while I went to the rain barrel with Grandma Ruth. We got buckets of rainwater and sloshed to the beds by the pine trees and dumped rainwater on the nasturtiums. Then we went in the kitchen and stuck our hands in the molasses cookie dough. It was heaven and it was as Polly defined it: home. My idea of home meant grandparents, people who had their children so long before that it was as if they never had any.

6.

Sex and babies. Five neighborhood girls all jumped up and down on our twin beds, squealing and tickling one another in the silky, rabbit warren mess of sheets that smell of childsleep between their crumpled ridges. When I burrowed into Gail's bed, I sniffed the Gailsmell while the others used my bed as a trampoline. Before Gram, alarmed at the squawk of the springs, had hauled us all downstairs, I'd stuck my finger up my underpants and found the hole, finger sized, then saw a color in my mind, blackish red, brought my finger out and smelled it, Ah! The whiff of me.

"All right now, all of you girls have to go home when you finish your oatmeal cookies. Come on now, girls, let's get a move on." My city grandmother had the quality of a business-like Shetland sheep dog nosing at the heels of the lambs she ushered out the door. "I'm glad to sit down!" Five girls, ages four to seven, were a handful. From her chair Gram leaned toward me and put her arms loosely around my waist. "Oh, you naughty kids! I'll have to make those beds all over again." She used "naughty" with benign acceptance. I knew she thought we weren't really bad.

"Hey, Gram, look what I found," I dared to say. I stuck my finger up my underpants into my vagina and brought my finger out, thrusting it under her nose. "Smell this!"

"Eeewwwhhh!" she exclaimed in delight. "What a cupcake smell!" Her eyes glistened with a kind of excitement, surprise, curiosity, and wonder. I searched her face for whether this was all right. I'd found the secret place she also knew about, and as far as Gram was concerned it was fine. "Let's go remake the beds," she said, corralling me and Gail up the stairs.

Because Polly had Gail by cesarean section, I thought all babies were born by emergency operation. It was only when Polly overheard me magisterially explaining this to Gail that she corrected me. I couldn't imagine a baby coming out of my vagina. It was only big enough for my finger! "Oh, you expand," my mother said. Expand?

When I was mad, I felt my whole body blowing up until I was the size of a wrestler. Did expanding feel like that?

One day Gram and I drove out to see Agnes, who shouldered open her ripped screen door while holding a hot iron in her good hand. Gram was on a scouting mission for Niagara Neighbors, and I was the excuse to stay just long enough to eye the mess Agnes was in and report back to other interested parties. Agnes had had a baby out of wedlock and lived on welfare. Watching her was hard because her withered arm hung loose as she pushed her good arm across the ironing board.

Her baby slept politely in a wicker laundry basket I myself wouldn't have minded curling up in. I was tired of being dragged around by Gram. Agnes lived in welfare housing, a kind of barracks where nothing was planted to obscure the cement foundation, and the grass was cut down to a yellow stubble, and there was no sidewalk leading to the ripped screen door. This was what happened when you got in trouble. Worse, people like my grandmother would come and throw old baby clothes on your ripped davenport and humiliate you with a lot of judgmental questions. My grandmother *was* someone I could ask questions of, and I did a substantial amount of quizzing on Agnes who was so skinny that her apron wrapped around her one and a half times. Her eyes were red, and her hair was thin and frizzy from a home permanent that had gone wrong. "It'll grow out," my grandmother said dryly.

"I'm going to marry a collie," I announced to Gram on the way home. You couldn't have babies with a dog, and that would insure my not ending up like Agnes. "Lassie," I stated, "I'm going to marry him." (But how would I ever meet such a celebrity as Lassie? I knew that, though they said it was a girl dog on TV, Lassie was really played by a male. Did such animals ever come to Buffalo? Would Lassie be dead by the time I needed to get married? I had heard there were *replacement* Lassies, a ghastly fact I could barely assimilate, though they might be useful.)

Now when asked whom I would marry, I could simply reply, "A collie, I am going to marry a collie." There on the windswept moor I would stand with my husband, a big, sandy mammal with its foreleg casually, protectively around my shoulder.

"So what kind of children are you going to have with a *dog?*" Gram asked, then answered her own question, *"Puppies!"*

"Maybe we'll have puppies," I said primly, "or we won't have anything. You can't have babies with a *dog.*" If only my parents were born as dogs. Oh, to be a feral child, brought up by wolves. And never have to continue the generations of fighting.

Is it strange for a girl of eight to be thinking about motherhood—or avoiding it—with such intent? But motherhood is what some girls only think of. When we came home I changed into my Annie Oakley outfit with my holster and gun. Soon Ted would be home and we'd have dinner, so Gail and I played in waiting. I sat and watched her maneuver Marilyn, her platinum blonde doll. Now and then I lazily shot the air with my pistol.

"I'm a bombshell!" Gail said in Marilyn talk. "I'm the blondest girl in Hollywood!" Gail strutted Marilyn down the carpet. "Vavoom! Va-va-va-voom!"

When Ted came in, Gail dumped Marilyn under the end table.

"Daddy, Daddy," she whooped, "let me ride on your shoe!" Ted shuffled over in his workboots and Gail climbed on, her tiny bare legs wrapped around the thick, foot-molded leather.

"Gail, tuck your feet in! Daddy could step on you!" I yelped.

"Nah, I ain't gonna step on her." She rode his foot, giggling, around the living room while Annie Oakley watched.

"Can I? Can I ride now, Dad?" Annie asked.

"Nah. We gotta eat."

7.

Out of the scallop shell of a weekend, Venus-like, Polly's friend Flo Skrypnyk rose to take me to a double feature, eat Creamsicles, and leap into the bushes behind a bus stop. Flo deeply desired to avoid the driver who had a crush on her. When we peeked out from the bushes, the bus had gone, and I was miserable to have barely glimpsed the black-haired bus driver, and tired, having had a day of five hours at the movies.

I wanted to go back to her apartment and rest (my mother would have had me resting hours before). How strange it was to wait for a bus when everybody I knew just went to the parking lot and got into their cars. Yet there was Flo, making us wait for the next bus because she was avoiding the driver, and also because she was not a mother and could not recognize when I was tired. I understood this, and felt a little scared and a little exhilarated because her ignorance of what I needed physically was more than balanced by being treated, regally, as an adult.

At last we returned to the little apartment where Flo lived alone, and I ate the dinner she prepared for us, nothing like the meat and potatoes Polly dished up. We ate salad and something called lasagna. Then she handed me a grapefruit which she expected I would cut up for myself. How amazing! Somehow I figured it out, getting a few scoops of the fruit for dessert. Weren't there any cookies? Flo produced a chocolate cookie from a package with a little gold stripe.

"I've earned my stripes," she said. "I've got my little place here, and my job."

"And you have Jacques," I said. Jacques was Flo's toy Pomeranian.

"Yes," Flo said, her muscled arm extending from the cap sleeve of her dress. Flo worked at Lackawanna Steel, beneath the smokestacks. She stood in a dark fiery place on the line and wore a protective mask, like blinders on a horse. She was strong as a horse, too, and as beautiful. ("Looks just like Jane Russell," Polly confided to me one day in the Dodge, "including the boobs!")

"And you have Wayne," I said boldly. Wayne wore a suit and paced past the assembly line. I knew because Flo arranged for my whole fourth-grade class to visit the plant and we all saw the molten steel and brought home free miniature steel cars. Wayne said hello to me because sometimes on Thursdays he drove to our house in his Thunderbird to pick up Flo.

"Yes"—Flo eyed me—"I have Wayne every Thursday." ("Once a week," Polly said, "like clockwork.")

"Never on any other day?"

Wayne once a week and cookies with a gold stripe. ("She makes more money than your father!" Polly said in awe.)

Flo got up to do the dishes so I was completely free to think up more questions. "Flo, do you really make more money than my dad?"

"That's none of your business," she said, flipping a little dishwater at me off her long fingers.

"How come you don't have kids, Flo?"

"I don't have a husband." She was wiping the stove off now.

"But you have Wayne!"

"He's not my husband."

"Do you want to marry him?"

"Molly," Flo said, turning round from her clean burner, "I like my life just the way it is."

She had Wayne every Thursday till he died, decades later. She had money to buy a house and retire. She had a muscle that flexed beneath her sleeve. And the bus driver, and double features.

"Really, Flo, don't you want any kids?"

"Here, catch." She threw me a tangerine. I'd never had one before. She showed me how to peel it and separate the wings inside so they looked like butterflies on the rind. "You're nice to have around every once in a while," Flo said.

I grabbed the compliment like a gold miner. ("Pure selfishness," Polly said. "A nice job and money and a boyfriend and she gets her hair done by Mr. Michael every week. My most selfish friend.") Look how Flo did on her own! I could grow up and not have children except for a girl like me to grace the weekend.

8.

"Stop wiggling your feet, Mols," Ted said. I had my feet tucked in the small of his back as we watched *The Ed Sullivan Show* with Gail and Polly in our new house. We'd hightailed to Tonawanda after Gram and Grandpa retired to their new apartment. "Mols, ya gotta stop moving your feet back there!" I wiggled from happiness at the thought of Monday—no gym! The brand new school in the brand new development didn't have its gymnasium finished, so I fled to art class in the cafeteria. Ted removed my stockinged feet and examined them during the commercial. "I like them socks, kneesocks," he said.

"You do-oo?" I was so shocked I said do in two syllables.

"They look nice on girls."

"On me?" I said me-ee.

"Yeah. Now stop wigglin' 'em."

Polly passed Ted the potato chips. They had their house, white with pink trim, and a naked three-foot maple tree (a "starter" Polly called it) in front. Gailie and I each had a room, and fifth grade stretched out like a cat before me purring, "art, not gym . . . art, not gym."

"Yes, this is where you eat lunch," Miss Cramer said, "but when you have art here, it's not a cafeteria. It's a sanctuary."

Twice weekly I entered the sanctuary and drew the still life in chalk, a green wine bottle and a garnet jug. Next to the jug was a white bowl with a blue Star of David in it—Miss Cramer's religion. "This is the sanctuary. Art is holy," she pronounced. It had certainly saved me from gym. Polly didn't believe in holy ("They trucked me to church three times a week! Wednesday choir and twice on Sunday!"), but I went to mass with Flo and watched her cross herself and genuflect. I wore a hanky hairpinned above my ponytail for a hat, and so did Flo. Were we holy? While she floated up to communion, I stayed in the pew.

"We're getting fat," Ted said to Polly when the June Taylor Dancers came on, "fat and forty!"

"Not me!" Gail chimed. She was a leggy thing who sprang into cartwheels during the number. "I'll never be fat!" Gail got better grades in our new school.

Polly passed Ted the fudge.

Much earlier that day Gail and I had eaten some of that fudge for breakfast while they slept in. Our kitchen, on Sunday morning with just my sister and me and Mitzi our dog, felt holy. For half an hour, it was a sanctuary. I drew on a piece of oaktag. The art class had to make the school calendar and my month was March. Miss Cramer had put the squares for the days in the bottom half and I filled the top with three green earlobes that were supposed to be a shamrock. Disgusted, I slapped the oaktag down on the other side and the stupid thing vanished. Then I had to sketch clusters of shamrocks around the margins to hide the butter stains from the fudge. A big blank space squatted in the middle. I had to fill it with something.

A poem could go there like in the *Golden Treasury* of poems at La Grange where each verse was framed in green ivy. Miss Cramer had said "Still life is poetry." I lettered lightly, erasably, *MARCH IS SUCH A PRETTY MONTH* then used the edge of the Courier Express Sunday Magazine to guide the next line, *FILLED WITH LOTS AND LOTS OF SNOW.* Didn't sound right. I stared so hard at the oaktag, my eyes had

to wander. Through the window was next door: the Marshes. Just one
letter away from the month of my poem.

Ruffled curtains, butter-yellow, framed their window like a sleeping
cap. The gray formica table formed a horizon below the sill. You could
lay a drawing pad on that table without fear of fudge crumbs. Mrs. Marsh
brooked no crumbs. I found that out when I came to collect for the
United Way and she was sponging off the table. Mr. Marsh smiled at her
and at me, then absentmindedly put his arm around her. He was like a
priest and she was like the nun, except they were married, as I thought
priests and nuns should be. Amidst Revere Ware with copper bottoms
and a clock that ticked majestically was the peace of the world that pas-
seth understanding. Mr. Marsh got out his wallet and gave me a dollar
for the United Way. Most people gave me a quarter.

("Hefty contribution," Polly said. "Well, they can afford it. It's just the
two of them—no kids.")

It dawned on me to make the snow line last, then rhyme something
else with it earlier. I lettered, *FILLED WITH LOTS AND LOTS OF SNOW*
lower down, then erased it above and wrote instead: *HAS THIRTY-ONE
DAYS, YOU KNOW.* All I had to do was think of the third line. It had to
rhyme with "month."

"Vonth," Gail said.

"Come on! It has to be a *real word.*"

"Squonth," she said.

"Stop it."

"Dunth. Punth. Sumpth. Womth!"

Warmth.

WE WAIT FOR WARMTH, I wrote. Too short. I added *IN MARCH.*
Then it didn't rhyme at all.

"Shit."

"Don't swear, Molly." Gail imitated Gram's snooty voice. "It doesn't
become you!"

"It's the shamrocks that matter anyway," I said stoutly. But I knew I'd gone "the extra mile" Miss Cramer talked about. Even if mine wasn't too hot, nobody else would have a poem.

Sunday night with Ed Sullivan, contemplating my calendar page, Ted in a good mood, and all of us watching, nearly approached being a sanctuary—except you couldn't draw a still life of it like you could in art class. There was nothing to make a still life *of*. Unlike other people's houses, we had no milk glass vases or little china Bo Peeps. Our surfaces, except for the potato chips in a metal bowl, were bare. Ted broke anything you put out for decoration. Not at first, but eventually he'd get mad and throw the porcelain frog, and then it would be gone.

After Ed Sullivan it was a drama with a miserly old grandfather.

"Heh!" Ted laughed. "Heh!"

"What's so funny, Dad?"

"That guy's like *my* grandfather."

"You mean Grandpa?"

"Jesus Christ, Molly, Papa's *your* grandfather and *my* father. You got no common sense."

"Oh."

Ted laughed again when the mean grandfather wouldn't give money for the crippled boy.

"*Why* is *that* funny?" I asked again.

"Because he's like old Granpop Peacock! The old geezer would heat pennies on the stove when I was a little boy, see?"

"On a *burner?* Heat *pennies?*" I was incredulous.

"Not on a goddamned burner! It wasn't an electric stove, it was a *wood* stove, for Chrissake!"

My mother interrupted. "Ted, for crying out loud, why would she know about wood stoves?"

"Yeah! Why would I?" I said defiantly behind the shield of my ally.

"Hey, Daddy," Gail said, "look at my socks!" She'd gone and put on kneesocks during the station identification. We all watched the miser and the crippled boy again.

"Heh!"

"So what about the pennies, Dad?"

"What pennies?"

"The ones on the wood stove!" I wiggled my feet in exasperation.

"It's nine-thirty. You guys have to be in bed!"

"But the program's only half over!" Gail whined.

"That don't matter," Ted said.

"Get your jammies on," my mother said.

"I won't." I shoved my feet directly into his sacrum. "Not till you say about the pennies!"

"Molly, that hurt! Don't be rough!"

"The pennies!"

We'd lost track of the program, but Ted watched the screen as he spoke. "Well, he heated them up on top of the wood stove till they were really hot, see? Red hot. And then he said I could have them if I could grab them. And it was the Depression, Mols, and a penny bought the world. I was putting rubber bands around my shoes to keep the soles on, so I really wanted those pennies."

"Where was Gram?" I asked.

"She was afraid of him," Ted wheezed. Polly got up and turned off the TV to force us into action. My father still watched the empty screen.

"Wait, Ma! What about Papa, Daddy, didn't *he* get you the pennies?"

"No sir! Papa's a coward."

I curled my feet under me and sat with the knowledge that they wouldn't help him. Gail was sloshing around the bathroom sink and Polly was getting the wash ready for Monday morning.

"Did you get any pennies, Dad?" I asked quietly.

"Heh. He stopped me from poking some off the stove with a stick," Ted said stonily.

"So, did you pick some up?"

"Hell no, Molly, they were *hot!* I woulda burnt my hands to a crisp."

If I were my dad I'd have gotten those pennies, somehow.

9.

"So I won't be here when you get home from school, girls," Polly explained at the kitchen table.

"Mitzi!" Gail shouted, and I swooped the dog's rear end onto the paper. Mitzi's habit was to get her two front legs on the newsprint while the pooping part hung off.

"Listen to me, girls, here are your keys."

"Our *keys?*" Gail and I said simultaneously.

"Because I won't be here when you get home from school," she repeated.

Gail was nine and I was twelve. It was the beginning of seventh grade. "Can't *somebody* be here, like Gram?" I pushed the keys back toward my mother.

"This is the new routine," she said firmly, pushing one key back toward me and handing the other to my sister. "Now, Gail, you'll get back first, around three-thirty, and Molly comes in around four. Your father will get here around four-thirty. He's working eight to four now. So you'll just have that hour alone before your dad comes home."

Daddy was going to take care of us? Cook dinner and everything? "But when do you get home, Mom?" I asked plaintively.

"Later, lots later, stupid," Gail said.

"So Daddy's going to cook *dinner?*"

My sister howled with laughter.

"Don't be such a hyena, poophead," I said. At the word *poophead* the parakeet squawked. Her name was Poopsie, after her first act, shitting on my father's brushcut. Poopsie and our lizard were going to be our only pets. Mitzi couldn't seem to be trained to poop outside, and when she went inside, she couldn't seem to get it right. Mitzi squirmed in Gail's lap.

"When's she going to the pound?" Gail asked numbly.

"Friday," Polly said.

"But when do you get *home* tomorrow?"

"After your father comes to relieve me at the store." Poopsie flew to my finger. We were friends, even though she was Gail's bird. And Mitzi was Gail's. She got them on her two last birthdays. Poopsie flew on top of Mitzi's head and the dog sat quietly, as if an angel had perched on her eyebrows.

"You mean Daddy's gonna leave us home?"

"Just for a few minutes. Till he comes to the store and I drive home."

Polly had bought a little grocery store. It was supposed to be just like La Grange, only it wasn't wood. It was cement blocks and the other half was a liquor store owned by other people. "They make lots of money in that liquor store!" Polly said. Now she was going to be just like her father. Only Polly and Ted had to borrow from the credit union to get started. We didn't have any money. *"If you weren't such a boozehound,"* Polly said. Ted was going to be good. He was going to come home from eight hours of work at the electric company and he was going to take care of us and he was going to work at the store, so Polly could come home.

"But Daddy can't cook!" I said in exasperation.

"He's not going to cook, poopface," Gail said, "Mommy told me."

"You be quiet, Gailie," Polly said. "Now, Mols, you're getting all grown up, and you can take on some grown-up responsibilities."

Gail threw Mitzi to the floor and screamed, "You're cooking, Molly! It's you! You have to feed us!"

I looked at my mother in disbelief.

"I'll have everything all set up for you, Mols," Polly said seriously. She'd had her hair done at Mr. Michael. She looked at us so directly that each of her eyes was like a tower beam.

"Do I have to?" I said.

"Yes, you do."

"I don't know what to do!"

"I'll tell you."

"Do I have to *every day?*"

"Every day after school," she said solemnly. Poopsie flew on top of her perfect hair. She lifted her off and flung out her hand and the bird flew back to its cage.

"You mean you're never coming home after school? We come home alone *every day?* Forever?" My legs twisted around the chair legs like ivy suckers.

"We're changing the routine, girls."

" 'We're changing the routine, girls.' " Gail repeated in repeat talk.

"Now stop that repeating everything I say," Polly said.

" 'Now stop that repeating everything I say,' " Gail said.

"I mean it," Polly said.

" 'I mean it,' " Gail and I both said.

"Oh, you girls!" Polly said, putting on a blue smock that said "Peacock's Superette" in red script on the front.

" 'Oh, you girls!' " we said.

"Girls! Girls!" Poopsie said.

"Starting tomorrow, so take your keys." We began to fight over our key chains. Mine was green and Gail's was pink. "I want the green one," she whined.

"Take it," I said suddenly. After all, I was grown up now.

There was more to it than cooking dinner. There was ironing a shirt for Ted to wear to the store. There was Saturday housework, vacuuming up the bird feathers and feeding the pet chameleon I'd won at the Erie County Fair. Polly'd let me take it home, and now it lived on the living room curtains. I had to get out a piece of paper and put a mealy worm on it. Then I'd cover my face while the chameleon chased it. Through my fingers I'd watch the lizard break the back of the mealy bug and eat it. There was also getting Gail to do her homework. And doing mine. Now I had a job (seventh grade) and a family.

"Sit down and do it, Gail." I pinned her to her desk chair. "Sit down and do it for"—I looked at my watch. I wore a watch now—"for twenty minutes. Then dinner'll be ready."

"But what if Daddy doesn't come home in twenty minutes?"

"We'll eat by ourselves."

"Hey, cool!"

She was nine years old. How did she learn to say *Hey, cool?*

"Come on, get started so I can go out and make the salad dressing." I'd already chopped up the iceberg lettuce. The hamburgers with onions were sizzling in the iron pan. Potatoes bubbled in the aluminum pot. All I had to do was smush some ketchup and relish in the mayonnaise.

Gail's homework was to glue color-coded bird stickers onto black-and-white outlines of bird shapes from blue jays to wrens. "Do you know how to do it?"

"Of course I know!" she said, grabbing the stickers. "Here!" She slapped the baby chickadee on the big fat father robin.

"Wrong!" I snapped, but she looked so downhearted that I took it back. "It's hard," I lied, "isn't it?"

"Yes," she said, soft as a bird.

The burgers burned in the pan and the potato water boiled out, but the rich smell of overcooking hadn't got to Gail's bedroom yet, so I had time to stare dumbfounded at what she couldn't do in fourth grade. I could've done that in second grade! Was she stupid? She was so smart at figuring out Polly and Ted. She knew Polly was going to make me be her mother before I did. She knew all about which teachers were single and married and she got all her friends into a baton-twirling group and I never could have done that. She couldn't be stupid. Maybe she was average.

"Well," I said, equally softly, "look at the size more than the color first. Don't pay any attention to the color." The color coding was a decoy in the instructions. "Match the big ones with the big ones, then the mediums and the smalls." I smelled the potatoes burning. "Bring it all out to the kitchen!" I screamed, and ran to hack the burgers from the pan and gouge the potatoes out for mashing. I threw the pans into the sink and turned to Gail. "Great!" I shouted. (She'd put the cardinal on the cardinal.) My father burst in, asking, "What's for dinner?" and handing me his lunchpail. I put it on the counter to wash later and started the salad dressing. Out the window was the Marshes' sanctuary kitchen. Here we had homework, lunchpails, and hamburgers the size of fifty-cent pieces.

"Jesus, what's that smell!" Ted declared. "You're not gettin' good grades as a housewife, Molsie. Them hamburgs look like dried shit!" He sat down. "Well, I'll eat 'em. But Christ Almighty you gotta watch that friggin' frying pan, Mols. You gotta grow up!"

"Sorry, Dad," I said, and meant it. Maybe Gail should always do her homework in the kitchen so I could teach her and cook, too. And then after I gave them supper, I'd iron Ted's shirt. Oh no, he'd need it right away. I should've ironed it just after school, but I forgot.

"Oh, Dad, I forgot your shirt! I'll do it right after supper!"

"Jesus Christ Almighty, Molly, you're makin' me late for the store!"

The phone rang. It was my math partner from school. I hadn't looked at the math. "Call you later," I mumbled, bolted my hamburger, and ran down to the cellar to iron. The shirt was a mass of wrinkles. I'd forgotten to remove it from the dryer.

"Hey, Mollleee!" Gail yelled from the top of the stairs. "Can you check my birds?"

Every day we came home after school to the smell of linoleum, the empty kitchen of the empty house that waited to be brought to life. It is mothers who bring houses to life, and ours was gone, though she'd left the table wiped and the counters clean. She'd left Pepsi and potato chips, chopped meat, stewed tomatoes, and lettuce. But it was all refrigerated, and none of it retained its smell in the cold. The house itself was cold of Polly's scent. She had left too many hours before. And I did not smell like a mother.

It was up to me now to keep us alive in the house, since Ted would probably try to kill us. Why else would Polly say, "Always put the knives away! Never, never use a knife and leave it on the counter. You can never tell about your father." Why did she roll her eyes toward Gail and say to me knowingly, "I told him I'd call the police if he ever harms a hair on her head." On the table lay her note with what to cook for dinner. If we wrapped ourselves in the apron of her instructions, would we smell like her? I was rank with fear and responsibility—the child-mother smell.

10.

Plunk went a Melmac bowl. *Thud* went a painted glass. Grandma Ruth stationed me at the foot of the big, marred walnut table at La Grange, then grabbed the bowl, went out to the fence, and picked the blackberries right into it. After she gave me the berries, she swiped the glass and cruised to the kitchen, lifted an enamel ladle from a white pail, and sloshed water into it. All the time I sat and watched her. I didn't have to do a thing. After she put the water in front of me, she sat down to watch me eat. I picked up each berry, the size of my fingernail, before I ate it. Sour! My grandmother dumped a spoonful of sugar on the berries. The timer chimed. She glided out to the kitchen where the heavy oven door squawked and the cookie trays clattered. Armed with a spatula, she shoveled molasses cookies, four inches wide and cratered as moons, onto sugared plates to cool. While she bedded them down in a tin between wax paper sheets, I got my gold-zippered white Bible with my name on it ready.

Time for Number 2. I slid from my chair and went to my room off the living room. Between the iron bed and the dresser was a white enamel chamber pot where I squatted and did my Number 2, holding Wild Rose perfume to my nose to help with the stink. Toilet paper was on the low shelf of the dresser. Then I clamped the lid. "Number two, Gram," I called on my way to the door.

"Don't forget the cookies!" she called back. "And watch for foxes!"

July buzzed with rabies warnings. I carried the tin of cookies and Bible in front of me ceremonially as I walked toward the white-spired church. It was 8:55 A.M. and the house at La Grange hummed behind me, all in place. I waved to my grandfather as I passed the gas pumps. He was in his ESSO uniform. I moved quickly past the orchard with the garden beds, looking for rabid foxes. Then past a house, past a barn, to the church. It was the second day of Bible School, and I already knew the routine. Hating the idea of camp, I was allowed to go home to La Grange. Gail was too allergic to come. She had hay fever and asthma, as did my aunt and grandmother. ("Not me!" Polly had crowed. "I'm strong as a Clydesdale!")

I used the back door to the La Grange Baptist Church, scuttling through the hall hung with choir robes and hurrying into the church itself, and down the side aisle to the hidden staircase. Our class was up in the balcony. There was Margaret, our teacher. She was a second cousin of mine—I was related to everybody in La Grange.

"Oh, you brought your grandma's cookies!" she cooed. "Thank you for taking your turn so early!" Everybody was polite in La Grange. Nobody took the name of the Lord in vain, let alone said shit or piss or friggin'. Each exchange was as fresh as the turn of a page.

Frannie popped in and then Judy, her half sister with the big boobs. My shy, dark second cousin Constance came, too. Cool Jack Stewart sauntered up, hands in pockets. And his half sister Bonnie Strathem weasled into the pew just before the Boyle boy with his sunburnt face and square freckled hands. Bonnie had been in a fire and the skin on half her face and neck and one whole arm was brittle as pork rind.

"Does it hurt?"

"I don't feel nothing at all," she said.

Her brother kept a long spear of grass in his mouth, almost like a cigarette. Five girls and two boys in our class. A boy like Jack Stewart

wouldn't have sat by me at Benjamin Franklin Junior High School, but
here I was cool. I was related to everybody! Plus I wore my turquoise
shorts.

"Let us pray," said Margaret. She stumbled through a made-up prayer
about Bible School and ended, "In the name of our Lord Jesus Christ,
Amen." Then she said, "Let us sing," and we sang "Onward Christian Sol-
diers" really loud. At Ben Franklin I was only a second soprano in cho-
rus, but here I let loose and sang the melody. We all sang the melody, and
Margaret sang the harmony.

"Is there anyone here who hasn't asked Jesus Christ to be their own
personal savior?" she asked when we finished. "Remember, you must ask
Him if you want to be saved and go to heaven."

Really? I had not asked. We were all silent. None of us raised a hand.

"Now," said Margaret, "maybe you asked when you were little boys
and girls, but now you're getting grown up. Jack, you're fourteen going
on fifteen. Judy, you're sixteen years old. How old are you, Molly?"

"Thirteen."

"Then you're all old enough to ask again. Call Jesus into your hearts."

None of us spoke.

"Jack and Bonnie and Red Boyle, this means you, too."

No one spoke.

"Before your noon meal, after we get done here and you play softball,
I want you to kneel by your beds and ask Jesus Christ to be your own
personal savior today." Margaret's voice quickened to our emergency.
"There's not a minute to lose!" She thumped her hand on the balcony railing and her pincurls flapped. Then, coolly, she whispered, "Onto our
projects, now." The God part was over and we hauled out our sandpaper
and plywood squares and little baby nails and tin crosses and shellac,
clambering over the pews. We were going to make Christian recipe
boxes for our mothers, and it would take us all three weeks. The wood
was pre-sawn, but we had to do the rest.

After the noon meal at La Grange the ladies with their crochet and embroidery flooded the dining room table with floss and gossip about my mother who tipped over outhouses, chopped off her hair, rode bareback, drove her own car, and grabbed a rich, deaf boyfriend who gave her a muskrat coat, then dumped him for my father. (Oh! I could have had a rich, deaf father instead of Ted!) Perching with the ladies, I learned how to do French knots, got bored, and flopped into my room to read. Squatting on the chamber pot to pee, then putting toilet paper on the urine and dumping in a few drops of Wild Rose to expunge the sharpness, then clamping the tin cover on, I thought of what Margaret said and pictured Jesus at the Last Supper. Shouldn't it have been the Last Dinner? There He was with all His boyfriends drinking and eating. If you didn't have Christ as your own personal savior, Margaret rasped at us, you'd go straight to hell. We wanted to go to heaven, didn't we?

When I knelt by the bed my legs stuck out so far I almost tipped over the pee. I got up and moved the pot. Down on my knees, the floor was hard. I moved the rag rug nearer the bed, and knelt down again. Should I close my eyes? No, I should clasp my hands and look up at the ceiling, raw board with nails in it—Grandpa had never finished the ceiling.

Dear Jesus, I prayed, *I'm asking you to come into my heart to be my own personal savior. Amen.*

Maybe I should have closed my eyes.

Dear Jesus Christ, I prayed beneath my lids, *please come into my heart to be my own personal savior. Amen.*

My heart, did it beat the same way? Yes, it did. I clamped my hands over my ears to feel the blood rushing through me. Was something there? I had said please and used both His first and last names. Nothing was happening! I bowed my head against the quilt. You don't feel changed right away, Margaret said, but some people did. Like they got struck by lightning. I must be having the gradual change. Getting up on my two feet made me sleepy. I plopped on the bed and really did sleep, waking in the afternoon heat, my cheek against a bump in the quilt. Was I changed? I lay there, feeling nothing new.

Time to walk across the road for Grandma. I traipsed to Mrs. Calofska's back door, played with some kittens there, and put a nickel in a basket before I removed a glass bottle of milk with a tin foil cover. I dragged the bottle home. I was famous because my grandmother put an announcement that I was attending Bible School in the *La Grange Herald*. Mrs. Calofska put a notice in that her nephew Oliver would come to visit his aunt that evening. Even my Grandpa Gillie, who never went anywhere, crossed the road after supper with Ruth and me to say hello to Oliver. Oliver was blond and my age and held two glass jars with lids, "For when it gets dark enough," he said.

We went into the farmhouse and looked at Ripley's Believe It Or Nots until it was dark enough. Then we crept through the night air. "Molly," Ruth called, "go home and get your sweater!" I shoved my jar at Oliver and ran across the road to plunge my arms into my grandmother's sweater, smelling of Avon's Lily of the Valley, and ran back and grabbed the jar. "What are we doing?" I asked him breathlessly. "Fireflies," he said. Out in the dark meadow the fireflies flickered on and off. In we went, the grasses biting my bare legs. "Like this!" Oliver caught one. I tried and couldn't do it. The fly's light went off just when I thought I could nab it.

"I can't!"

"Sure you can. Watch again!" He was taller than I and lanky, like Jack Stewart. He was here for the week but refused to sign up for Bible School. I tried again and couldn't do it. It was like asking Jesus Christ to be my own personal savior. "They go off at a slant when the light goes out, so snap it up to the side and get the lid on and hold it tight." I tried again. My jar lit up with two of them! "Hey, you got two!" Oliver whispered. Then we tried again and got more. Our jars were lighting up like store windows.

"Molly!" Ruth called, and I pretended not to hear her.

"Your grandmother's calling you," Oliver said dutifully, and I said, "Oh," and ran back to her with my jar. Oliver came after.

"How do we feed them?" I said.

"What for?" Oliver asked.

"Well, we don't want them to die!"

"They ain't gonna die, we're gonna let em out!"

Oh, we're going to let go of them, I thought with disappointment, the same letdown I felt when Aunt Roberta once said we had to put back the little perch we caught on our lines, followed by the same feeling of freedom from my trophy. I wouldn't be responsible for killing the fish, or now, for having to keep the bugs alive. Everything was on its own, including me, buzzing in the universe.

Each day of the week was a tad different: laundry day, watering the gardens day, Frannie and Judy come pick me up for the lake day. In the mornings Ruth wrote in her diary and I went to the church; in the afternoons Ruth sewed and I read; some evenings Oliver and I caught fireflies and played with the kittens. On others Ruth looked up with her moist eyes and said, "Are you bored?" She looked as sweet as a Swiss cow. "You are bored," she concluded, "so why don't you write me a poem?" Then I obliged her with haikus. I'd learned how to write them in seventh grade Language Arts and dillydallied over the three lines of five, seven, and five syllables—a lot better than rhyming my shamrock poem. I knew you had to write hundreds just to get one good one—like capturing a firefly out of the field.

The flow of the days was light and even, like the skies of heaven in the Bible books. Jesus Christ had not come into my heart, though I asked Him every dinner hour, and on Friday, I gave up. *This is like Santa Claus for older people,* I thought, picturing Buffalo and the smokestacks and Peacock's Superette with Polly hidden inside it and Gail scrunched over her Barbie and Ted sacked out on the couch with the TV on. I was the visitor from another planet, the city, and like extraterrestrials I knew more than the humans at La Grange did: I knew they had heaven, right here, all to their own.

11.

As if somebody stowed six slabs of bacon in a lingerie drawer, the six bottles of beer in Grandma's refrigerator assaulted me when I opened the door. What were *they* doing there? I'd meandered in from the orchard where I'd spent the early afternoon looking up into the branches of an old, old tree with my notebook and my pen. I was writing a story about a girl looking up into the branches of an old, old tree. Maybe the brown bottles were some kind of birch beer. . . . No, they were Carling's Black Label. Voices in the garage. Quick to the spy hole.

The spy hole was a round piece of telescope glass that Grandpa Gillie embedded in the wall by the telephone that was so old it didn't have a dial. You had to get the operator to place a call. If you climbed on a wooden stool and looked through the glass, you could sweep the whole store, all the red shelves of candy and the blue pop machine and the newspapers and the bags of flour and sugar and the cans of motor oil on white shelves. There was such a crowd out there! My mother and my father, Aunt Roberta, and Stanley and Lucie Calofska from across the road, and my cousin Howie, and the minister! He left immediately, though. He was just paying for gas. The others stayed. Something grabbed the hem of my shorts. It was my sister. "Hey, Mol."

"What are *you* doing here?"

"We came today instead of tomorrow. Daddy wanted to. Mommy got Flo to take the store."

"Daddy put beer in Grandma's refrigerator!"

"He put a lot more in his stomach than in the fridge," my sister said. "Is he drunk?"

Gail giggled. In her white sleeveless blouse she looked cool and soft, like a stuffed animal you'd want to buy and know it would be your favorite. "Drunk as a skunk!" she said.

My silent cousin Howie came in to meander around the dining room table and look us up and down. He was Gail's age and wore overalls with a bib and hardly ever talked. He was in the pipsqueak class at Bible School. "Any cookies?" he finally said, round-eyed. The three of us raced to the kitchen to the glass cookie jar with its tin lid. Molasses and peanut butter in fistfuls.

"What do you mean, we're going now? Aren't we going to stay for supper?" I asked my mother in the bedroom.

"We're not staying. We just came to get you."

"But you weren't supposed to come till tomorrow!"

"Well, your father wanted to come today." Polly rolled her eyes.

"But, Ma, I'm not packed!"

"Just throw your clothes in the suitcase, Mols. We'll wash 'em when we get home."

"You mean I'll wash 'em," I spat at her. "Why can't you sell the store? Why can't you just be home?"

"Don't start that, Molly."

"But I can't go! I haven't said good-bye to any of my friends!"

"Call 'em on the phone, Mols."

"Jack doesn't have a phone!"

"Is Jack a boy?"

"Yes!" I screamed. "But he's not my boyfriend!"

"Just pack, Molly. Fast. Gail's waiting in the car."

My grandmother came into the bedroom with two lines across her forehead. She was wearing her green flowered dress and her stockings and her brown shoes. She was dressed to meet the world as she always was, dressed for Saturday, when so many visitors came because they stopped for gas. "Oh, Pauline," she said to my mother in a quavery voice, "I had everything all ready for tomorrow! I've got a nice chicken to roast, and gravy, and mashed potatoes, and nice peas. I baked fruit pies. Oh well, I'll pack up the pies for you. I wish you'd have called, Pauline. I could have popped that chicken right in the roaster." It wasn't a chicken you buy at the store. It had its neck broken by Mrs. Calofska who swung it around her head like a boomerang. Then Ruth plucked the feathers out of it and threw the head to Mrs. Calofska's cat.

"Here's your suitcase, Molly," my grandmother said. She opened the green bag on the bed.

"Just throw your clothes in, Mol," my mother said softly. Polly looked as if she had just thrown her clothes *on*, dressed in stretch pants and a floppy jersey.

"Oh, Mom," I said, my wail surprising me.

"Whass everybody doin' in here!" Ted burst in.

Polly took him by the arm. "We're just getting Molly packed," she said.

"Well, son, you took us by surprise!" my grandmother said.

"It was time for a trip!" Ted crowed, backing out of the bedroom. He held one of the Carling's Black Labels crooked in his arm. He was wearing Bermuda shorts. No man in the country wore them. They all wore overalls, or long pants with shirts for church.

Skinny Aunt Roberta peered round the door. She bobbed her permed brunette frizz excitedly up and down saying, "Here's your birthday present!"

"But my birthday's over with," I said sullenly.

"Birthdays go on all year!" She handed me a striped box with a white ribbon. The box matched the lime stripes on her cotton sundress, all the pleats on the bodice sewn into neat lines.

"Can I open it?"

"Sure you can," both Polly and my grandmother said simultaneously.

I tore at it hard. It was taped up with so much Scotch tape it seemed bandaged. When I got the box open, there was even tape on the tissue paper. Inside the tissue was a blouse, white, with blue embroidery. My aunt had bought the blouse and my grandmother had embroidered it with blue daisies, blue stems, blue leaves down the front placket. It was really a corny blouse, but so starched, so white, the satiny stitches shone like keys to a secret. It would glow in my closet on Pilgrim Road, where we were going, going in minutes.

My voice caught when I thanked them, and we sailed right on into leaving.

"Here are Frannie and Judy and Jack's addresses," my grandmother said, "and here's your Christian Recipe Box."

"You can write them when you get home," my Aunt Roberta said.

"But that box was for you, Grandma!"

"Oh I know you love the box you made, I put a cookie recipe in it for you. You use the box at home and make some cookies."

"Thanks," I mumbled. I really did want the box I'd spent three weeks sanding and varnishing.

"Now wash your hands," my grandmother said. "I'll finish packing for you." I hadn't really even started.

The kitchen was cool and empty. Out the window were pink hollyhocks, and beyond them, the vegetable garden. I dipped the metal dipper in the enamel pail of water Ruth had pumped. I poured the water in a white enamel basin. I splashed my hands and soaped them and splashed again and wiped them on a long striped towel. There was water all over the floor.

"Come on, Mol!" Polly yelled from the car. My father was in the driver's seat, swigging a beer. My sister and cousin sat in the back seat. Aunt Roberta made my cousin get out. My grandfather came and made us all get out. He lined us all up against the car and took our picture. Then Gail and I climbed onto the prickly wool back seat of the used turquoise Chrysler, and Ted and Polly sat in the front, with one more un-opened beer between them.

Ted finished the one in his hand as we sailed down Route 242, weaving past the corn and oats and timothy.

"Don't touch that other beer, Ted, you're driving!" my mother ordered.

Ted drove faster.

"Slow down!" we screamed from the back seat.

He made deep dips in his zigzags.

"Take the slow way," Polly begged. That meant the back roads.

Ted turned at the entrance to the Thruway. It was so hot that we kept the windows open even though our hair blew and we couldn't catch our breaths for fifty-five minutes.

By the time the car prowled off the Thruway exit, the afternoon heat, like fur, had covered us up, even though the windows were wide open. The earth held the high temperature, even as the shadows began to lengthen a little. By 4 P.M. we were sleepy, and lazy, and suffocating. "Move over!" Gail cried. "Don't make your leg touch my leg!" I moved obediently on the wool seat. I didn't know the difference between her leg and the upholstery, we crawled so with heat. After we parked in our driveway my father fumbled with the keys to our side door. "Here, I'll do it!" Polly said.

"Goddamn, no, I'm getting it. Ain't you got no patience?" He dropped the keys onto the hot cement of the stoop. Polly picked them up. They tussled over the keys and Ted got them, holding them over his head. "Gotcha!" he cried, pirouetted damply, and opened the door. The first blast was the mild, cool air from the basement, but then the inner door opened and the second blast, much hotter, barreled into us. "Dogs from hell!" Polly said.

"Hell's kitchen!" Ted said.

"What's hell's kitchen?" Gail asked.

"Where the devil cooks," our father explained.

The heat created palpable air from the ceiling to the floor. We parted it as we went through the house, Polly opening windows, Ted flying into the bathroom, Gail heading for her stuffed animals, and me keeping going, going through the living room, past the bathroom, through Gail's room to my room. I opened all the windows on three sides and threw myself down on the bed. Where was my bumpy cotton chenille spread? In its place was a wool blanket, scratchy and blue. It itched my knees, my arms, my cheek as I lay on it, unable to move, sunk into it like quicksand, itchsand, my body dove down, down through circles of heat-sand into sleep.

"Did you actually fall asleep?" Polly stood at the door an hour later. I woke with a rash on my neck and face. "Here, give me those dirty clothes, I'll wash them," she said gently. "There's a breeze outside now, why don't you go ride your bike?"

Oh, my bike, I'd missed that at La Grange! Stumbling out to the living room, I heard my father from the bedroom. "Go to hell, Polly!" he was shouting.

"You go to hell!" she said back.

Where was Gail? "Where's Gail?" I interrupted them. There was no point in waiting for them to finish. The argument went on forever. Even the heat of their bedroom didn't stifle them.

"She's down the street at Betsy's," Polly said. "Are you sick, Mols? You never sleep in the middle of the afternoon." It was a La Grange habit, when everything seemed to stop after the noon meal. Sleep. Another place you could go.

A place you could go when you couldn't leave. "I'm OK," I said crankily. "It's too hot. Can I have a fan in my room?"

"Go in the living room," Polly said. "We've got both fans set up in there." We only had two fans. "Or go ride your bike and get a breeze."

It was 6:30. "Aren't we going to eat?"

"Molly, you slept right through dinner!" Ted said.

I had never done that before. There were sandwiches on the pink and turquoise Melmac dishes on the table. That was supper. I grabbed two and went out into the end of the day. It was cooler out there. The lawn rolled to the fence. I rolled my bike off its kickstand, a sandwich in my mouth, and one in my hand. I rode down Pilgrim Road, then Ogden Street, then Floradale, eating the sandwiches and wishing I had a drink. Wishing I'd stayed in La Grange. Summer school was next week. I was retaking Algebra for a better grade. Why was there a wool blanket on my bed? Where were Oliver and Jack and Frannie and Judy and my teacher, Margaret? Ruth and Gillie would be sitting under the maple tree on their Adirondack chairs. In the orchard the rabbits would be out on one side, having their dinner, and the woodchucks would be out on the other side, having their dinner. I finished my sandwich in solidarity. But I wouldn't be there again to stay for a whole year. The days fell before me like flakes of burnt skin. Bonnie Strathem, Jack's half sister, burnt in the barnfire. Like her arms.

A stop sign was coming up on the corner of Floradale and Ogden. I must have gone around the block again. I pulled to a neat stop and leaned my foot on the curb to wait for a car to mosey through the intersection. On the lawns, sprinklers came on, and people called from their backyards. The smell of wienie roasts came up through the thinning heat, and to waste time I looked at the sky. The sun wasn't setting yet, but it was low, and behind clouds. The clouds filtered the rays into streaks that fanned out into the sky, the heavens. There was a short fat streak, the thumb, and four distinct thinner streaks, the fingers. They were the Fingers of God. I had seen them at La Grange. They had followed me, coming right down into Sheridan Drive. I didn't have to ask the stupid son of God to be my own personal savior. I hadn't done a thing, and the Fingers had come to me. And if they were at Sheridan, and I was at Odgen and Floradale, then I must be in the palm of their Hand! It was heaven, reaching straight down to me, and I stayed at the stop sign, even when a car came up and offered to let me go. I waved. They thought I was waving to them. I was waving to . . . God, sort of, but not really, God the Father, why would he have any interest in me? He was nicer than Jesus Christ though. It really was the Fingers I waved to, that there might be Heaven in Tonawanda.

12.

Wienies roasted on the backyard grills of Pilgrim Road, but our hot dogs were boiling in a pot on the stove, as they had every Wednesday for the past year. That's how I made them according to the weekly schedule. The July shadows lengthened on all the suburban lawns. Gail and I were now eleven and fourteen. Ben Franklin Junior High was over for me and Kenmore East Senior High wouldn't begin till after Bible School and summer school where I would take math again, just like the previous summer. We listened to the swish of each car as it slowed down so that the kids playing baseball in the street had time to disperse, and each slowing down caused us a prick of anxiety because it might be our father's car. The later it became, the more certain it was that he would be drunk, but what he would do was not certain. His dinner heated on the stove, drying out in the pans. We chewed with a mix of summer doldrums and a kind of haste to finish before he came. Then we wouldn't have to eat with him. When we finished, it was still light out. Gail put her dishes in the sink and went out to play baseball. I did the dishes, washing the knives first, just as Polly told me, then continuing on with the rest. ("Dry those knives and put them in the drawer before your father gets home. Never leave a knife out!")

Molly obedient, Molly good, she never left a knife out. Molly wasn't obedient or good because of moral fiber, but because her dad might kill her. Her mother emphasized that her father might do this. That's why Molly put the knives away. *Wash them first.* I slopped through the suds, drenching the scatter rug below the sink. Poopsie squawked in her cage. The sun hung lower in the sky. This time when the sounds of the baseball players dispersed, the car wheeled into our driveway. I dropped the plate back into the dishwater, grabbed the towel, and immediately wiped the knives. Then I pushed them into the drawer, shut the drawer, and turned around. "Hi, Dad. Dinner's on the stove. Want to eat?"

His face was rough-red as a piece of ham. "No, I don't want nothin' to eat," the face said. The arm of my father picked up the saucepan full of creamed corn drying out on the back burner from being set continually on "Low." The arm of my father flung the pan of corn at the wall. The dull creamed corn dripped down the pink kitchen wall.

"You don't have to have corn, Dad. I made you some pork chops."

"Don't want no pork chops!" The workshirted arm of my father picked up the iron frying pan from the big front burner on "Low."

"Dad! Don't throw it!"

He didn't throw it.

Remember what you said just now, Molly, I thought, *and remember how you said it. The timing. Remember how you got him not to throw the pan. Maybe you can do it again.* While I organized these thoughts in my mind he lumbered to the corner cabinet.

In the cabinet was a lazy susan filled not with food or dishes but with files of receipts for the quarterly taxes of Peacock's Superette. Pink and yellow receipts, hundreds of them, clipped together, rubber banded, stuck in between notebooks, little pads with columns of figures, and rolls of adding machine paper with columns of figures.

As the arm whirled the lazy susan faster and faster, the receipts came flying out. But they didn't fly fast enough. The arm of my father, then both his arms, started grabbing the receipts and hauling them down onto the counter, then onto the floor. The kitchen was awash in receipts. Some stuck to the creamed corn on the pink walls, some fell into the frying pan with the chops on the stove.

The frying pan. I should have let him throw the pan. Next time, remember to let him throw the pan. Remember. Don't say anything. Let him throw it.

Because this was worse. The side doorbell rang.

Ted was swearing, "Fuck the store! Don't want no dinner!" And mumbling, "Fuckin' shit, fuckin' bitch." He waded through the receipts toward the kitchen table. All this time I'd been moving around the kitchen, keeping at a safe distance. I made no move to clean anything up. If I began to clean it up, I'd have to turn my back. And if I turned, I wouldn't see him come to kill me. And so I watched in fascination at the destruction. Ted's legs marched him toward me. I backed up. He pivoted toward the kitchen table. The doorbell rang again. Ted was still swearing. He planted his legs as two columns. His arms choked the tabletop, tipping it over. Salt, pepper, napkins, and his place setting flew off the table. *Molly, be glad you cleaned up the other dishes. And put away the knives.*

Then my father was down on his knees, bracing them against the upside down table, wrenching off the table legs one by one. It was a solid hardwood table. I'd learned about adrenaline from the doctor who treated my allergies. *What amount of adrenaline is coursing through him?* I wondered blankly. The doorbell rang again. He continued swearing, "Cunt, cunt," and methodically braced himself to break the last table leg. So I backed into the foyer and closed the kitchen door just as Ted took a table leg and beat it like a club against the tabletop on the floor.

It was Susie at the side door. "Wanna come out and hang around, go to the drugstore?" Susie was quick-eyed and skinny as a spool. Polly nicknamed her Spindle. Her legs were spattered with what looked to me like cigarette burns. She said they were mosquito bites she scratched and made worse. I stared down at the dish towel in my hand. Behind the door Ted grunted as he methodically beat the table. His work-booted feet

made a swishing sound as he shuffled through the flimsy carpet of receipts. How much could she hear? What would she make of it?

"I can't. Go with you. I . . ." *Think of something normal, think of a regular excuse, what regular parents do to normal kids.* "I'm grounded," I shouted enthusi-
astically as I located my lie, "I've got to stay in and do the dishes. He's
making me." *Imagine, doing something dumb and wrong and normal, and then getting punished, and then having it be over.*

Behind the kitchen door it was over temporarily. No grunts, no
swearing. Then, "Molly," he ordered, "get in here and clean up this goddamn mess."

"You see? Lookit, Sue, I've gotta go."

"Yeah. Well, see ya."

Inside I eyeballed Ted with every ounce of censure I could muster.
"Oh, Dad, what's Mommy going to say?"

"Don't worry about your mother. I'll worry about your mother. Get
into your room. I'll take care of this." Then he was pale and repentant. I
knew he wouldn't do anything more. He was ashamed and cleaned it up
by himself.

After Ted left for Peacock's Superette, I crept back out to the kitchen,
thinking of calling Spindle, but I stood there instead, marveling that the
kitchen floor and walls were clean, the receipts piled back into the corner cabinet. Of course the knives were put away earlier. I'd seen to that.
And he hadn't broken the chairs. Our four hard maple chairs stood
against the wall, waiting like a police lineup.

It was far too dark to play baseball now. The kids outside were playing a flashlight game. Then parents began to call them in, and my sister
wandered home. Though I'd left kitchen lights ablaze, I sat alone in the
dark in the living room with only the light of the TV. "Hey, Mol, what
happened to the table?" Gail asked when she found me. "I saw Dad dragging the pieces out to the garbage."

"He broke it. He broke up the table. He threw his dinner at the wall and broke the table."

"Jesus. Those chairs lined up—they look like Goldilocks and the three bears," Gail said in awe.

Later our mother arrived. "What the hell happened to the kitchen table?"

"Dad broke it."

"No wonder he was such a lamb at the store," our mother said.

"What really happened here?" Polly asked the next morning when she opened the door to the cabinet where all the receipts were shoved in disorder.

"Dad. He did it when he broke the table."

Polly didn't ask me to tell her more about it, nor did I volunteer. She simply took in the information, groaned, and started reorganizing the receipts. "This will take me a week," she muttered. She did not say he was wrong, she did not say it was his disease, she did not say she was sorry I had to be there during it all. She treated it like a horrible fact of life, a hurricane you had to clean up after.

This is how it would stay, I thought. And if this is what family meant, I didn't want one. Now plenty of teenage girls say this to themselves, but change their minds later. I said it, but I wasn't sure changing your mind was always allowed. After all, Polly hadn't changed hers. She determinedly left the house at 10 A.M. and returned at 10 P.M. These days Ted usually didn't get to the Superette to relieve her. He'd stopped being good. I was being good for all of us.

13.

"I'm going out with this great guy tonight," Gail whispered over the minute steaks I had burned. "Don't tell Mom, Molly, you're always such a tattletale." I was a tattletale; she was right. "He's coming over at seven and we're going to the Falls." Niagara Falls was not within walking distance.

"How old is this guy? Does he drive a car?" I asked.

"Sure he drives. He's nineteen. He goes to night school, isn't that cool?"

"Cool . . ." I said, nonplussed.

"He was at the JV basketball game. He likes basketball."

"Likes basketball?"

"Yeah, but Molly, don't tell Mom, what he really likes is cars. He likes to drive 'em."

"Cars?"

Now my sister was a JV cheerleader. I had coached her for hours before the tryouts. I hadn't been chosen as a cheerleader in junior high, but like a teenage stage mother I'd decided that my Gail should rectify my inabilities and mistakes. And so I'd hounded and nagged her until she learned a great routine and was honored with a position on the squad. She was too hip, though. She smoked; she never did her homework. I was a rotten mother and worse as a sister. I just couldn't keep an eye on her. I couldn't even answer my mother's questions about her.

"Molly, why does Gail hide her underpants in the back of her drawers?" Polly asked me one Sunday when she was relieving me of doing the laundry.

"Don't ask me, Ma, I'm going to the library, OK? I have to finish my history project." I was a sophomore now.

"Gail, how come I don't have your underwear? Go into those drawers and get your underpants!" She opened her top drawer, fished around behind the sweaters, and plucked out her panties.

"Why aren't they in the hamper with the rest of the dirty clothes?" Polly queried.

"I don't know," Gail said. "They just aren't."

They just aren't. Polly seemed to take this for an answer from her when she never would have taken it from me.

"Look, I better call Mom and tell her you're going," I began, but Gail mocked me.

"Better call Mo-om," breaking the word in pieces, like a saltine.

"The guy's nineteen! He's three years older than I am!" I squawked.

"So who says you have to be the oldest thing around here? This guy is cool. Wait'll you meet him. He knows Mom, too. He hangs out at the store sometimes." The only guys who hung out at the store were dropouts. Polly collected them.

"Keep an eye on your sister," Gram always said. "Be vigilant. You can never tell what will happen."

She looked to me as the mother I hated to be. She told the truth to me, more or less. And whatever truth she told increasingly horrified me. She was blonde and sexual and loved danger. Personally, danger left me cold. I was endangered enough waiting for Ted to come home.

"That's him!" my sister squealed as she heard a muffled noise at the door.

"How could it be him? I didn't hear a car drive up." I still listened for my father's car in the driveway every night. I listened for how he drove, whether the turn was reckless and the brake was jammed on at the last minute, or whether it was a smooth, panther-like crawl, the turquoise Chrysler oiled with only a couple of beers. Late, later, after countless shots of whiskey with beer chasers, meant either rage at full force, or maybe only a dead sleep, or maybe a few slurred questions tucked around an insult and then the blackout. A couple of beers maybe meant OK, he'd get changed and go to relieve my mother, but it also meant fuller consciousness, questions, Where was my sister going? What was I doing?

My sister was unlocking the door and speaking to a figure in the dark she didn't ask into the light of the hallway. She left him standing outside in the cold while she ran for her coat and grabbed the keys to my mother's used pink Plymouth that was mysteriously harbored in the rivulet of our driveway. How had Polly gotten to work, anyway?

"You're taking Mom's car?" I was horrified.

"I told you, Molly, he likes cars. He loves to drive. He's a really great driver, too. We'll be back before they know it's missing."

"Put those car keys on the hook!" I hissed as she swung out the door. She knew I wouldn't tackle her on the front steps. She knew I'd be afraid of the nineteen-year-old boy. She knew I was confused and couldn't decide whether I was her mother or her sister, and she knew I wouldn't tell Polly because I was supposed to act like Polly. And somehow she also knew that my mother's car would be there for the taking. The Plymouth wheeled out of the driveway with the wild teenage daughter I couldn't control.

Ted reeled home, obedient to some unknown-to-me command from my mother that he pick her up at the store and bring her home. I said Gail was at her girlfriend's house. Just after he left, Gail came back with my mother's car, and there the two of us sat, watching *Adventures in Paradise*, when my parents drove up at 10:30. How had Polly gotten to work without a car, how did Gail know this, and how had my father so easily understood the arrangement? Nothing I kept an eye on stayed still; it vaporized. Yet I had to keep my eye on my sister, and especially on my father. If I took my eyes off him, he might kill me.

Ted, the luckiest man in Buffalo. *How can he be alive when he drives like that?* It had been about a year since I started trying to get him into Alcoholics Anonymous. I campaigned to my mother every morning in the car. We'd sit there freezing while the car warmed up, and I would beg her to leave him. "We'll be free, Ma! We'll never have to see him again!"

"There's plenty you don't understand, Mols."

"I understand this! We're in a hell hole!" The car was toasty as a parka by the time we got to Kenmore East Senior High.

"I'm picking you girls up for a fish fry tonight," Polly announced as I clambered out. "Flo said she'd relieve me at the store. Your father can drink himself up and us three'll go out to Ricky's where Ann Louise works."

"Us two," I said gleefully. "Gail's got horse lessons." My sister was in a baking group that sold brownies at lunchtime to get the money for horseback riding lessons. After a series of allergy shots she'd been allowed to ride.

"She's not getting that horse. We can't put gas in the cars, let alone get a horse. Well, tonight I guess it's you and me, Mols."

It would be just us. And the Formica tabletops and linoleum floors of the fish fry place. And the baked potato and the salad and me and Polly all alone, having dinner with no one to cook for and no one to clean up after and Ann Louise to serve us. Heaven on a plate.

"If you ever get pregnant like Judy with the boobs in La Grange, you come right to me—OK, Mols?"

"I'm not getting pregnant like Judy with the boobs, Polly!" I was indignant as we sat in the booth waiting for our fish while car headlights flashed outside in the cold dark beyond the big restaurant windows. "I don't even have a boyfriend!"

"But if you ever do, Mols."

"Will you drop this subject, Ma? We've got something more important to talk about."

"Oh?"

"Your husband. You have to leave him, Polly."

"You know nothing about this, Molly. Why, no one ever was divorced at La Grange!" My mother's eyes were wide and green.

"He's an alcoholic, you know. It says so in the *Buffalo Courier Express.* Walter Winchell's column gives you ten questions and if you answer yes to any five you're an alcoholic, and Ted has at least nine!"

"Oh, Molly, eat your fish."

"Your husband is an alcoholic, Polly."

"What'll we have for dessert?"

"Hot fudge sundaes!" The heat of the restaurant had steamed up the windows. Polly and I had coffee. I was allowed to drink it now. And the vanilla ice cream and steamy chocolate arrived underneath the whipped cream and maraschino cherry. Tomorrow was Saturday. Sleeping in. The week was over. I'd made it through only cooking four meals. Polly had rescued me. There we sat, our waitress, Ann Louise, beaming at us. "You girls joined the clean plate club!" she said.

"Hey thanks, Ann Louise, and I guess you'll see us on Monday for dinner, too." Ann Louise, Flo's sister, was Polly's second best friend. She was skinnier than Aunt Roberta, and, according to Polly, looked just like

Ava Gardner. Ann Louise had two kids, too. She'd been a waitress all her life. (*"And saved every nickel she ever earned,"* Polly would say enviously.) Both Ann Louise and my mother lit up Lark cigarettes from my mother's pack.

"Well it'll be good to see you again. Ricky will be cooking. That means you'll get extra-big portions!"

"Flo said she'd relieve me at the store so I can take Gail to the doctor," Polly said importantly.

"Is she sick?" both Ann Louise and I asked.

"I'm taking her"—Polly lowered her voice and continued—"to the gynecologist."

"No!" Ann Louise widened her eyes. I narrowed mine. It had to be something to do with those underpants.

"Gail's got something wrong up there."

"How do you know? Did she tell you?" Whose daughter was she, Polly's or mine?

"That's none of your business, Molly, keep your nose out of this."

On Sundays Peacock's Superette opened at noon, so the four of us had breakfast at home. Polly cooked. Ted was sober. Poopsie squawked and ate Rice Krispies. We all read parts of the *Buffalo Courier Express*. The ten questions that were in Walter Winchell's column were in the Sunday paper, too!

"Here, Dad," I said. My pulse popped in my wrist. If Polly wasn't doing it, I would. Whose job was whose, anyway? We weren't going to be helpless. "Listen, here are the ten questions that if you answer yes to any five you are an alcoholic." Our elbows were in the toast crumbs. The cups had little rings of cold coffee at the bottoms. "Come on, Dad, you could answer most of the questions yes." Ted looked at me the way he looked at Gram, fear in his eye.

"It says here that you should join Alcoholics Anonymous if you can answer yes to any five!"

"I'm not that bad!" Ted said.

My sister skittered away from the table, but to my surprise Polly stayed. After I rehearsed my plea again, and my father rehearsed his answer, she said, "You're hurting your father."

"Kids!" he said. "You have 'em and they turn on ya."

Not me, they weren't going to turn on me because I was never going to have them. I was going to get out. Soon this would be none of my business. I was going *to sail*.

14.

Neither Spindle nor I had been rushed by a sorority. Spindle became a creep, but I escaped creephood by being yearbook editor and by, as Polly put it as she sipped her instant Maxwell House and ate a peanut donut, "not being a sheep." I would have loved being a sheep, but instead I had Spindle, who looked up to me, actually, down, since she was way taller than I was, and she believed every word I said, just like a little sister, except that she was my own age. In fact, by the time I had reached my junior year, I hadn't saved a single real friend. All the phone calls and checking in to see if we had gotten our periods that charged my group of girlfriends in junior high were gone. The years of friends squealing on the couches of our living rooms were long over. I had no group but those artificial clubs institutionalized by the school. The main problem was: I could not invite anyone home, even Spindle. I especially could not ask her, to whom I had lied horribly and unconsciously.

"I hate my father," she said as we trudged through the ice of an unshoveled sidewalk, thrown shoulder to shoulder. "He drinks too much beer and he's mean. Mean to me and my brothers. He's not like *your* father. I know how much you like your father. I know how nice he is to you, Molly. You probably don't even understand how I could hate my father so much."

Absolutely stunned, I stammered, "I . . . I . . . can . . . sort of understand, Susie," then said, "I mean, my father isn't *that* nice."

"I know he like brings you presents and stuff, like when he comes back from business trips and everything."

BUSINESS TRIPS! Oh God, how much had I lied?

My mother dies. My sister is sent away. My father stops drinking, becomes an executive, and buys a penthouse apartment where I keep house for him, and wait in glorious solitude above downtown Buffalo—the traffic spinning below me, reading on our charcoal gray sectional couch surrounded by our shell pink walls—for him to come home.

How much had I actually told her? Carefully, I questioned her. When I referred to my mother and the store, Spindle nodded. At least I didn't tell her my mother was dead. When I mentioned my sister, Spindle talked about her sister. OK, sister here, not sent away. "I'm going home," I snuck into the conversation, "to Pilgrim Road."

"Where the hell do you live but on Pilgrim Road?" Spindle snorted. She was tired of this ridiculous conversation. She only thought my father was kind and didn't drink. Well, that was the main part of the fantasy anyway. Like urine spreading through the seat of my pants, the realization, fast, warm, embarrassing and untellable, spread through my consciousness: I had fantasized, and I had *told.* I couldn't distinguish reality from fantasy. I was crazy. I had lied. My father drank. He was mean to my mother. He was just like Spindle's father. I was just like Spindle. I was a creep, too. And I was crazy. At least Spindle told the truth. I was lying. There was no shell pink room.

Except the one inside me. Was I crazy? OK, I hadn't lied all that much. Only to Spindle. *God, don't see her anymore, avoid her. At all costs don't walk home from school with her again. Stay longer after school. Work on the yearbook, hide in the stairwell, do anything.* Now I would have no friends at all, not even a creep to hold in contempt.

The room inside me was empty. There was just that faint glow of pink in the air around the trees that means eventually, after two more months of mud and cold and disbelief it will ever come, there will be spring. With spring came my self-imposed deadline. I was going to be asked to the Junior Prom. I was going to get dressed up in something those sorority girls never thought of and I was going to go. And not alone, either. I was going to get someone to ask me. This was reality and I was going to face it. *No more fantasies, Molly. Forget the penthouse. Get going. It is February 19. The Junior Prom is in June. You have three months to get a boyfriend and keep him until the Junior Prom. So do it.*

Michael Groden was the smartest boy in my class. He had the kind of mind that snaps back like a brand new window shade. He had gotten perfect scores on both his Math and his Verbal PSAT's. No one in the history of the school had gotten perfect scores. Aside from doing the impossible, he was Jewish. Polly said Jewish men were nice and always took out the garbage, bought their wives diamond rings, and *did not drink.* I wasn't going to go after a fraternity boy. That was a lost cause. But not just anybody was taking me to the Prom. I didn't think I was very pretty, as my sister was, off in the wilds of junior high, but I was going after Mike Groden anyway. I was going after him and I was going to get him. I would focus on him as I focused on my fantasy, but he was real. And I was going to get him, because he was lonely. His loneliness was a force field around him. His hands jerked and shook when he answered questions in his nervously fierce intelligently shaking voice. I was going to set my hair, and put on makeup and reach out to him. And he was going to fall.

How glad I am that we are fallen. Fallen in the back seat, fallen on the high school lawn. We have fallen on the plastic seats of the couch in your basement. We have fallen on my living room floor. I have reached you. And I have brought you home. Polly was always at work now. Gail was always out. Ted stayed later and later at the bars. It was . . . a little bit safe . . . I was calculating. I was loved, so together we calculated . . . what would we do if my parents appeared? I did not tell him all the really terrible stuff. What was I, crazy? I couldn't even tell myself that terrible stuff! But in all the calculating I had not counted on falling myself.

Mike Groden, your shirts smell so good. When we dance my nose fits under your shoulder bone and I drink in the smell of Tide soap and skin underneath. Skin. I had one. He had one. We had borders to our bodies. *Oh, honey, I wear a black dress to the Prom and carry a rose instead of a corsage and you cooperate.* We were smart. I was not wearing pink carnations and a pink pouffy dress. I was an artiste. (An artiste of what it didn't occur to me to determine. An intellectuelle.)

Steady Mike Groden worked after school and bought a car. A car was my equivalent of Polly's diamond ring. He delivered me to my stream of dentist appointments. This was my equivalent of taking out the garbage. He carried a condom in his wallet, just in case.

Gail was off with the cheerleading squad. Ted was at his bar. Polly was at the store. Late spring. Mike Groden stood at the screen door on which I had posted a note: *Come in. Lock the screen door behind you. Then go to the kitchen table and find another note.* I heard him come in from where I was ensconced: in a bubble bath with nearly three times the recommended dose of bubble juice to achieve the right effect—covered in stiff whipped foam as in a *Playboy* photograph. Mike Groden in the kitchen read the next note instructing him to proceed to my room and take off all his clothes.

"Molly, are you here?"

"Yes, yes," I whispered, "I'm here in the bathroom, but don't come in here!" (He wouldn't have *dreamed* of coming in.)

"Where's your parents? Are we alone?"

"Yes, we're alone. They won't be home for hours. Do what the notes say!"

Take off all your clothes but your underpants, come to the bathroom.

And so he did. And so his eyes popped out of his sockets because there I was, naked in the tub.

"What if your parents come home?"

"Well, I don't think they will, but we'll have to listen for them and then run to my room."

"I'd better go get our clothes to have them ready just in case, Molly."

I knew he was right. What on earth had I been thinking of to trust fate so? When I'd looked in the full-length mirror on my closet door at my seventeen-year-old body trying on my swimsuit for the coming summer, I thought of the Empress Li Ching Chao who lay with her orchid boat open. *How ripe I am*, I thought. Ripe for what I wasn't exactly sure.

"Let's just wash each other first. All over. Then we'll get out together."

"OK," he said as I gave him the washcloth and the soap.

He was real. He was as real as my father, and as different from my father as he could be. When he touched my shoulders with the soapy cloth and proceeded down my breastbone and around each breast, I remembered Aunt Roberta. Twelve or thirteen years before, she gave me a bath one night. How extraordinarily lightly she swiped the cloth over my arms and legs. "Howie's always covered in scrapes and bruises and scabs from the rough way he plays," she said. "I wash him very lightly, so he doesn't hurt and so all the bruises can heal." I was astonished.

"Does he get *clean?*" I asked her.

"Clean enough." I thought you got clean only if you really scrubbed, and held my aunt suspect, but loved the sensuous treat of elaborate care and the safety of the big towel she wrapped around me before she led me off to bed and thoroughly undisturbed sleep. And here Mike was, so lightly easing the cloth down my belly and around what the Empress Li Ching Chao called my orchid boat . . . and here I was, trying to slide my soapy cloth around his back and down his spine toward his buttocks and to reach underneath to his balls and then to what Lawrence called his cock, and trying to do it gently, like Roberta did.

15.

Her oxblood Kotex landed in the waste can. Polly rose from the toilet, took another one from the box, fixed it into place by inserting one end into the back tab, then the other into the front tab of a little elastic belt that came with the box. She didn't believe in Tampax. "That dinky little thing? Why, it'll get *lost* up there!" Polly was naked except for the elastic and the menstrual pad. Her breasts pointed directly down to the belly which, when she sat back on the toilet, sat itself comfortably on her thighs, like a globe of the world in its special stand. Gail sat on the edge of the bathtub, trying to extort money for her cheerleading outfit. I leaned on the bathroom sink, looking into the mirror, holding my hair up, then back.

"I don't know, Gail," my mother said, accompanied by a loud stream of pee, "we've got to save money for Molly's college stuff. If your father doesn't drink it all up." Then she wiped herself and flushed and sauntered across the hall to the bedroom where she put on her extra-large white cotton underpants and cotton bra. "Come on, kids, get going or you won't get a ride to school! I've got to open up the store on time."

Pauline's door was usually open, and she shared the musk of adulthood, the tinny smell of monthly blood and Arpège.

"Look, Molsie, I gotta get your sister to school and open the store. Are you going to get dressed or what?"

I stood before her with half a head of rollers wearing her bathrobe, a royal blue tent with satin ribbing that Ted had presented with a flourish a couple of Christmases before. But Polly almost never wore it, preferring her nakedness, even in winter. My face felt stiff and blank as a plate. "I don't think I can do it, Mom, I just can't do everything, apply to colleges, I don't even know which ones, and get my schoolwork done . . ." I whined in a stiff white voice. *And leave you. I just can't leave you.* It was the voice of a plate, rigid and breaking.

"Well, everything always gets done . . ." Pauline began.

"No it doesn't!" the porcelain girl screamed. "I can't do it all!" *I can't take care of my sister and my father and go to school and apply to college and be the yearbook editor and have a boyfriend.*

"Look, Molly-ooch, you're gonna go to college, by hook or by crook." Polly watched my face. "Let's not have a nervous breakdown here. I'm going to take your sister to school and then I'm going to come back for you because I've got to get to the store or I'm going to lose business. The Pepsi truck gets there right when I open."

Polly was a mass of flesh and hair and polyester pants being pulled on and a turquoise blouse. Where were her eyes? Her dressing was a drawing of a shade. With the final donning of the blue smock that said "Peacock's Superette," she drew that shade completely. What was she thinking in there? Her eyes were searching my shiny, tearful blankness, yet her own matte blankness held no reflection at all. The side door slammed. It was Gail, getting into the car. The side door opened. Gailie yelped and came back for her books. Then they both hustled out together. The side door banged more gently, Polly pulling it shut. Then the farts of the pink Plymouth starting.

Get dressed, I said to myself. *Put in the rest of your rollers. Get out your makeup base. What have you got first period?* I was going to be late. Polly would have to write me a late note. Inside, I felt a tightening so strong, so sphincter-like, that I held my breath until suddenly there was a loosening so reckless I thought I would break into a thousand pieces from the force of it, or drown. I reeled to my bed with a roller in my hand. Sat down on the bed, held my sides, and rocked back and forth. I could not stop rocking myself and could not stop the tears that broke my face into something human.

"Help me!" I called out loud in the empty house. "Help me, please help me, please." A part of me was horrified to be calling out. It was like speaking up in class when the teacher hadn't said your name. *I'm going crazy,* I thought. *I'm going to need shock treatments like on* Dr. Kildare. To another part of me the cry sounded lovely, a litany of beseeching. It was a kind of praying I could only do in emptiness.

"You know that you can come to me if something gets very very bad, don't you?" my mother had said. But wasn't this very very bad right now? It must not be, or Polly wouldn't have said *if.* It must not be very, very bad yet. *Do your hair. Get dressed. Go to school. Decide on the colleges,* I said to myself. *Get the applications. Write the essays. Meet the yearbook deadline. Go to the dentist for your root canal. Make dinner for Dad. Slice up the vegetables. Cook the hamburger patties. Iron him a shirt. Tell Gail to do her homework. Write down all the details for the senior honors historical research paper. Make an appointment with Mike to drive to the University of Buffalo Rare Book Room.* I'd chosen option A, high honors.

"Please help me," I whispered aloud, then called, "Help me," then screamed, "HELP ME," words that ricocheted. Why not scream? No one could hear me. I rocked back and forth. *There IS something wrong with me,* I thought. *I'm not stable. They're all adults, my mother, my teachers, the college counselor, they must think that I can do this. There must be a way to do this, if this is what they're asking of me.*

I heard Polly's car roll up the driveway, but couldn't seem to move from the bed. I was still wearing her bathrobe and holding the roller in my fist. "Come on, Mol! Hop in the car!" she called from the kitchen.

I didn't answer, but with a force of will that surprised me stopped rocking.

"For crying out loud, Molly," Polly said as she barreled into my room. "My God, you're not even dressed." She stopped, horrified. "Why aren't you ready?" she said to my swollen face, a little tomato on a slender blue stem. "What's a matter, Molsie?"

"I can't go to school! I can't do everything!" I blurted out. "I've been crying and crying and I couldn't stop!"

"Listen," Pauline said, turning on her heel out of my room toward the bathroom and the medicine cabinet, "listen, the doctor gave your father something for times like this. Here!" she shouted from the bathroom. "I've got it!" Pauline returned to me, huddled in her blue bathrobe on the side of the unmade bed. "You look nice in that robe. Here, they're tranquilizers."

"Ma, are you kidding?"

"No, I'm sure they're all right. The doctor told your father that they were just for times like this."

"But they're for *Daddy!*" When he was maundering drunk, sometimes he, too, was unable to stop crying. Was I like him then? *I am not.* Was I that bad? Was this very, very bad?

"OK, take half of one. Half. Here. Open up the capsule. See? Empty half of it out on a piece of paper, then take the other half." Pauline handed me the capsule.

I held it in my free hand. My other hand still clutched the roller. "I'm going to wait awhile," I said, as if sleep logged. "See how I feel. I'm not sure yet."

"All right, Mols. I'll write you a note for a whole day off school. Take the tranquilizer if it gets really bad. The Pepsi guy is waiting for me, I've got to go."

"OK, Ma, I'll call you later."

After she left, I put the hair roller into the pocket of the robe and went to the living room to watch the morning shows. During the first one I tossed the pill back and forth gently between my hands. Then all at once I put it in my father's ashtray. *I'm not like him, and I'm not taking his pills.*

The programs rolled on till noon. Then I turned them off and went into the kitchen, still full of breakfast dishes. A small pan and bread and butter and Velveeta cheese. A slice of baked ham and a slice of tomato. I grilled a sandwich, poured myself a ginger ale, and ate looking at the comics in the morning paper. Then I trailed to the bathroom.

Think. Think. You've got to write the application essays. You've got to make the deadlines. You've got to. Polly was blank about the choices. "Don't they help you with that in high school?" she had asked. "What does that college counsellor do, anyway?" *But should I go? Should I leave you? What about Gail? What will Gail do alone? She's going to be all alone with him!*

You have to go, a reedy voice said inside me. *To get out of this house. Out of Buffalo.* And I was going, I had my hand on the bathroom door to prance out with my head held up, then remembered I hadn't showered. I coaxed myself into the shower.

Hair lank and wet, the rollers forgotten till the next day, I lay on my unmade bed. The chenille bedspread, wool blankets, and faded pink sheets were messy, furry, and soft; I masturbated, dressed, and began to read a novel, not for school. I was all alone. No one could ask anything of me. I was sick today, mentally ill just for today. The panic had lifted so thoroughly I thought it would never be back. I'd had my call answered, my prayer. I'd caught my breath. Of course I was going to college, I would find some way to choose one and apply. Polly was right. Everything was going to get done.

"Hi, Ma," I said after the eighteenth or nineteenth ring. (Polly didn't answer when she was cashing out a customer.)

"Didja take it?" my mother asked.

"Take what?"

"The tranquilizer."

"Nah."

"So you must be better."

"Yeah."

"There's steak in the meat compartment of the fridge for dinner," she said.

"Yeah, I know, I found it."

"Molsie, everything's going to get done."

"Yeah, I guess it will."

"I've got a customer."

"Well, 'bye."

"See you later!" She hung up the phone. In the blankness of hanging up the heavy receiver I pictured her wiping her hands on her smock before she started ringing up the groceries.

A skinny gray house with white gingerbread, Victorian remnant surrounded by parking lots: bookshelves built in every room. The Saturday after my breakdown Mike and I drove all the way to Rochester to forage in used bookstores. This place was my favorite because of the slenderness of the house and, inside, the willowy cases with their thin, thin books. I had four authors in my hand: Issa, Buson, Basho, and Shiki, the haiku masters. Each book, with its motif of bamboo or chrysanthemums, had a three-line poem perched on its pages, like a series of frogs on small flat rectangular white stones. Holy pages. I bought them all with the money I had, and afterward we went and had French fries and held hands in Rochester where we knew no one and could pretend it was Paris.

ii.

T H E

P O E T R Y

W 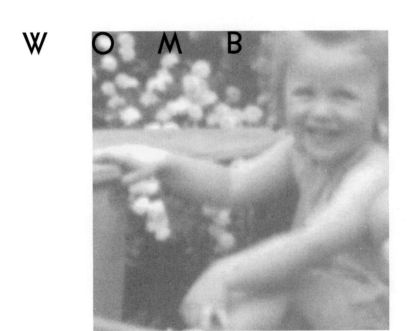 O M B

16.

When I stood in the linen line in the basement of
my dormitory on a Sunday night, I discovered the most important fact
about college: sheets. My suitemates, Maggie and Lily, two sophomores
who had adopted me, grumbled about having to stand on line for them,
but I loved it the way I loved standing on line in the dining hall. To be
served food I never had to cook myself by pleasant dumpy ladies with la-
dles, then, each Sunday night, to be the recipient of angelic wrappings,
clean linens that I had not washed, or struggled to fold, or left in the
dryer to become a wrinkled, itchy mess felt like heaven. The Sheet Angel
was a benign, doughy lady in a flowered housedress who looked as
though she went right home and made peanut butter cookies for her
grandchildren.

I had stepped into a pop-up book full of scenes where parent-figures
made decisions behind closed doors to keep the children from their
adult worries, of children's secrets that grown-ups miraculously knew
about and pretended to ignore, affably watching from behind the newspapers they read on their davenports, or just out of eyesight on the
wraparound porch, drinking their iced tea. Even the plain, lowest-bid
construction of the State University of New York seemed to have the
charm of a book, down to the cul-de-sac suite at the end of the hall I'd
lucked into: three tiny rooms off a tiny common area that my suitemate

Lily had commandeered. All that fit in these cells were our single beds and desks. Maggie Mack barely had room for her cello, and Lily Allisman barely had room for her famous behind. We each had a medieval slit of a window, and the little common area had no window at all. Like living in an appendix to the great intestine of the state university dormitory system, it was happily, uselessly cut off. There we each lived our secret lives, Maggie doing little but practicing the cello, Lily doing everything—on the phone day and night with anti-war efforts and assignments for the campus paper not to mention the assignments for her double major, Education and Sociology—and me eating and laughing and having time to dress myself, doing my work lazily and steadily. I had come to college to retire.

Maggie Mack was tall and big boned. Her large blonde head rested on square shoulders. Her wide hands easily gripped the neck of her instrument, and her square, flat-bellied body wrapped neatly around the torso of the cello. Two tiny blue eyes sometimes blazed from her ruddy face, though often they were hooded with concentration. Lily Allisman was delicate as a sprite, with brown curls and brown eyes in her pip of a face. A shock of white hair sprouted at her forehead, just like my mother's. Lily's slender arms, slender shoulders, small breasts and slight upper torso perched on a large pouf of a derriere. Crudely nicknamed "All-ass-man," she looked like a wood nymph with a permanently attached toadstool to sit on. Only a few sophomores had been dumped with extra freshmen; Maggie and Lily seemed to take it as a badge of honor. Now they, from sophisticated downstate, had an upstate pet to train, though I was nearly untrainable. I even got up routinely for breakfast, and went to all my classes. Sized in between them, with my wispy brown hair and long legs, they sandwiched me into their lives.

When Maggie's practicing and Lily's volunteers cluttered our common area, I packed up for the library. In the library was a poetry room.

No one was ever there. All the books were thin and all the poems perched like black islands on white pond pages. The saggy old couch let you sit on it for hours before the door squeaked open and someone else came in. I always slipped out then. For the poetry requirement, I'd signed up for a course with a real poet, and now I was required to write a poem myself. I figured out it would be six stanzas: two for Polly and Ted and Gail and me in Buffalo, two for us all in Tonawanda in the new house while Polly was at the store, and two for me now. I carried the poem with me. I got the first two stanzas fine, and felt a kind of horror and relief when I got down the next two. There were four lines to each stanza, one for each member of our family.

But now I was at the end, and I couldn't get it. Maggie and Lily were in it, and Mike who called every Saturday night from Dartmouth, and the Sheet Angels, and the mashed potatoes in the dining hall, and the very couch I was sitting on, writing the last two stanzas. It was all too much!

The poetry room was like a chapel. The couch was like the altar. I'd looked in the mirror that morning and seen my face smiling. For a moment it seemed like a mask, yet I knew I was real; the smile was for nothing in particular except that I was not at home. But Gail was home. I had abandoned her for college as surely as Polly had abandoned us for the store. How selfish could I be? The stain of selfishness spread through me to my fingers, which lazily moved the pen. I could not get the happy ending of the poem. Who was I? I was nothing but wrong to leave them all. I didn't deserve to be in this poetry room. Perhaps I didn't deserve to live. Maybe I should just die. I saw the bare tree on the windy hill in my mind. I would hang there. *Get realistic, you jerk*, I said to myself. *It will have to be pills.* I could always go to the Snack Bar and cop enough pills to do me in. Tiny pills, like wild strawberries in my palm. There! I would put the strawberries in the end. I'd have Lily and Maggie and me eating strawberries in the cafeteria, just the way I'd started the poem in the kitchen in Buffalo. I was making art, the well-wrought urn I'd heard so much about in class.

In the late fall I took the bus to Rochester, changed for the bus to Albany, changed for the bus to Rutland, Vermont, and changed for the bus to Hanover, New Hampshire, thirteen hours. There was only one place in the vicinity of Dartmouth College to lose your virginity, a run-down clapboard inn with space heaters and crinkly plastic shower curtains and brown toilet paper. Mike and I had to hitchhike there. He was small and dark and thin and Jewish, like a dense little cat's-eye marble in a basket of tennis balls that were the Dartmouth boys—thick-necked, blond, and beery. He hated it. The senior confidence we'd both wallowed in had disappeared. We were frightened freshmen now. But he'd gotten the condoms and I'd gotten my bus ticket. I knew that I was supposed to be transferring my orgasm from my clitoris to my vagina, like Freud said, but I also knew it wasn't happening, so I was probably defective. I was going to have to make the best of it.

Exhausted from the four buses, I got my first migraine, and lay on the worn bedspread with a cold washcloth on my forehead while Mike periodically came over and held my hand.

"Let's take a shower," he coaxed. "Here we are, away from everybody."

"OK, but listen, are we going into town afterwards?"

"Well yeah, we have to. There's no food here, and I saved up to take you out to dinner."

"Oh, Mike!" I screeched irrelevantly, the washcloth falling over my eye as I rose, reeling from the migraine. "What am I going to do about my hair!"

"Your hair's fine."

"But it won't be if we take a shower! I'd have to curl it and wait for it to dry!"

"Nah, you'll look fine."

"No I won't!" I stormed from the tiny, breathless hurricane inside my head. "I'll look terrible!"

He turned on the shower. "It's nice and warm," he called, coming into the room and standing next to me. I reached up and he reached down and we held each other on the bed as the sound of the water lulled us. We kissed and moved against one another with our clothes on, and he unbuttoned my blouse and I unbuttoned his shirt and we moved off the bed and stood. Knowing he'd never get the back undone, I unhooked my bra. We stood in our pants and looked, even though we had seen each other before, and I wished my nipples were pointed and hard. And then we tried to take each other's jeans off, and began to laugh when we wiggled out of them, but this was serious. We walked naked toward the shower. *Remember every minute!* I admonished myself. *Oh God, my hair!* I broke for my suitcase, grabbed my pink shower cap, and squashed it on my head. "OK I'm ready!" I said, and we slid into the now lukewarm shower.

"I guess we let it run too long," Mike said.

But we washed each other until the water was cold as an outdoor pool and the sky outside deepened toward sunset. Finally we turned off the nozzles and got the skimpy towels and half dried ourselves before we rushed to the bed and threw ourselves under the covers where Mike fumbled with the condom. The rubber and tinfoil together smelled like bug repellent. My nipples had hardened and so had his penis, though I had barely touched it. It rose of another volition. I'd tossed the shower cap on the floor—at least I had my own hair on. Our pubic hair, straight when dry, had curled with moisture. We were ready to have Mike lie on

top of me, and so he knelt on the bed—we'd thrown off the covers by
then—and solemnly he peeled on the condom. "How did you learn to
do that!" I exclaimed.

"They tell you on the package."

"Oh." He was ready, and he lay down on me and was strangely heavy,
even though I'd opened my legs. After a while he found the entrance and
moved his penis inside me. I thought, *We're doing it!* and tried to move my
hips and groan and whisper a little, in a fake way, knowing I should.
Then we synchronized just as we did when we walked down the street,
left legs out, then right legs out, in unison. Only now the unison was a
core of us, like a pear. I lost myself for a moment in a picture of a green
pear, and then Mike stopped moving.

"I came," he said. "Did you?"

"Women aren't supposed to the first time," I whispered definitively.

At first Polly had mailed me wacky packages: a whole cartonful
of Welsh's Fudge Bars, another of sardines in mustard sauce. But then the
packages stopped coming. Hadn't I thanked her enough? God, I was
selfish. Hadn't I written and thanked her? Is that why they stopped? A
pile of letters from my sister lay trapped under a paperweight on the corner of my desk, whimpering to be answered. Gail said it was bad. I
really was selfish. Something must be happening to stop the packages.
How bad was it back there? Was it very bad yet?

Soon I had hardly any news at all, not even the letters from Gail
saying how awful it was at home without me, but I did get the note
from the Financial Aid Office. Polly and Ted had neglected to fill out
the financial aid forms for my sophomore year. "We filled them out
once, wasn't that enough?" my mother said when I finally called home.
"Can't you do something about it there?" I floundered into the Financial
Aid Office and found from the avuncular officer that I was eligible for

scholarships I hadn't known about. The college would pull me behind its veil.

The dormitory bathroom with its row of toilets and sinks offered holy privacy late on Saturday nights. There I stood, luxuriously washing my face all alone, waiting for Mike to make his weekly call, pretending that a phone date was just as good as one in person, when Maggie and Lily burst in.

"Amy is packing," they whispered at me. "Amy is leaving the school right now."

"Right *now*? It's one o'clock in the morning!"

"Amy's getting married. Gary's going to marry her," said Lily, adjusting her corduroy bell bottoms.

"Amy's in trouble," Maggie whispered, her eyes widening.

"Amy's pregnant," said Lily, the realist.

"Leaving school forever, you mean, permanently?" I asked in astonishment.

"Well you can't live in a dorm with a husband and a baby, Molly," Lily said in exasperation.

"Is she"—I hesitated—"is she thinking about . . . ?"

Maggie finished my sentence for me: "Not having it? Getting . . ." Now Maggie hesitated.

"An abortion?" I said for her.

"Absolutely not!" Lily declared. "He wants to marry her! They want the baby."

I thought of Agnes on welfare, the one Gram dragged me to see so long ago, standing over her ironing board with her baby in a laundry basket. But unlike Agnes, Amy was so pretty, her thinness so chic, and now she would be ruined by Gary Wexler, himself so hip, so lithe. His body would not change, but hers would. *I would rather die*, I thought, no, I *would* die, my spirit so squashed that it would bleed from me, and then I might try to take my own life. I remembered Sylvia Plath, sticking her head in an oven while her two babies slept in the next room. *Those babies*, I thought. Later when I learned of Gary Wexler's suicide, I took it as a confirmation. A spirit so crushed could not have gone on, I reasoned. A cloud over the couple had released its poison vapor. He had hanged himself with a belt from a rafter of the converted barn on the commune where he and Amy were living with the baby and Gary's teenage brother. It was his brother, the runaway, who had crept up the stairs to find him.

My selfishness, which had become a self-attention, and sometimes a kind of self-respect, had begun to harden around me like a scab. But beneath the crust I was wounded and could easily imagine killing myself, just to feel free of my burdens. I knew I really was not the same as Gary Wexler, yet something in me was afraid of becoming him. What was happening at home now that I was gone? Was it really bad? *It must have been bad for Gary*, I thought briefly, then turned my thoughts to the living room on Pilgrim Road. How did Amy feel about having a baby, living with her parents, now? How bad would it have to be before you *never* wanted to feel again?

Mike, holed up at Dartmouth with a fearful look in his eyes that never seemed to leave them through my next two visits, and his visit to me, seemed to have a secret panel in his voice that refused to open, although he dutifully dialed me every weekend. Nothing could remove the Plexiglass wall I felt between us, as if we were having prison visitations. I couldn't *reach* him. Or he couldn't reach through the glass to me.

Boys brushed against me in the cafeteria line, in the bookstore, and Maggie and Lily urged me to come to the dances, and I went, and danced with the boys who ate in the dining hall and slumped in their chairs in my classes. Like ground water that ebbs in hot summer, Polly, Gail, and Mike seeped away. I abandoned the dry well, stashing my sister's unanswered letters in my underwear drawer, skipping the Sunday calls home.

But I did call Mike and, after three consecutive tries, finally managed to break up with him the cowardly way, long distance.

"But, Molly, it's almost summer!" he choked out in our last conversation. "We almost got through it!"

"I can't," I rattled, "I can't, I can't."

Spying disdainfully out our window at a panty raid a few weeks later, Lily interrogated me, "So what are you using?"

"What do you mean?"

"For birth control, dummy."

"Well, Mike used condoms."

"But now you don't *have* Mike!" she said exasperatedly. "And you can never tell." Amy and Gary had unnerved Lily as much as they unnerved me. Every morning she ceremoniously clicked the dial on her birth control pills, popping a pink one into her rosebud mouth as the three of us left for breakfast. I was a good influence on them, they'd decided. All of us ate breakfast together now and sometimes even Maggie went to classes, that is, when she didn't have an extra studio with the cellist-in-residence. More and more she disappeared with the wild-browed maestro.

At Lily's insistence, in preparation for the squads of boyfriends whom she supposed were poised to descend, I made an appointment with the local gynecologist who looked like a grizzled sheep with granny glasses. The disc of pills he prescribed for me was different from Lily's; it dispensed white and blue in a twenty-eight-day sequence. The quarter grades came out, and I was fine, and my scholarship secure. The literary magazine wanted me, and my petition to take Independent Study in creative writing was granted. Everything rolled in sequence for me, and for Lily, but Maggie had two Incompletes.

"What are you still doing here on this campus?" Lily demanded of her. *"Why* aren't you going to music school where you belong?"

Maggie looked up in protest. "But I love studying with Piotr!" He was the maestro. She called him by his first name now. Her lessons had doubled.

"But what if you want to be a professional musician?" Lily persisted. "Why are you hanging around at a liberal arts school?" Maggie had hung around high school in the same way until her college counselor telephoned to the Admissions Office and filled in the application for her after the deadline for everybody else.

"I'm playing my cello, All-ass-man," Maggie said, "and I'm going to finish my Incompletes next quarter and play in Aspen this summer. So get off my back."

Lily was continually on everyone's back. The literal pain in the ass, Maggie called her. She was just like Gram. Had Lily not been busy planning anti-war rallies with military zeal, she could have *been* in the military, a wood nymph in mufti. But Maggie with her cello was like a great boulder in the middle of Lily's stream of organizing. Lily simply had to part and rush around her. I knew why I fit in with them so well. I loved Maggie's single-mindedness and her art; I loved Lily's life by the book and her zealous organization. They let me go my own way through their examples, even if Maggie was vaguer and more aimless in the rest of her life than I could ever be, and even if Lily exhausted me with the direness of her taking charge. We shared our meals, our makeup, our movie passes, and our gym lockers. We'd combined our lives, the three girls at the end of the hall.

Lily was Papa Bear, and I was Baby Bear, and now Maggie would really be Mama Bear, because she had never bothered to make the appointment with the sheep-faced doctor. She finally told Lily and me over the cafeteria pot roast one Sunday night that she was three weeks late with her period.

"I'm surprised you even keep track," Lily said.

"Even *I* keep count for *that*, All-ass," Maggie said.

"Oh, Maggie, you've got to get to the gynecologist!" I cried.

Of the three of us, only Lily had a car, her father's cast-off battered gray Lincoln. Two days later, after Lily made the appointment, we took Maggie for the pregnancy test.

"Are you telling Mr. Spiderbrow?" Lily demanded the next week when Maggie hung in the doorway in her nightgown, whispering the positive results. "Are you telling him? And if you're telling him, are you having it?" Piotr the spikey-browed cellist was married.

This time I yelped for Maggie. "Lily, come on, give her time to decide!" I knew, though, that Maggie never decided anything except what piece to practice next. She was wholly focused on that wooden mother's shape, the cello.

"You haven't got much time. You're almost eight weeks pregnant!" Lily's voice rose.

"I don't know . . . I don't know . . . ," Maggie whimpered, then put her jeans on over her pajama bottoms and, without combing her tousled hair, padded out to the Film Society with us.

"I'm not telling him," Maggie whispered to us in the dark as the credits to *The Seventh Seal* rolled. "I'm not telling him."

"Well, at least you decided that," I said softly.

"But what are you going to doooo?" Lily wailed.

"Shut up!" both Maggie and I hissed.

Lily lowered her voice. "If you're going to want, if you're going to need . . . If I've got to get the phone number . . ."

"Maybe." Maggie said "maybe" as if it were a statement. "Maybe get the phone number, Lil."

The next day Lily cruised the Snack Bar for phone numbers. And the day after that I went from table to table in the cafeteria asking for contributions. It was like collecting for the United Way in the suburbs.

Brown sooty apartment building on the West Side. Down to the basement, as to a bomb shelter. A kind of blitz in progress. The blitz of men with our lives in their hands in a legislature far away. Who was the man in shirtsleeves who ushered us with hissed whispers into the suite of basement offices painted an unsterile-looking green? He was disgusted that there were three of us. He wanted one patient and one driver only. It *was* like a war. We were the resistance who showed up despite crossed wires. Why was he doing this? Why was he risking his license? Or had he lost it already? Was he a doctor at all? All the time I thought of him as a possible butcher, but he was also a savior. Lily and I knew he had to be a real doctor because of the way he ordered us around. "I don't have a nurse here! I can't! You, here, wash your hands, then hold these." Lily washed her hands in a little sink and held the kidney-shaped aluminum bowls.

Pregnant Maggie was led to another room I couldn't see into very far. Lily followed behind to hand the doctor the bowls. I stayed in the outer room, which was an examining room with a little sink where Lily washed her hands. In a moment the doctor appeared at the door telling Lily to sit down. "You, make yourself useful!" he said to me. "Take these and wash them out in the sink." He held two kidney-shaped pans full of blood. I only saw blood in them, no bits of anything like a fetus before I turned my head away. "Go sit down," he whispered with sudden sympathy. "I'll do it."

And so he performed a perfect abortion and saved Maggie's life in a basement suite, rescuing our friend who made the mistake we could have made, might still make, as the war went on, winter after winter. He had done a neat job, taking $500 in cash in 1967, and the three of us turned loose onto the streets where, in a strange elation, we drove to the Village to wander among the jewelry shops on this, my first trip to New York.

In our flowered dresses we searched among the storefronts for what we all wanted to buy: filigreed rings that opened up, Lucretia Borgia–style, to reveal a secret compartment. When we found them, we forked over $20 apiece, and then drove in Lily's rust-finned Lincoln north of the city, up into Dutchess County, to Maggie's parents' blue-shingled nineteenth-century house where Maggie and I spent a safe weekend, after our day of espionage, though Lily's duties weren't done. She sped on to Troy where her mother lay, an invalid, in the turreted town house where Lily grew up with her beloved, incompetent father, older sister, and half brother. What was left of the Allisman lumber fortune had been spent on Yale and Wellesley tuitions for them, while Lily was dispatched with a few bucks to a state school. Her dad had moved in with his rich mistress, and Lily had organized a sibling council with her sister and brother, the agenda to scare up caretakers for their mom.

Maggie's only weekend duty was to pretend that nothing had happened, and mine was preventing the family dog from scarfing up her bloody sanitary napkins from the wicker garbage basket in the bathroom and revealing all to her four sisters, one of whom at least would surely tell Mr. or Mrs. Mack, who spent the weekend on two parallel chaise longues with a wine bottle on a glass table in between.

17.

But it was Maggie who told. She told Piotr the wild-browed married cellist, after all. And with the telling she came face-to-face with her talent. The maestro got her a late, post-deadline audition at Julliard, and when she was accepted, she left her Incompletes unfinished, went home for the summer, and transferred to Julliard for the next fall. Everything had changed. When Lily and I came back to school, we had to give up our little cul-de-sac for a regular dorm room. So the campus paper and the literary magazine were helped to run from our buzzing headquarters, the lonelier without Maggie, though she arranged to take the bus up many weekends, and Lily drove more often to New York, where her cousin's family had an apartment. We loved staying there when we visited Maggie. It was vast and empty, kept almost as a crash pad for a family that came to the city once or twice a year. Like our dormitory suite, the Upper East Side apartment in its white brick door-man building was like a big book with blank pages, bound on one side by the distant authority of the richer branch of the Allismans. Now I had a place to go, because I couldn't go home.

"He was standing at the Marshes' fence, Molly, and then he was running like a quarterback, like he had a football under his arm!" my sister shouted on the phone from Flo's house. Polly's best friends, Flo and Ann Louise, had bought a house together after Ann Louise got divorced.

"Where did he run to?" I asked incredulously.

"He ran straight at the pool!" In a fit of energy a few years before Ted had put up an above ground swimming pool with metal sides, wasting half of our backyard. Nobody swam in it, just as nobody had skated on the ice pond Ted had carefully made a few winters before on Saturday mornings, when he was the most sober.

"Then he crashed into the pool, Mol, headfirst!"

"Oh my God, did he knock himself out?"

"Molly, no, he did it again! He did it lots of times! He just bashed his head at the pool, drunk as a skunk, till he was bleeding and everything. Then Mom was afraid he'd come after us."

That was when Polly packed a bag and hustled Gail into the Plymouth and headed for Flo's.

"Is Mom there?" I asked Gail. "Can Mom talk?" From my darkened dorm room I pictured Polly with *her* head bashed in, too.

"Are you OK?" I asked breathlessly when Polly's cigarette hoarse voice came over the line.

"Yes, Molly," she said. "Your father . . . your father's got a concussion and we're staying with Flo and Ann Louise for a while."

Then Flo got on the phone. "Your mother called the police, Molly," she said matter of factly. "They hauled your father to Mercy Hospital. But he's out now. He's staying with your grandparents."

I heard a commotion in the background. Gail's excited wail and my mother's low-pitched cautionary syllables. According to Flo my father's car was going past the house. Gail grabbed the phone from her.

"Molly, he's going around the block again and again, screeching his brakes when he gets to us! Flo's calling the police if he doesn't stop! Wait, they're making me get off the phone so they can call the cops, Mol. We'll call ya back." Gail hung up. I pictured Ted rubbing his butted head, tears streaming down his beerswollen face, stumbling back to the Marshes' fence, zigzagging his way toward the pool, then pictured him holding his concussed head in the Emergency Room. I imagined Flo and Gail and Polly and Ann Louise gawking out the living room window at Ted's Chrysler prowling, then screeching. A fear seeped into me like gas beneath a locked door. No matter how many locks I put on the door that I had shut against them, the gas streamed in. I coughed and coughed till I calmed down and reached for a cigarette. To Lily's dismay, I had started smoking. Larks. Polly's brand. I got my pajamas on and went to bed and smoked, uncensored, in the dark since Lily was out. But Gail didn't call back.

Oh, Dad, did you take your tranquilizers? Everything had become really, really bad. *If you had stayed, they wouldn't be like this,* I thought guiltily.

When the call didn't come the next night, or the next, I didn't call Flo's house. I didn't call Gram's. I floated through my classes and drank chocolate milk shakes in the Snack Bar.

"That's your third milk shake in three days!" Lily observed.

"Yeah," I said.

"Want to go to New York this weekend?"

I had a big paper to write. "Nope," I said.

"You're quite a conversationalist these days," Lily said. "What's wrong?"

"Nothing. I have this paper to do."

Lily left for the weekend and the sanctuary apartment high above the city, and I stayed home. I wrote the paper in the poetry room, though it was a history paper. Then I ate double mashed potatoes for dinner, alone in the dining hall. After the Film Society I went alone to the Snack Bar and had another chocolate milk shake with vanilla ice cream. By Sunday morning I called Flo. My mother and sister had reunited with my father who was all better and everybody was back on Pilgrim Road. "Just like nothing happened!" Flo exclaimed.

Just like nothing happened. *It was nothing,* I said to myself. Yet that night after Lily came back, full of chat about Maggie's performance and moving to New York for the summer because none of the Allisman cousins would be using the apartment, I still floated. Not flesh anymore, I was made of the poison gas that had infiltrated the room I had tried to lock against them. I'd only opened the door for mashed potatoes and milk shakes and movies to be sent in and closed it quick before the gas could come. But it seeped in anyway. *It was your fault,* I said to myself. *You were the one who left home.* Lily buzzed like a honeybee from suitcase to closet to telephone to desk to telephone while I tried to read Thucydides. Just after midnight she sat down on her bed. "Hey, you made the bed for me!" she said. She'd finally noticed.

"Yeah."

Suddenly she leapt from her bed and came over to mine, sitting down next to me, angling her tiny bell flower of a head around to look me directly in the face. "Molly, you look like you have the flu."

"I'm fine," I said.

She put her thin arm around my back and rested her tendril hand on my other shoulder. "Oh, Mol, I wish you'd tell me what's wrong."

Her touch was as light as the touch of a sweet pea vine, and as tenacious. My back, stiff as a wire fence, returned to flesh, and I began to cry. When I could speak, I said, "I'm sorry!" But Lily still held on to my shoulder, so I said, "It's all my fault!"

"What is, Molly, what is all your fault?"

"Everything!"

"Molly, do you think you can say more than that?" Then the story of Ted came up to my lips, but stopped. "It's my parents," I said. "They're fighting and my sister's there, and it's awful." I couldn't speak the details. Instead, an idea came to me. "Oh, Lily, I can't go home this summer, and I don't know where to go!"

"But I've got the apartment!" she said gleefully. "You can live with me!"

When I dragged myself home during spring vacation to assess the damage, suddenly Polly was filing separation papers, and Gail was threatening to run away. Polly had begged her to stay in school, just to finish the year, because they were moving out. She was really doing it, divorcing Ted. My father was still in the house, though. The divorce was like a secret from him. I learned all I learned in the garage-like storeroom of Peacock's Superette. It was dank as a cellar, even though it was above ground.

"Daddy and I are getting separated. But first I've got to sell the store. Then sell the house. And find a job. And a new place to live."

"I'll testify!" I said stoutly. "I'll take your side in court!"

"You won't have to do that, Molly. It's filing papers with a lawyer. It's paperwork, like taxes." She was forty-eight years old and leaving Ted after twenty years and selling the store. Polly had not looked for a job since she was twenty-six, working at Bell Aircraft during World War II. Though she had run her own business, she had none of the low-level office skills entry-level jobs required.

"Where's Gail going to go to school?"

"Wherever I get a place to live."

"But where are you looking?"

"Near Flo."

"But don't you want me to come to court or anything? I can come back from school and go with you! Don't you want me to look at the apartments?"

"You don't have to, Molsie. You finish school. I'll take care of things here."

"Are you sure?" She had needed me for everything before, but now the rotten store and our house would be sold, and just Gail would live with our mother and it would be everything I had wanted but not in time for me to have it. Gail would have it.

"Then I might not come home for the summer, Ma," I said.

"We'll see," Polly said, her voice rising from low in the belly of the blue grocer's jacket.

"My roommate has a free apartment in New York for the summer. My faculty advisor said he would help me get a job."

Polly's face had a kind of unmoved knowing about it.

"Can't you just stay home and work?" She spoke from her throat, in a growl-like cry.

"I can live free in my roommate's cousins' apartment they keep just for when they're in New York, except they're never in New York, so I can live there." Polly was silent.

"They're rich," I continued, "that's why they never use it. But Lily has the apartment this summer. So I can live there, too."

"Can't you work in Buffalo," Polly blurted out, "like you did last year?"

I was silent so long I felt I was in an outdoor place of silence, like the garden at La Grange. No customers came in. Peacock's had been losing customers to the supermarket down the boulevard. Her question hung in the air like a barn swallow, swooped, and was gone.

"I'm going to come and visit, later on, Mom," I said softly, "if I have the money, when you get your new apartment and stuff. Then I'll try and come up from New York."

Gail's promise to stay in school lasted as long as it took me to ride the Greyhound bus back to finish my semester. She surfaced at the home of an old teacher of hers, who invited her to stay until the school year was finished. She stayed to take a high school equivalency, but disappeared again. Polly wound up with work on an orthopedic floor of a big city hospital, filling out the doctors' orders at the desk. She'd gotten herself a job helping to heal broken bones. I didn't have the money to go back to Buffalo to see her that summer, and I couldn't have asked her for any. When we talked on the phone she was worn out and full of fear about the debts that had to be paid from the sale of the store. She wondered if she could even afford an apartment, maybe she should just move in with Flo and Ann Louise—they had offered—but she thought if she had an apartment of her own, then Gail would want to come home. "It's a good thing you've got your scholarships," Polly said.

"Hey, both you and your mom are looking for jobs at the same time!" Lily said when she showed me the friendlier-sized *Village Voice*. I'd ridden with her to New York, thinking I'd have the job that my faculty advisor arranged, though he hadn't really arranged it, and after I recovered from the stunned fact that I, too, was without a job in a terrifying city, I became even more overwhelmed from reading the Help Wanted ads in the *New York Times*. But the *Voice* had an ad for an East Village au pair girl. I was the fifth to call but the only one to show up at the 8:30 A.M. sharp interview with the parents, a bead and incense seller and his wife, an actress. After they hired me to baby-sit their two little boys, I bought a piece of orange and purple psychedelic cotton and made a short, sleeveless dress by hand which I wore like a uniform. Every day I strolled the children past the drug dealers and the opened hydrants pouring water into the streets of the East Village. In the evenings I took the bus to the air-conditioned apartment on the Upper East Side and worried why my period hadn't come, even though I had made a visit to a gynecologist and had a disc of pills.

I must be pregnant, I thought. But how could I have made a mistake? I had taken every last pill in the baby blue rotary dial—on time, every morning. Maybe the pill hadn't worked. The boy I thought had made me pregnant had gone into the Peace Corps. Every day I practiced being a mother, and every night I worried I would become one.

For my birthday Lily wanted to take me for a ride on the Staten Island Ferry. She made tuna fish sandwiches on whole wheat bread. We rode the Ferry back and forth twice. The wind blew. I had tied a scarf around my head, à la *Glamour* magazine. The water was blue, the Statue of Liberty was green, lower Manhattan was grayish, greenish, blue.

"How did you tie that scarf around your head like that?" Lily asked. "You always know how to do these things so well." She was so kind, and so pleasantly cool against the heat of the city, far away from her committees and campus campaigns. With the solicitude of a student nurse she asked me, in a tone she must also have used at her mother's bedside, "Have you written any more poems?" It was what Grandma Ruth had asked me in her letters.

"I'm working on one." It was a poem about the boy far away and me in New York on my twentieth birthday, the last day of June 1967. I knew I could not take care of a baby. I did not want to leave college. I did not even want to baby-sit in Tompkins Square Park. I wanted only to eat tuna fish on the Staten Island Ferry as a friend helped me know who I was. The wind whipped the scarf around my head, and it whipped her curls across her face. "If my period doesn't come, I'll have to have an abortion," I said loudly into the wind.

"Well, let's hope it comes," she said, cupping her hands over my ear, " 'cause I don't want to take you to that doctor." As a belated birthday present I woke in a hand-sized circle of blood.

Chicken legs were 69 cents a pound in the D'Agostino's on Second Avenue and 74th Street. I wore my specially knotted scarf around my homemade minidress. Nestled in my underpants was the string from a Tampax. I pushed my cart among the blondes in beige linen with pearls and sandals throwing filet mignons and salad greens into their carts. A girl, also blonde, but a shaggier, dirtier blonde, came up the aisle toward me. She was barefooted. She wore a black spangled flapper dress and ropes of jet beads and carried a khaki duffel bag. "Hey, Mol," she burbled, "it's me, I ran away!"

Gail had borrowed bus money to come to New York. She had gotten a job at the candy counter at the Fillmore East, just a block from where I picked up the two boys I baby-sat. Into the mild murmur of the Upper East Side supermarket, she spoke in a loud gravelly voice, even louder when she said, "And believe me, we don't just sell M & M's! It's the best candy counter in the Village!" She winked one bright eye, just like a macaw.

Ran away? On borrowed bus money? Here? I ushered her out of the D'Agostino's, where our doorman had told her to find me, not daring to look around me at the checkout counter, the burn of embarrassment increasing as I approached our doorman again, of whom I was very frightened. I was sure I would be tossed out of the apartment I had no real right to live in anyway, bringing up a barefooted girl in an antique dress to the nineteenth floor. We entered the sparsely furnished Allisman place, with its odd blend of gold-rimmed china, but crummy stainless-steel cutlery, and Egyptian cotton, deep-blue towels, but ratty bedspreads.

"Hey, you live here? Cool! But it's too far uptown. I like it downtown, Mol," Gail said. I was quiet. I more than anything did not want her to ask to crash in the apartment I barely had a claim to. "Hey, Mol," she continued, "Gram could've worn this dress! Isn't it cool?" She did look cool. "I can't stay long," she said. "I've got to be at Max's Kansas City! All these great people are there, Viva, and everybody. Wanna come? I left Buffalo, girl, Leslie Fiedler helped me. And now I'm at the Fillmore."

"But Mom said you left two months ago!" Had it taken her two months to hitchhike from Buffalo to New York?

"Girl, it was an ape-fuck, no kidding. I went to California, Molsie. Hey, I'm going to introduce you as my little sister. I'm going to bring you to Max's and maybe Andy Warhol will be there with Viva and I'll say, *Here's my little sister!*"

I looked down at my feet. A panic began rising in me, a kind of toxic carbonation, almost fizzing through my limbs and up my neck into my head. "I'm really tired, Gail, I might . . ." I trailed off, ". . . have to come another night."

"Yeah? Well, whenever you want, baby sister! Hey, I'm never wearing shoes again! I'm gonna let big huge calluses grow on my feet and I won't feel anything through them. People weren't meant to wear shoes! Are you sure you don't want to come to Max's? It's really cool there. We can sit with Viva!"

I looked down at my homemade electric purple and orange dress. It was out of place in the D'Agostino's, but it would be even more out of place at Max's Kansas City. It really was a kind of nerdy psychedelic dress. "I'm tired. I just got my period. I thought I was pregnant," I began to confess.

"Me too!" she crowed. "Only I had to pay to get out of mine. I had to pay high, Molsie." She stopped. "Hey, you got any tea or coffee or caffeine thing?" She followed me out to the kitchen where I put the teapot on to boil. "I called Mom from San Francisco," she said, "and I asked her for five hundred dollars, and you know what the bitch said?"

She was calling Polly a bitch. Calling our mother a bitch. "She told me no. She wouldn't help me."

How alone Gail must have felt out there. How alone Polly must have felt, going to her new job at 6:30 A.M. and looking for an apartment at night. When she had the apartment, she hoped Gail would come home. Would I tell her where Gail was?

"So what did you *do?*" I asked. My eyes must have been round as coat buttons. Gail had had to have an abortion. And I had not. She asked *our mother* for the money. Why not the boy?

"Bill and Dan paid for it."

"*Two* of them?"

"Yeah, and Cassie and Belinda took me there and stayed with me. I was fine. The doctor had those bung-out eyes, like a frog. They called him The Gardener. But I'm all right. That *cunt*, she could have sent me the money. Hey, Molly, I need a few bucks now. You got any money? This is a really nice apartment."

She called Polly a *cunt*. Had I ever heard the word I'd only read in D. H. Lawrence spoken out loud? Oh, yes, I heard it in my father's voice. Ted calling Polly a cunt. You cunt. Bitch. It was Ted speaking through Gail's lips, like a mass of something, bruise-colored, growing. . . . He was coming out of her mouth, like pus.

"Well, yeah, I . . . I have the grocery money. Fifteen dollars. Here."

"Hey, thanks, well, I'll pay you back when I have it."

I was going to have to borrow bus money from Lily. It was all I had until they paid me the day after tomorrow. There were enough groceries till then, unless Gail stayed.

"I gotta go to Max's. Sure you don't wanna come? Somebody'll pay for your dinner. I always get someone to pay for mine."

"No, really, I'm just going to stay home."

"OK, I'll call ya, or maybe I'll come up here and visit ya in the next coupla days. I gotta work at the candy counter the next coupla nights. We got some great shit down there if ya want any. I can cop for ya."

"Great," I said. No way on earth was I buying drugs at the Fillmore East. My sister and my father never got caught at anything. But I would. I'd look up and the room would be empty and all I'd see would be the veiny yellow eyes of a policeman.

Then she hopped out to the elevator and was gone. When I told Lily later, I realized I didn't even get a phone number from her, let alone an address. Of course, I hadn't wanted them. The little blue vein that had pulsed wildly at her temple was now pulsing wildly in mine. *I should be taking care of her. . . .*

18.

In the two years since I had broken up with Mike, I had fallen into four sexual dalliances, a bout with mononucleosis, and twenty or thirty head colds. Now in the spring of my junior year, I procrastinated in the corner room Lily had managed to commandeer, hunching up my shoulders to see how my hair would look longer, obliterating for whole ripe moments the job of four papers due.

"You need a break, Molly. You need to get out," Lily said when she bustled in. The sought-after corner room had its own bathroom. We moseyed toward the mirror over the toilet to put our makeup on. It seemed that Lily wanted to fix me up with a graduate student section advisor whose name was Jonathan Stewart Mull. *John Stewart Mull.* Immediately the mnemonic song from Phil 101 pinged through my brain,

John Stuart Mill
John Stuart Mill
Oh, what a pill
That John Stuart Mill!

I had a birth control pill in my hand. I hadn't had sex in three entire months. Still, I ate the pill.

"He wants to take you to dinner," Lily went on, waving her mascara wand.

"Dinner?" In 1968 on that campus, no one was taken out to dinner.

You were taken to the boy's apartment to sit on the floor, and after you smoked hash and listened to Ravi Shankar, you crawled onto a mattress with a paisley bedspread underneath a Peter Max poster and tried to have sex.

"He's a *graduate* student, Molly," she admonished me. "He's sophisticated. He's from *Manhattan*."

"What does he look like? Is he smart?"

"Of course he's smart, he's a graduate student!"

"So what does he look like?"

"Molly, one thing you've got to promise me," she began, then was joined by another voice. It was Maggie at the door with a duffel bag and her cello. "Promise *us!*" They laughed. Lily and Maggie had met Jonathan in New York. He was a pal of Maggie's new boyfriend, our new young music professor. The maestro had abandoned his classes for a world tour, and this young pianist, unmarried and with two small, neat eyebrows, was his emergency replacement.

"I'm not making any promises till I know what he looks like."

"Promise us you won't drop this guy, Molly, he's too nice, he's too sweet, he really needs a girlfriend," Maggie said.

They loved him. He had driven Maggie and her cello up from New York. Then he had run errands for Lily and the campus paper. In the Snack Bar he put their food on his tray and carried it all to the exclusive graduate student side and sat down and invited them to sit down, too.

"You're not telling me the thing I need to know."

"He's cute, Molly, really, he's nice-looking," Lily said.

"But."

"But what?" they wailed.

"I don't know, but you're not telling me something."

"All right, he's a little heavy," Maggie said.

"He's a little overweight," Lily concurred, "but he's adorable. Really. See? Here he is in the newspaper." She unfolded the local paper and pointed to an ad for new hot water heaters. There was a bearish looking man with black curls above and a mustache below dark almond-shaped eyes. The dressing gown he wore gave him an Edwardian air. The smile was Russian prince. "He's like Sebastian Cabot!" Maggie chimed, referring to the portly, sophisticated TV actor, who was also a chess-playing intellectual, connoisseur, and gourmand.

By the time I agreed to a date with Jonathan Stewart Mull, I was scared and alone. Rather than face a summer in New York again, I had chosen to spend it as a dorm counselor staying on campus, watching over my freshmen charges and taking a course or two I didn't really need for credit. Lily was graduating and off to get her Master's degree in Education, a shock to me and Maggie, since we were sure she'd try to get a newspaper job. "It's time to get practical!" she had announced. Maggie was still at Juilliard, but playing at Aspen for the summer.

Now in a restaurant with Jonathan Stewart Mull, I was being asked if I would like a drink. He wore a jacket and tie. I wore my only silk blouse. I didn't have the slightest idea of what I wanted to drink. "Well," I said slowly, "why don't you order something for both of us?"

"We'll have two Cinzanos on the rocks, each with a twist, please," he said easily to the waitress in his light, firm, pleasantly knowing voice. I didn't know what a Cinzano was. His voice had slipped around me like an arm around the waist of a satin party dress. I felt as if I were wearing such a dress. It was as if we had been left there by parents supervising us from afar, parents who wanted us to have *advantages*. I liked the dinner very much.

I liked having the hock of his arm around me in the front seat of his used car. He was both hip and genteel in his tweed jacket. He huffed benignly at the wheel as he invited me home with him, to a house on the widest street in the upstate river town. He had asked his roommate to remove himself for the evening. His roommate had been obliging. First we sat on his couch. Then we repaired to his bedroom.

We took off our own clothes, mostly, since he was so big that I couldn't get his shirt off after I unbuttoned it. His undershirt sported grease stripes, like jail bars. He had washed the undershirt, but it had not dried sufficiently, and so he had put it in the oven, though he had forgotten about the oven racks. The shirt had brownish prison stripes of casserole remnants on it. Jonathan made light of it. He wore his mistakes as lightly as he wore his tweed jacket and as suavely as he ordered the vermouth. I said it was fine. He took off the shirt. I was in my bra. He looked like the Buddha, with a great roll of fatty spirit around him, inset with an enormous navel. I had never felt so small. Thumbelina-like, I pirouetted in my bra. We took off my skirt. I left him to his pants. They were enormous, and black. Without them he stood naked as a bison.

We lay down together, but we did not make love. Instead we had a kind of nude pajama party under his duvet. I had never seen a duvet before. Even his bed was cosmopolitan. He was Jewish, he told me. Mull was modified from Mullinsky. Stewart from Stein. Jonathan was really Jacob. Jacob Stein Mullinsky. Jake Mullinsky. He was a completely different person than he appeared to be. He had gone to private school. He had already spent years in psychoanalysis and he was only twenty-three. Since we'd been talking more intimately than we'd been touching, I ventured the premature question, did he ever think about having children? Oh my God, that was too far off even to consider, he said. *Very good*, I thought. If you hadn't even thought about it, then you couldn't very much want them. And if sex also seemed distant and diffuse, then you really couldn't want to produce them, could you?

Shortly after our date, Jonathan began calling every day, and one afternoon asked if I would iron his shirt. Ironing was beyond him, he said. The maid had tried to teach him, but he hadn't gotten the hang of it. "Certainly," I said, ignoring the disgust I felt at having to do it. "Bring it over to the dorm." After I took out the floor's starch-infested iron, I slid the shirt onto the ironing board. It was bigger than any of my father's, but it wasn't a workshirt, of course—it was a buttondown blue oxford. When I spritzed it with water, it fell off the board in a heap. I grabbed it up and repositioned it, though it skidded across the starchy board and fell again. Finally I grabbed a sleeve and let the rest of it dangle on the floor. Each swipe of the iron made another crease, and another, and another. The collar was scalloped with creases, the front placket askew, the back yoke bunched, the seams around the pockets puckered.

"I'm not very good at this," I said, handing him the shirt, drooping off a wire hanger. "My mother made me iron my father's shirts." Jonathan looked down in amazement. The shirt bore the same resemblance to a freshly ironed buttondown that a plastic hamburger on a museum pedestal bore to one off the grill. "It looks like a pop sculpture," he said in appalled wonder.

"Really," I warbled, "I hate ironing," then addly lamely, "I wish I had done a better job."

"Well, why didn't you tell me you hated it?" he asked legitimately. "I guess we'll just have to send our laundry out."

Our laundry? Later that night Jonathan suggested we live together for the summer, to try things out. "Oh yes!" I said to the man who would send our laundry out to be magically cleaned and pressed—and paid for. It was just like getting the sheets every week in the dorm! When I thought of our tentative, sibling-like sex, I thought to myself, *You can't have everything*. Then we called Polly and Gail in their new apartment to tell them we were moving in together. My sister was actually finishing high school, and my mother had sold the store and the house. They both listened, Gail on the extension, and my mother groaned, "Well, Molly, it's OK with me, but . . ." She fell silent.

"But what, Ma?"

"But just don't get *involved*." To her, it seemed possible to live with someone and stay uninvolved.

"OK," I said.

A year later Jonathan and I were married in a homemade wedding in the house of graduate student friends of ours. My college advisor gave me away, and the faculty poet read Ezra Pound, and Polly drove down from Buffalo and Gail took the bus from New York where she was working at the Fillmore again. Grandma Ruth and Grandpa Gillie were too frail to come. I refused to invite my father, who had moved to Florida. "I'm not going to meet your father?" Jonathan asked.

"My father would ruin this wedding, Jonathan," was all I said. But if Ted didn't come, neither would Gram or Grandpa Peacock. My family had shrunk to my mother and sister. It was Lily and Maggie who helped buy the gallons of fresh shrimp and fussed over my daring crimson velvet gown.

Like creatures lost in the woods, Jonathan and I depended on and watched out for one another. How grateful I was not to be alone! Jonathan was as big as a door that fit snugly into its frame. When I dreamed that poison gas was seeping round the doorframe and woke up panicked, I saw him in bed and reminded myself how airtight he could make life be. And so his presence began to shield my fear, and I in turn gave him my attention, which he craved. We grew like hermit crabs into each other's comfy shells. He enjoyed dispelling fear for me, and I enjoyed his ease, his humor, his confidence that things were usually all right, after all, what could go wrong? Everything in Jonathan's manner denied any knowledge of ugly family behavior. To me he was a home, a womb, and like my mother he didn't have a clue as to who I was, only Jonathan had more of a reason: I hardly talked about my childhood.

Why should I? I had a nice job doing student counseling at the university and a nice husband who drove me to work in our new car. I would work, and Jonathan would get his Ph.D. And then it would be my turn to write poetry, but I wasn't writing any poetry now. I was learning to cook nice meals and watching the Watergate hearings and Mary Tyler Moore. I was falling asleep on the couch after dinner, after work, then getting up groggy and going to bed to read Agatha Christie. And Jonathan was there across the room sleeping with the TV on and there across the bed reading Dick Francis mysteries. Weekends of our first year of marriage were dreamy, full of friends' houses and moderate dope smoking and flirting with Jonathan's graduate student pals. If I possessed feelings I stored them with my poetry books. It was aesthetics, epistemology, ethics we talked. And at work it was students' feelings. And at parties it was the feelings of know-it-all graduate students.

On Saturday mornings Maggie, who drove up for weekends with her music professor, sometimes went out with me for breakfast. We ate at Perkins Pancake House, discussed our disdain for Lily's ordinary career choice, and dissected our dreams. One night I dreamt about a strange pet, a cat with a purple plume on her head and a monkey tail. This pet had special complex caretaking instructions to insure its survival, and I'd failed to take care of it. Racked with guilt from my neglect, I found the animal dying, maybe already dead, and I woke in a panic.

"I'm probably going crazy," I said matter-of-factly to Maggie, slurping my maple syrup.

"You should have more sex," she said.

Jonathan and I had sex on Fridays.

"You know, I'm wrecking my hormones on birth control pills. I feel like such a cow. I'm practically mooing from bovine bloat!"

"So why not get rid of them?" she asked.

Why not? It was 1973. The consciousness-raising group I'd joined was reading *Our Bodies, Ourselves*. In a cold conference room one weekend some women had demonstrated the use of a plastic speculum so that we all could learn to look inside ourselves and see what was there. One of them, whose name I never learned, got up on a freezing conference table, slipped off her slacks and underpants, and inserted the speculum into her vagina. "This isn't easy for me to do," she hissed at us, "so come up here quickly and take a look." All the women in the room, maybe forty of us, lined up and gawked.

Fascinated, I bought a disposable plastic speculum from one of the women in my consciousness-raising group who had volunteered to go to the local medical supply house and get them.

"You're *buying* one of those?" Maggie was disgusted.

"Why not? I want to look!" And Jonathan did, too. We got a flashlight and looked inside me, after the trial of getting the stiff plastic speculum in. Neither of us had ever looked at me like this, straight on. I had never seen a porn magazine or a split beaver photo, never read a description of a woman in that position. There I was. We saw where the hair stopped and the folds began. We started laughing we were so nervous and then I was embarrassed and wanted the speculum out. Jonathan still held the hand mirror and the flashlight in one hand, so he began to unhinge the speculum with the other. But it was stuck completely open, like a dislocated crocodile jaw.

"Maybe I should get out a wheelbarrow and wheel you to the emergency room!" He laughed.

"It's not funny!"

"Stop crying, Molly, crying isn't going to do anything."

"This thing isn't stuck up you, it's stuck up me!"

"Try not to wail. I'm getting it, I'm trying not to break it or I'll scratch you."

"This was a terrible idea! Maggie was right!"

When I relaxed, he slipped the thing out, no harm done.

In fact, it amazed me that simply seeing my sex made it possible to take charge of myself. In a newfound spirit of feminism, I was off to see the gynecologist, requesting a fitting for a diaphragm. Soon I had my shell-pink half globe to fit inside my magenta insides, a cap to don, a physical barrier against the sperm, so specific and unmysterious. Sex with these diaphragms was planned, intentional, and sexier because of the acknowledgment. I liked the silkiness of the creams, the wetness of the jellies, the pure practical physicality of the act of inserting the springy pink circle and checking my cervix, like a nose pressed against the diaphragm's screen. I was in charge of protection, of reproduction; it was my responsibility, my joy.

The diaphragm became a kind of pet: to be fed and cared for, to be kept clean and refitted and replaced. The lavender plastic case bobbed along in the company of my wallet, my checkbook, address book, calendar, Kleenexes, makeup, pens, and the balled-up bits of tissue that littered the inside of my purse. I cleaned out my handbag countless times, devising pitiful new ways to organize it, but always there was the plastic diaphragm case and in a separate pink plastic bag, the spermicidal jelly. Why didn't I leave it at home in the bathroom or by the bed? As if it were alive, I gave it my constant attention.

And now by our third anniversary Mrs. Molly Mull—young wife with an interesting job, flair for conversation, moderate sex life, and great fear of feeling—had put an end to the eccentric, emotional, poetry-writing Molly Peacock. She was not going to be like Anne Sexton whom she had met at a drunken party before Sexton committed suicide. Or like John Berryman, whose tobacco-stained vampire fingers jittered at a podium in a lecture hall where she had gone to hear him before *he* committed suicide. Molly Mull, intent on leading a normal life, had calmly chloroformed the poet she was. Now, instead of writing two poems a month, she came down with something. Two years' worth of illness equaled eleven sore throats, seven hacking coughs, fifteen head colds, two flus, three bouts each of tracheitis and bronchitis, nine allergy alerts, and four sinus infections. When Mr. Mull finally asked to be released from nursing duty, she had to let him go visit the friends they'd been supposed to visit together. . . .

———

Alone I sniffled in my ratty nightgown. I ate my soup alone. I let the dirty tissues pile up on the couch where I dozed in front of the TV, feeling I'd entered a blessed state of empty-all-around-me that I hadn't felt since the poetry room. Like a cat in blankets I slept all Saturday night on the couch and on Sunday woke up with a poem in my head. It swam there like a goldfish. Without thinking I grabbed Jonathan's yellow legal pad and wrote it down. Happiness spread through me like water or light, elemental. That night, showered and dressed, I read it to the relaxed, returned Jonathan, who was so delighted I was actually alarmed.

I wrote another poem the next weekend, and the next, and the next, until I was doing it all the time. I sniffled and wrote, I hacked and wrote. At pencil length Ted got drunk, Polly abandoned us, Gail took drugs. Reality crafted into artifice made it all safe. Poetry had become a fetus in the womb of recall. Jonathan was very impressed by my cautious attempts to publish them.

I could give birth to a poem, but I did not want to give birth to a child. Babies were real. All that was monstrous and unpredictable and demanding would be released with the birth of real children. But that was OK, because even by the time we'd been married three whole years, we didn't want them.

"You'll change your minds." Gram announced.

"Well, you have lots of time," Polly said.

"You can have them later, Molly!" Flo declared. "Now get more education!"

Jonathan tired of graduate school and thought of doing something "real." "I want a regular life," he said. Did this secretly mean children? I secretly knew I wanted an irregular life, the life of an explorer, far away from the motherhood and the family I was terrified to replicate. Polly, Ted, and Gail already bulged inside me, leaving me without my own outline because their very being had stretched me into something lumpy and mis-shapen. And with every poem I wrote, I grew more afraid that I was going crazy. Jonathan, meanwhile, was growing more and more frighteningly normal, now bringing home a paycheck from his new job. Just short of his Ph.D., he'd fled his department for a job at a foundation. Now he gave away money during the day, and at night we shopped for another new car.

But slowly my ambition, amphibian-like, climbed out of the muck of my fear. I began to want to be a writer more than anything, to want to be who I would be. When I had published five poems—and when we had been married five years—I was listed as a poet in a national directory, and this put me on a mailing list for art colonies. But the minute I got the idea to apply to one, I began to feel pains in my ear, the very place my gills would have been, had I actually been a creature who could live in two elements. No doctor could find anything wrong with me, yet by the time I tore open my acceptance letter, one whole side of my face had paralyzed from Bell's palsy.

From my paralysis I watched Jonathan, intent on changing. He began a diet, and grew as ambitious about how he wanted to look as I'd grown about being a writer. Daily he transformed, becoming less and less of himself, the man I married. With palsy medication, I went to the art colony, and Jonathan continued at Weight Watchers. The private tailor he'd found to make his outsize pants was about to lose his best customer. By the time I got home, Jonathan's metamorphosis was shocking—my big Hansel had become small, and was getting smaller, just as my Gretel's need for him was diminishing, and probably his need for me. Where had he gone?

Our need to wrap ourselves in the cocoon of our sibling marriage had peeled away with each poem I wrote and each pound he lost. We really were going to be butterflies, if we could just make our way out. Jonathan already had his wings.

"I can't seem to fix the way I feel," I whined to him.

"So get somebody to help you, Mol. See a therapist." There was

Jonathan, fixing himself by losing weight. Why did I need help? Didn't I do everything by myself?

In a kind of dream state I called the office of the campus psychotherapist, Ruta Arbeiter, a woman I'd often observed in campus meetings. She had short black hair curved to her head and a tiny waist that made her hips look ampler than they were. In her office I saw again that she possessed a reactive face: her eyes brightened, her mouth widened, her eyebrows rose in response to my words—an ideal reader. She was the soft-lipped mother I needed, though I would have disclaimed that I needed one, since I already had a mother, and my mother and I were completely alike, and I didn't have a father, oh well, I mean I had one, but I wasn't anything like him, and he didn't matter, I didn't take after him in any way, my sister, now she was just like my father, and I was just like my mother, that's the way it was in our family, no there isn't anything about me that's from my father, I'm completely my mother's girl, I'm good, I'm responsible, I'm wondering if it's bad enough yet to leave Jonathan, because, really, my marriage isn't bad, not the way my mother had to leave my father, I mean, he was going to kill her, and Jonathan wasn't killing me, it was just that I'd tried to kill something in me that had woken up instead. . . . It was a complete shock to me when I looked up and announced, "I want to leave my husband."

Jonathan and I had helped each other emerge into what we could barely admit we were: a thin energetic man, and a seriously ambitious woman. The pudgy Hansel and the vague Gretel fell from us like carapaces. Polly had led me astray with her axiom that people never change. They do, all the time. Intently we both applied to graduate schools in cities half a continent away from each other, and when we were both accepted we had to face the fact that we were going, literally, our separate ways. We didn't recognize each other, or at least I did not recognize Jonathan, and I barely recognized me. The crumbs we had dropped on our journey were unnecessary. We weren't going back.

19.

Little Ruthie the attendants called my grandmother in the nursing home when they braided her hair and tied little ribbons around it. She was their pet. Hard of hearing all her life, she turned stone deaf in the home, and then blind, too. When I would visit, she gripped my hand as if she knew me by vibration. Sweet tempered, she let attendants prop her in a wheelchair in a pink housecoat Polly provided, while at the opposite end of the same nursing home in another wheelchair sat my grandfather, tears continually streaming as he gave my mother imaginary sets of orders for stock at La Grange Garage. Meanwhile, Jonathan and I were drawing up separation papers, and I was waiting to hear if I'd gotten into graduate school at Johns Hopkins. When Grandpa Gillie died, Polly instructed me not to bother to come to the funeral, and I obeyed. "Don't come," Polly said swiftly and clearly. *This death belongs to me,* she seemed to say. Just after Gillie died, Aunt Roberta was diagnosed with stomach cancer. She, too, was dead within months. "You don't have to come here, Mols," Polly said, warding me off with the fierce flatness of her voice. Ragged and fearful, I stayed where I was.

But when I heard her "Don't bother!" on the phone after she told me my grandmother had died, I disobeyed. Ruth had belonged to me, too. Gradually I had tucked benevolent pieces of her inside me, like drying flowers inside the leaves of books, forgetting them until they fell out in my hand as I turned a page. Curiously I was not sad or lonely at her death, because she had taken the time to cut herself into pieces and tuck them here and there in the continuance of my life. Leaving the Baltimore rowhouse apartment I'd recently moved into, I climbed in my car and drove furiously north to the funeral, getting there in time to read a poem and greet Ruth's friends, most of them my mother's age, daughters of the quilters and embroiderers and gardeners and Bible readers who were her pals.

Before I could think or feel too much, I was driving back to Baltimore to catch up on my first semester. The student I called to get the lowdown on the graduate seminars I missed was Sean, the lanky, opinioned Irish American poet I sat next to in class. He smelled of apples and wool. I'd watched his long, spidery fingers pass a fountain pen over his notebook to produce the curliqued script the priests taught him. More and more I desired to be that paper the long hands caressed in their urge to produce meaning. Perhaps I could be what he meant. Ridiculous. Sean Byrne was far too young—twenty-two years old, the age of the students I had counseled in the job I left to come to graduate school.

He met me at Helen's, a Fell's Point bar, where we were served by the bartender, Helen herself, who, I thought, looked like Lilian Hellman. He sat his high, round rear end on the leather stool and spoke to me in his cultivated bit of a burr, though he'd grown up in Wisconsin. He was wonderfully fake, as full of artifice as his poems which, he told me, surely would be ranked with Yeats. With a wicked memory for detail, Sean recounted the seminars over a coke. He didn't drink. Nothing, he'd decided, would come between him and his page, certainly not the Irish virus. When he took a break in the evenings from writing—and every poet should, he felt—he did it according to his rules: one coke, never dessert, nondairy vegetarian dinner. And he had other rules: no cars, they clutter up your life with going places. No smoking. I wondered if one of the rules was no sex, as I sat drinking a Virgin Irish Coffee. God, it was cold in there. A Chesapeake chill had settled on the city. My mind wandered to Ruth in her best blue dress in her coffin, cold, and Jonathan out in Chicago in the public policy program he'd decided to attend, the wind cold on him, then the damp chill of Baltimore. *I must be getting sick.* I shivered.

"Cold?" Sean asked.

"No, I'm fine."

Far away in freezing Buffalo, Polly in her thin hospital smock wrote doctors' orders. I thought of her bare feet in her loafers long ago. . . . And Gail had suddenly taken to writing one- or two-word notes with no return address on postcards of snowy Catskill outposts like Bearsville and Woodstock—*Hi!* surrounded by a heart, or *Hi Molly!,* nothing else. Ted, too, had sent a letter that made me shiver, though the postmark was Florida. He'd gotten married to a wonderful woman, he said. But another letter a few weeks later said it didn't work out. I coldly determined not to answer either of them.

I rubbed my hands up and down my shoulders at Helen's bar, and spent more of my fellowship money on another Virgin Irish Coffee.

"I wish I had my sweater," I said, then felt what seemed like every cell in my body collapse when Sean threw his long arm around me, as if I were his favorite Irish setter. I nearly whimpered, dog-like, as I looked up from my notes.

Brilliant cloth rolls off a bolt . . . only to reach patches so threadbare that the bolt can't be used. That's how my life was unrolling, I thought, in patches—some whole, some worn right through. *Make something out of the bright swathes,* I thought. *Let the thin spots roll past. Let me make a piece of my life right here, starting in this bar with a man who orders a coke instead of a beer.* Could a life be made from piecework, like my grandmother's coverlets Polly had given away? First she had cleared out the store at La Grange, selling off car parts and groceries, then she scourged the house, dragging to the dump drawersful of old dress patterns and piles of fabric triangles, squares, and tiny octagons Ruth had cut for quilt reserves.

Polly had a horror of redheads like Sean, even though her favorite grandmother had flaming red hair, domesticated in braids. "I checked your head daily, Molly, to see if you'd come out a redhead. Thank God you didn't!" Bringing a redhead into the house was like opening an umbrella indoors. "We're the black Irish, Molly," she said to me always, "fair skin and dark hair, the darker the better. I wish my hair was so black it was blue, like Elizabeth Taylor's."

I had light brown hair—where did that fit in? I wondered as I drove my flame-headed boyfriend of one month, three shopping bags of Christmas ornaments, and a fresh turkey up from Baltimore through the icy Poconos, along the frosted Susquehanna, then, north and west through the hills, past the vineyards, into the apple and dairy country of La Grange, where black and white cows mooed in the snowfields and fruit tree branches were delicately inscribed with snow. Sean no longer objected to cars, as long as they belonged to other people. In the trunk we carted a Christmas tree, a long-needled pine so conical in shape, so plump at the bottom and sides, so slender at the tip top that it could be situated at any angle in any room and decorated with the hammered tin angel ornament I found for its crown. The windows of the house at La Grange Garage were already steamy with interior heat as we drove up in the dusk and began to unpack the car.

"We're going to make a wonderful Christmas!" I announced to Polly. "This is Sean!" Polly blanched at the red hair sneaking out from the tweed poet's cap he affected. "And Gail and her boyfriend, Ed, are coming tomorrow, and Howie, too." I had called them several times, coordinating arrangements. We were going to have a real Christmas, us, the next generation, at La Grange.

"I'm not going out into that snow and help you unload, kids," my mother announced. "I'll just hold the door." She was wearing a pair of sweatpants and one of my dead grandfather's flannel shirts. Behind her, the dining room looked beautiful, the newly refinished sideboard and china cabinet gleaming. But bare. There were no poinsettias or Christmas cactus.

"Christmas city," Polly said dryly as the bags of ornaments and holiday flotsam came by. The Christmas ornaments were part of my booty from the divorce, as was the temperamental car I was driving. Sean lankily, sexily, innocently introduced himself to my mother and handed her the fancy dates and figs and apricots I bought for him to give her. "Well, thank you," she said. "You know I haven't got any money and I said no presents. I haven't got any presents for you kids."

For years she had been declaring no presents. And for years she had not bought a single one. She meant it. She wasn't giving a goddamned thing to anybody, and didn't want a goddamned thing *from* anybody. But I couldn't believe it. Maybe she had gotten me a little something. I was thirty-one years old, but I craved a gift from my mother as if I were ten. Just as Polly saw me with thick black hair when my head was covered in fine fieldmouse down, I could not accept that she wanted no part of birthdays and holidays. She sent both Gail and me a card. That was all, and all, she said, we could ever expect. She was husbandless, motherless, fatherless, sisterless, dollarless, and she intended to be holidayless, too, whether I wanted to make Christmas or not.

Of course I had pulled out my credit card and gotten presents for everyone, including my sister, who was on welfare, and the mysterious Ed, and my cousin Howie, Aunt Roberta's surviving son, who was probably more solvent than any of us but was so paralyzed with indecision he couldn't decide what to get for himself let alone for anyone else. I had bought a braided rug for my mother, and an electric broom to clean it with. It wasn't a personal present; it was really for all of us, something to put a little warmth under our feet.

Warmth in our hearts was an entirely different matter. Polly still had two days left to go out and buy something, I thought—maybe she would relent and get me a private little gift she could press into my palm when no one was looking.

"I see those packages, Molly-ooch," she said, using an old nickname for me, "and I don't have any packages for anybody. That's it."

By this time Sean had leaned the Christmas tree against the wall in the tiny living room and had begun looking around the gerrymandered house that connected to the garage. Gillie had built the place with just a dirt foundation and no running water. I showed Sean where the pump was, and how he could pump water to fill a bucket to flush the toilet, and how he could wash in the morning—in the narrow kitchen which led to the garage. The toilet had been fairly recent, lodged in an old closet. But everything that got washed—bodies, dishes, laundry—had to get scrubbed in tubs in the kitchen. Christmas dinner, a production under any circumstances, would have a nineteenth-century cast to it because of the slop bucket continually being emptied and the water continually being pumped. The sheer physical outlay of it was housework raised to a power of three, like doing dishes and pressing weights in between loads. Little Ruthie had had great biceps.

Electricity we did have: a bare bulb operated by a long string hung in each room, though the living room had outlets and lamps. The floors were linoleum. The white-curtained windows went all the way to the floor and the white woodwork gleamed. On each deep sill were geraniums that had bloomed year round in Ruth's day and cactus that bloomed in January. The windows were positioned for the best possible light, and the daylight washed fancifully printed wallpaper in a happy bath.

There were oak chairs and an oak rocker. There was an upright piano by the old couch, and stacks of sheet music. And there was a farmhouse smell full of apples, rainwater, and baked goods, though no one had baked a pie in the place for years. There was a hint of gasoline in the air, too, since the pumps were right around the corner. The ceilings, coffered with plain white-painted wood, were low. It was a handmade house with nothing elegant about it except the elegance of what anyone makes with their hands. Outside was a blackness as deep as the back of a black Angus bull.

"Why the hell did you bring that Christmas tree, Molly? You'll never learn! You're allergic to those things!" Polly exclaimed to my back. Then she turned to Sean. "Why I remember getting those trees out of the house as fast after Christmas as possible, my daughters were so allergic to them. Gail, now she had shots, but Molly wasn't as bad, so she didn't have shots. You'll see. She's still going to sneeze her brains out. And roses, she's allergic to them, too. My mother was awful allergic, and my sister, she had asthma, and Howie, he has it, too. I seem to have gotten away with it." She lit a cigarette. "Molly, throw that tree out right now, and put those poinsettias in the back room away from everything."

"Forget it, Ma, I'm not that allergic. We're going to have a wonderful Christmas." We had hauled the tree through the snow, into the house, and now snow puddles were all over the floor.

"Get the mop," Polly moaned.

"We're having it, Ma, we're having Christmas. We're all here and we're all having Christmas. Take this." I handed her a bag of chocolate-covered sponge candies.

"My favorites!" she crowed. They really were, too. "Well, you kids clean up and keep that tree in the living room." She had given in, temporarily.

Howie, my cousin and man of few words, drove up. While Polly made us all sandwiches, I hugged him awkwardly and introduced him to Sean, who immediately admired the new Swiss Army knife Howie had dumped on the dining room table.

"Didn't you want the Ford, Howie?" I asked him immediately. When Polly cleared out the garage, she'd had Howie's beloved model A towed down Route 246. It wasn't really Howie's; it was Polly's own first car, but Howie had played in it all his young life.

"Nope," he said. At least I'd gotten a syllable out of him.

"She asked you if you wanted it, didn't she?"

"Yeah," he said, "she did."

"But you didn't want it?" I asked incredulously.

"Nah, not now."

Polly brought in the sandwiches on dreamy soft rolls and watched us eat them. Sean, always looking for material for his narrative poems, pumped Howie for details and Howie ceded information bit by bit. He'd finally finished college after Aunt Roberta died, but now he had no job and milked cows for his dad and hated it.

All Howie's high school friends had left for jobs in Buffalo. He followed my mother around like a lost duckling in a flannel shirt. And sometimes he imprinted on me, like a baby brother, educated but aimless in his jeans and baseball cap. There was a cozy unspeakingness about him. He liked to arm wrestle and track animals. He was supposed to like hunting, but he was not interested in shooting.

Sean tore open the boxes of Christmas ornaments, and Howie fished around in the tissue looking for the missing hooks while Polly scowled and smoked. Howie was at his most purposeful looking for things. In the woods he'd notice the broken twig, the half-buried spoor, tracking what had been there and now was out of sight, like his mother. Aunt Roberta had died so quickly I had only visited her once in the hospital, where she'd talked about how women could wear pants to church now. *You don't discuss clothes if you're dying, do you?* I thought wrongly, then remembered the blouse she had embroidered for me when Polly and Ted had precipitously arrived in La Grange to return me to the suburbs when I was ten. She had given me a piece of wearable sanctuary. And the following summer she had given me a birthday party, with confetti angel food cake.

In the hours it took to decorate the tree, Sean and Howie and I regressed years: Soon we were arm wrestling and Sean was making me guess what my present was, not as an adult game paraphrasing childhood, but as a real game. Then we shined a light on the wall of the dining room and played shadow finger games. But Polly outlasted us, reading a Louis L'Amour western and eating the chocolate-covered honey sponge and looking up periodically saying, "You're going to start sneezing, Molly. You never should have brought that tree in here."

I began to feel achy. My sinuses were clogged. I had driven eight hours and decorated a Christmas tree and it was two in the morning and I was making the figures of dogs and birds in shadows on the walls with my lonely cousin and my redheaded boyfriend. Polly was staying up to oversee us, in a way she had never overseen what I had done when I was younger. The issue of where Sean and I would sleep had been glossed over. We would sleep in what had become my room. I had simply instructed him to dump our bags there. Gail and her boyfriend would take the living room couch and a cot. There was another bedroom, but it was full of dust and junk and treasures. "I have to get some sleep," I announced, so Howie went home, and we turned out the lights in the dining room. Polly stayed in the living room, smoking and reading. My room was off the living room, a few feet from her chair. Sean and I traipsed to the kitchen to go through the elaborate procedure of brushing teeth and washing faces without running water. I showed him the art of less soap, less water, and how to use the slop bucket. We gagged when we brushed our teeth. Then I sneezed.

"I heard that sneeze, Molly," my mother called from the living room.

I wouldn't give up. All I had to do was hold out till Christmas Day. My eyes had begun to get puffy and my throat was sore. We gathered up our toothbrushes and toothpaste because there was no place to leave them in the kitchen. Then Sean and I traipsed past Polly to my room, got into bed, and waited for Polly to shut off her light and go to bed herself. She had been staying to make sure we were asleep, but we were not asleep, we were waiting for her to go, because we wanted to make love. I was exhausted, but I knew that sex would bring me back to the adult I was, from the five-year-old I had regressed to. I shushed Sean, and we lay breathing quietly in the dark until Polly finally shuffled to her room.

I felt for my diaphragm among the tumbled clothes and bags we had not organized or put away. Got it! Then I felt for the tube of jelly and squeezed my usual generous amount into the middle, slathered it around the edges and some even on the reverse side. I was slow and thorough. We would completely enjoy this safely protected sex. Then, quietly, I got into bed and urged Sean to be very quiet and we were, we were stealthy and delighted that we were making love in my mother's house until the burning began. When Sean's penis pressed against the diaphragm an excoriating burning began in my cervix, then radiated into my vagina. *This has got to be psychological,* I said to myself. *You have a burning sensation because you are making love in your mother's house.* So I ignored it until my vagina felt like it was being cauterized, and Sean said, "I can't come like this, Molly. My penis feels really weird."

His sudden affirmation made me squeal, "Get out! Get out! There's something wrong!" I knew I was supposed to leave the diaphragm in for hours afterward, but I reached inside me and tore it out to relieve the pain. Sean pulled the string on the lightbulb so he could examine himself in the glare. His penis was covered in aqua goo. I held the diaphragm in my hand. It oozed the same aqua color. My vagina burned the way iodine burns on a cut. "God, what *is* it, Molly?" Sean beseeched me.

"Crest," I said, "Crest toothpaste. I grabbed the wrong tube in the dark."

"Jesus Christ, I've got to get this shit off me!" Sean ran toward the kitchen and started dousing himself with water, splattering the whole kitchen floor. I followed, wondering how I could flush the toothpaste out of me. I splashed ineffectively, needing some way to direct the water into me, but the only thing I could think of was a turkey baster. There one was, in a drawer, but the ancient rubber bulb of the baster was cracked, thank heaven, because I hadn't wanted even to think about the dried crusts of old gravies inside the thing. I was lying on the floor and Sean was pouring glasses of water into me, then going to the pump and pumping another bucketful. Of course Polly was wide awake. We'd turned on the kitchen lights and her doorway was nearby. And we'd begun to laugh. After the first couple of glasses of water the burning softened and I began to heave with relief. Now Sean and I were naked in a flood of water holding our sides from laughing and Polly's gravelly voice was asking, "What's happening out there? Can't you kids keep quiet? What are you pumping that water for?"

"Well," I began to blurt out the truth, "I put, I put," then collapsed into gales of laughter with Sean, acutely aware that my great scheme for affirming my adulthood had turned into the most adolescent flaunting of my sexuality, and with a redhead, to boot. I had not succeeded in rescuing myself from regression. I was still five years old. I was caught, and I told the truth. "I put *toothpaste* in my diaphragm, Mom! And it burned like hell, so Sean and I have to get it out of me!" All I could picture was a child racing across the living room naked in front of company, being chased after by an adult holding tiny pajamas.

"Make sure you clean up that kitchen floor, Molly. It sounds like Noah's flood out there." Sean held out his hand and pulled me to my feet. I got the mop and cleaned up. It was 4 A.M. on Christmas Eve, and Sean and I went to sleep. We did not make love again at La Grange, punished by our red, raw genitals.

Late that afternoon Gail arrived with homemade potholders and aprons, muffins and breads, a St. Bernard named Brandy and the grizzled Ed. He must have been Ted's age! But he didn't look like our father at all. For one thing, he had shoulder-length white hair.

"I'm growin' all our own food in Ed's spare lot, Mol," Gail chirped, "and livin' in his cabin with him and Brandy!" She pointed to the St. Bernard. "Ed's my old man now. Mol and Mommy, meet Ed. He saved me from the Fillmore!"

" 'Lo, everyone," Ed said, hauling out his guitar and singing, quite sweetly, a French folk song, telling us between verses that though he had the same given name as my father, he was called Ed, not Ted, and that was a world of difference, he assured us, since he was the exact opposite politically and socially. Then, before he revved up his Woody Guthrie, he crooned a ballad he'd made up about how he dragooned Gail from the Fillmore and hauled her to Woodstock to dry out.

And saved me, I thought, *from always thinking I should save her.* Gail had made clear sense when she had talked to me on the phone from Ed's. Usually when she called from the Fillmore pay phone she was incomprehensible. Her new life and my new life with Sean and Polly's new life after Ruth and Howie's new life after Aunt Roberta had given me the idea for Christmas together, and now here we all were. Red welts of allergic reaction spread across my face and wrists. My eyes watered. My nose was too stuffed to sneeze.

Gail always kept herself busy in Polly's presence and immediately got down to making a pumpkin pie. Even Polly got into the spirit of cooking and the three of us chortled and grinned through our tasks while Howie fixed the TV and Sean and Ed talked politics between songs. Suddenly I sneezed, loud as a tiny clap of thunder.

"It's that goddamn Christmas tree. Get that thing out of here!" Polly said when she looked up at me. "You're going to be sick as a dog, Molly. My Lord, you're sick already. You're sick in the head to bring that thing in here."

"Forget it, Mom," I said, holding the Kleenex box to my chest as if it were my pet. My sister and I were orchestrating Christmas. Polly had no say. We were having a great dinner and a terrific tree.

"When are we going to open our presents?" Sean asked. He was terribly proud of the box for me that he had wrapped by himself in an un-Christmas-like hyacinth pink.

Of the two types of Christmas present opening families—the Christmas Eve openers and the Christmas morning openers—ours was a morning family. My father had been sober in the A.M. "Let's open 'em up tonight!" my sister gleefully suggested. "Let's change everything around!"

"Great! Let's change everything!" I agreed, though Polly had remained unchanged. She had declared *no gifts* and she had stuck to it. There was nothing from her to anyone under the allergy-provoking pine.

Gail and I had planned a Christmas Eve supper and a Christmas dinner. There were squashes and cranberries and walnuts and dates and tangerines and mincemeat and shrimp and turkey. The bought things were bought by me, the garden things brought by Gail, or bartered for by Gail and Ed since they'd had to stop every hour to let their car cool down and walk the St. Bernard, and in the process they would meet people and exchange a squash for a zucchini nut bread, or some potholders for a bottle of wine. Howie brought over apples and pears from my uncle's orchards.

We had our Christmas Eve feast and Ed and Howie cleaned up the kitchen for Christmas Day while Sean shoveled snow. It was snowing and snowing. It would be a country fairyland outside on Christmas morning. Everything was just the way it was supposed to be. Midnight. "OK, everybody, we're opening the presents!" Sean crowed.

Polly seemed genuinely pleased with the braided rug and even more pleased with the electric broom. Gail loved her store-bought sweater from me, and for the next ten years I tried occasionally to wear the vest she knitted for me thinking that surely what looked so good on the hanger would look good on my body, but it never really fit, and that, of course, is the story of this Christmas. For Sean I had carefully selected poetry books exactly to his taste, and in turn he gave me the present he was so proud of: a stuffed rabbit.

"Doesn't it have silky ears!" he crowed. He had given me a toy. He had not given me perfume or earrings or poetry, but a carefully selected stuffed animal he would have loved himself, a present he might have given his mom when he was ten. The rabbit looked at me with reproachful eyes. I was desolate and knew it was my own fault. I had corralled everyone to come for Christmas at La Grange when they were all better off in their own worlds. No one but Polly belonged here. But what would *I* have done? Found Ted in a bar in Florida?

Well, I could have stayed home alone and bought a dozen red roses to congratulate myself, but that wouldn't occur to me until the following December. Humiliated, ashamed, thwarted in my fantasies and empty of what I really wanted, I reached for the Kleenex box and began to sneeze. My eyes ran, great gobs of mucus welled up in my sinuses. If only I could have broken down and cried. But I was stuck in the bud, wanting what I would not get, and just beginning to be deeply sad. Soon I would learn to create other families out of friends whom I tried to see for who they were, and who tried to see me in return, but now I was awash in unconscious tears, that I would eventually snort into being. And so I sneezed until the sadness rolled allergically from my eyes, until my face was as red as an infant's from squalling, and I couldn't stop. I had gone through a quarter of a box of tissues and Sean was patting me on the back as if he was trying to burp me. Polly was saying again and again, "It's that goddamn tree you brought into this house! Every Christmas since you were a little girl, Molly, you have had an allergic attack around Christmas trees! You should have brought an artificial one. Get the damn tree out of here!"

I couldn't catch my breath. I heaved and heaved, reddened to such an alarming color that Howie and Gail and Ed and Sean became frightened and started agreeing with my mother.

"Maybe we really should get rid of this tree, Molly," Sean said.

"I am *not* allergic to pine," I insisted, blowing my nose.

"Let her have the freakin' tree, man," my sister said. "Look, blow a nice joint of maryjane and chill out, Mol."

"Gail, your mother's right," Ed pronounced. To hear this pronouncement from a perfect stranger swung the room in my mother's favor. Even the St. Bernard barked in assent.

"Mol," Howie began, "I think we better get out the ornament boxes." I sneezed.

"Give in, Molly," my sister yelped. "Come on, I'll roll ya a joint."

"Oh no you won't!" Polly insisted on no drugs in the house. She was afraid of the law. "There's a nice bottle of scotch in the kitchen. Have a little of that."

I sneezed.

"Come on, Mol," Sean said gently.

My cousin handed me an empty ornament box. I reached up and pulled off the top star, then everybody rose to help dismantle the Christmas tree that had been up all of twenty-two hours. By one A.M. the tree was shoved point down in the mound of snow built up from Sean's shoveling. I almost got in the car and drove back to Baltimore that night, but was overwhelmed with exhaustion and simply went to bed.

Church was long over by the time I got up the next morning, having slept the sleep of the dead, and dead I was, tired of my desires and empty as a cardboard box. Polly and Gail had taken Christmas dinner into their hands. Polly preempted the turkey and stuffing; Gail was working on the sweet potatoes. Sean was setting the table per Polly's orders, and Ed was outside directing Howie in a big truck with a snow-plow. They were plowing out the cars. The sky was as blue as a tour-maline. The snow shone in glazed white drifts of grainy crystals, like dunes. The upturned stump of the Christmas tree flailed, as if it had, in embarrassment, stuck its head in the sand.

I was a child again, defeated. No sex. No present. No tree. Now, cowed and only sniffling, the big sneezes over, I would get a mother being a mother. She was dressed and had her makeup on. I couldn't even brush my hair. I sat in my bathrobe and watched Sean set the table with my great-grandmother's china and silverware. Gail handed me a cup of coffee and a slice of coffee cake.

"Merry Christmas!" she chortled.

The kitchen was occupied, so I took a pitcher of water and soap into the cold, unheated garage and washed in privacy. I stomped back to my room and dressed. Forget the week, Sean and I would leave the next day when Gail and Ed did. Reduced to silence, I accepted my assignment from Polly: fruit salad. Since I had first learned to use a utensil, I'd always made the fruit salad. Then I whipped the cream for dessert. Two o'clock came and a huge Christmas meal was laid at the table. Mother's food. We ate it and it was delicious.

After second helpings, after dessert, after several of us had volun-teered to clear the dishes, then sunk back into a post-dinner stupor, after Polly and Gail and Ed lit their cigarettes and the post-Christmas lethargy stretched lion-like across the gravy-beaded plates jeweled with bits of cranberry sauce and orange squash, and Howie lazily stuck his finger into the whipped cream bowl for a prolonging fillip of cream, a slow, steady, insistent, invasive banging began on the front door. Outside the snow was high and crusty, the kind of snow that buoyed up the walker, making it slippery because of the ice on the crust. And here a person was knocking on the door, and the person must have come on foot, for no car had driven up. It was about four o'clock in the afternoon. It would be dark by five-thirty, but the late afternoon had an extra brightness to it because of the glare off the snow.

"There's a strange man at the door, Ma," I said. I could see a wizened little face like Rumpelstiltskin through the large window.

"My God, it's Fergus," Polly said, leaning herself around to look. "Well, open the door and see what he wants."

There on the stoop stood Fergus Buxton, a short, slender, ancient man with an Irish cap and a tweed jacket over two gray sweaters. A frayed gray wool scarf was wrapped around his neck and the bottom half of his face below his red, broken-veined nose and brightly rheumy blue eyes.

"I knew your grandfather!" he chirped. "I'm Fergus Buxton from down the road! Ain't you gonna let me in?" He half terrified me. I was in an Irish fairy tale and the little man on the stoop wanted in. Was this where, if you wished the wrong wish, you were turned into a salmon for the rest of your days? If I let him in, would we all get the gold or would we eat the cake of sin? I just stood there, looking at him. He had on baggy woollen pants and cracked leather shoes and a pair of moss-colored wool gloves with the fingers out. No boots. No winter jacket or overcoat. "Well it's cold out here, girlie! I knew your grandma and your grandpa. I've lived down the road there all my life." It must have been way, way down the road, because I knew every farmhouse in the vicinity. It must have been miles down the road.

"Here you go, Fergus." Polly was behind me at the door. "Come on in the house and get your Christmas dinner. Walk all the way down, did you?"

"I came out for a little nip, I did!" Fergus exclaimed.

"Now, Fergus, you sit down at the table and have some food before your nip," my mother firmly suggested to him.

"Come here, Fergus, sit down and warm up next to us." It was Sean, pulling up a chair for the ancient, bowlegged man as he wobbled toward the table. Gail made him up a plate of food from what was left on the stove.

"Hey, Fergus, so you knew my Grandpa Gillie, did ya?"

"Now you're a pretty thing!" Fergus looked longingly at my blonde sister.

"Just keep your hands on the plate, Fergus," my sister teased him, and the old man burbled with laughter, the way a wise salmon in a tale might laugh.

He seemed a magic man with secret powers in his frail, tweedy, doll-like torso and arms and legs. Sean was fascinated. An artifact had walked through the door. Sean began asking him questions and Fergus started telling how he escaped his niece. Fergus and his wife had had no children of their own, and after his wife died he'd had to surrender himself to his brother's daughter. His niece and her husband and their children were keeping him, and not that they weren't grand to him but nobody had a little nip for Christmas there, they were all born-again teetotallers, but Fergus felt Christmas wasn't Christmas without whiskey, so he had fled the place and walked to La Grange Garage.

My mother edified us all by explaining which house it was that Fergus had walked from. It was on a back lane nearly four miles away by road, but closer across the fields. He had trekked across the fields on the crusty snow for over two miles without boots or a coat. He was shiny as a coin from his exertion. He dug into the turkey my mother had insisted my sister cut into little bits. Fergus didn't seem to have his teeth with him. "You've got to have some proper Christmas cheer," he announced for the twelfth or fifteenth time.

A bottle of Cutty Sark scotch had been sitting on the sideboard until my mother briskly removed it when Ed guided Fergus to his seat. "Now, Fergus, I'm truly sorry, but there isn't a drop in this house," Polly lied.

"Oh and I thought sure your dear father had some right here for the holiday. He always did before."

"Well, now Gillie's dead," Polly began.

"I know that, my mind's not gone!" Fergus snapped. "Bless his soul."

"But we don't want you to go without your holiday cheer, Fergus," my mother suddenly said, "so we'll take you to the Tavern in Perry!" The Tavern in Perry? This was how Polly would get Fergus out of the house. The Tavern opened on Christmas night for a cup of wassail for the community. Howie looked horrified. Only drunks and Catholics went there.

"Polly Wright, you were always a good girl and your father, bless his soul, always loved you!" Fergus declared.

"We'll take you for a Christmas nip on my father, Fergus, we'll buy you a nice drink, but only one and then we'll take you home to your niece. She's going to be worried about you, Fergus, so a little cheer and then home and tucked into bed."

"Hey, everybody, get your coats on, we're going for an adventure!" Gail shouted.

"Well, now I'm all ready," Fergus declared. He hadn't even taken off his scarf.

"Hey, Fergus," Sean said, "where's your coat and boots?"

"I'm fine as I am," Fergus stated. "I'm ready to go."

"Sean, go out in the garage and find my father's rubber boots. We'll give them to Fergus," my mother commanded. "And, Ed, you go out there too and find Gillie's plaid jacket. That'll be good for Fergus, too."

Polly was mobilized. Fergus was a friend because he was a buddy to her father. But he was an enemy because he wanted a drink. Yet she was going to get him a drink, just as she had provided her husband with drinks, in a motherly appeasement. Fergus stood before her bundled in my grandfather's outer clothes, ready for his Christmas nip. By now it was almost dark.

I did not want to go to Perry Tavern, a wood and neon whiskey road-house that reminded me of all the bars my father haunted. There would be a few frizzles of tinsel over the bar, like all the rathouses where every man's workshirted back was my father's.

And now my father had reappeared in the shape of Fergus Buxton, who was regaling Sean and Ed and Gail with stories of the mythical Fergus, aide to Irish King Cuchulain. A sudden panic at how everyone rallied to meet his need twisted inside me, and then a disorienting fear of everything being wrong and nothing, *nothing*, I could do to fix it came over me like the burlap bag a woodsman in a fairy tale would use to capture an unsuspecting girl. Inside I fought like the girl in that bag, though silently, as I put on my boots and coat and scarf and hat and gloves and went out to my mother's car. She was driving all of us, crammed together, with Fergus between herself and Sean, who seemed to have adopted the little man who might have been a friend of Yeats himself. Howie and I and Gail and Ed all squashed ourselves in the back seat. Gail and I fought like eight-year-olds. "Move over, Molly! You're on my coat!"

"So get off *my* coat if you want me to move," I whined.

"Girls, girls!" Polly growled from the steering wheel. The neon lights of the tavern were up ahead. She slowed the car and parked and everybody crowded in. I was swept along as the whiskies and sodas were poured and knew, as they all found a table and Bing Crosby sang "White Christmas," that we were in for the long haul. The whole tavern began singing "White Christmas" and Fergus toasted my family. I felt for the niece who somehow had inherited Fergus and wondered whether she was calling the sheriff. But the old codger reigned.

"Fergus, Fergus, how are you?" rang the tavern and three different rounds of drinks were sent to our table. My eyes filled with water and my chest filled with smoke and my head filled with panic as the ceiling lowered and the bar moved toward me, the girl clutching her glass of ginger ale.

"Give me the keys, Ma." I fished in her pocket. "I'm going to wait out in the car. You said *one drink.*"

"Oh, Molly, for God's sake we won't be long," Polly said.

"You're buying into this, Polly!" I squealed.

"Don't make a big deal and it won't *be* a big deal," Ed intoned, crossing his arms sagely. Thank God he'd forgotten his guitar.

"Join the fun, Mol!" Gail piped up. "It's a Christmas party!"

Sean threw back his second club soda. Even Howie had another beer between his two silent paws.

"You said *one drink,*" I repeated as I grabbed the keys and leapt out of the tavern into the dark and snow. I got in the car, turned on the ignition, and rolled down the windows with the heat on, not wanting to asphyxiate myself. Sean rushed after me.

"What happened? What are you doing?"

"What am I doing?" I parroted back. "I'm waiting in the cold outside a bar for an old man to have a drink, then another and another. I'm waiting outside a bar on Christmas Day like I've waited for my father all my life, that's what I'm doing!"

"Well you won't have to wait long, Molly." Sean said. "Fergus is so old he'll be drunk with half a shot. Come on back in, Mol, and be with the rest of us."

"I can't, I can't, I'm gagging and the walls feel like they're moving to crush me."

"Stop being a baby, Mol. Come back in and have a drink with your family." As Sean turned to go, he snorted in exasperation and asked me the question that Gail and Ted and my friends had asked me so many times, "Why can't you just have fun?" Why can't you *laugh?*

A sense of humor comes from perspective. Danger is one-dimensional. People in danger don't laugh. Yet Fergus was not Ted. I knew I was not really endangered now. But the threat lived inside me. It had entered me long ago, like a spirit from the Land of the Shi, the land of Faery. I was as trapped as a girl inside a tree, helpless to free myself. Now Sean and I would fight and all would really be ruined, even the barely constructed life I had just begun.

"I know you want to talk to Fergus," I said, "I'll be fine," sending him back into the watering hole. After an hour of turning on the ignition and turning it off when I was warmer, I left the car and went to the tavern window. There I was joined by Howie, who'd come outside to get away from the cigarette smoke.

"Polly's afraid he'll pass out," Howie reported.

"Polly is just sitting there, encouraging him," I said.

"There's a lot of beer bottles lined up on that table." Howie was impressed.

We watched Fergus get up and stumble. Sean and Ed lugged him toward the men's room.

"Remember when my father came to get me from Bible School, totally sloshed?"

"My mother was scared," Howie said, "scared shitless of your father."

"So was I." Through the window we could see Sean and Ed lugging Fergus back to the table. "Oh, Howie," I continued suddenly, "your mom gave me the nicest, weirdest blouse that day!"

Howie tapped on the window to get Polly's attention. "I don't want to talk about her," he said to me emptily.

"Well, why don't you go back in and see how much longer they'll be?"

Soon Polly was getting the car keys from me, and Ed and Sean were hauling Fergus to the front seat. I crawled in the back again with Gail and Ed and Howie. Gail had apparently been attacking Ed in the tavern. Ed told her she was lucky it was Christmas and he wasn't going to give her what she deserved. Polly was at the wheel, slowly driving toward Fergus's niece's house.

"We're all drunk as skunks!" Gail warbled, though Polly was less so. I wouldn't have dreamed of insisting to my mother that I drive. Insistence would have led to commotion, and besides, I had a ludicrous, unfailing sense of being protected in my mother's hands.

"Next year, it'll be just you and me," I said at breakfast the next morning. We were the only ones up. Everyone else was too hung over. "We can have a quiet Christmas. No presents. Maybe we'll even eat out. No cooking."

"We don't have to go that far!" my mother protested, and smiled. We were mother and daughter again. Next year I would leave everyone else far behind. I would not bring sex into her house. I would not bring a Christmas tree or ideas from magazines about what to cook and how to serve it. Gail and Ed and a St. Bernard would not invade her. I would make no demands as I sat quietly by her side so I could have her, so I could drink her up.

My mother sat reading and smoking at the dining room table while Sean walked through the house to make sure we hadn't forgotten anything. Howie was out in the snow with Brandy the St. Bernard. Gail and Ed were just waking up. I shoved the bags in the trunk and our coats in the back seat along with the reproachful rabbit. I wasn't cut out for this: family, boyfriends, marriage. I couldn't help thinking of my father, no longer a symbol, but only a man out there. Where was he? In a bar on a beach in a tacky Florida town.

Whenever we closed up La Grange, we turned the water pails upside down to drip dry. They would see no use till someone came in the spring. By then those pails would be so dry that every mineral deposit would have its ridge. Inside they would be yellow brown, like buckets of desertland. They'd be home to spiders, their webs filled with the exoskeletons of bugs.

The thought of a life alone entered my head, and it was a calming thought, a soft thought. It had a clean, calico brightness to it. A life alone. I was going to be alone and write and end up an old lady admired by my students and leaving my money to an art colony. What's so bad about that? But how would I tell my mother? Really, I wouldn't have to. My fantasy of a life alone was modeled on her. Happiest by herself with a book, a chocolate, and a cigarette, her chores done, her world contained, the phone unanswered, letters unresponded to, alone in a dry pail of silence. When I held to myself the cherished idea of *ma vie seul,* I was determining to live the best of my mother's life, childless, manless, friends and relatives at bay. In bed with my books, I'd be cut away from everything, like a picture in a locket. Safe in the borders of a golden heart, I would breathe. I'd never be stuffed up. I'd simply be.

To be, and not always to react, to exist without organizing people futilely or resisting being erased—that was the present that couldn't be given. The taking of air into the lungs, then the expelling of it, as any animal does, was the gift so basic it could never be exchanged. Breathing unaware, without gulping or crying or heaving, was *being able to live.* Wanting this so deeply felt like a huge greed inside me. Greed rhymed with need, didn't it? And freed.

"I have a voracious lust for freedom," I said to Sean as we sped down Route 246, nearly dry now with a morning of traffic and sun.

"All writers need privacy." He yawned.

"Not like I do."

20.

I was not having children, I was pruning the family tree. This was it. Now I would live alone, cook alone, drive alone, and do my new job solo. Being paid to be a visiting poet was like a dream to me, and when the Delaware Arts Council invited me to be such a personage after my graduation from Johns Hopkins, I packed immediately. When I realized Sean thought Wilmington was too ugly to live in, my relief popped open like an automatic umbrella—he was moving to Vermont! With a miraculous down payment from Polly, I bought myself a Toyota and found an apartment from which I launched my new work. Days I taught alone, relating only casually with the teachers whose classes I visited, and nights I wrote alone, bathed in the rainwater of calmness, never intruded upon, growing greener, and brighter, and, even one day, happier, deep inside a landscape I had carefully fenced for myself, into which only the privileged were allowed. These privileged were my adult education students, who were so grateful for my attention to their writing that they asked me to continue their classes privately. I entertained them twice a week in my apartment, bookcases studded with the bunches of flowers I bought myself weekly, rewards for my attempts to stop smoking.

I was going to be addiction free, I'd decided. Slowly I taught myself to write a poem without cigarettes. And slowly I taught myself to write the kind of poem I'd always wanted to write: dense, sensuous, with rhymes. Without friends or a lover, I had endless amounts of time, and used it to learn how to write sonnets. These determined structures and rhyming words many people would find limiting, but to me they were poems with happy barriers. So I happily, sloppily made them, like a child with crayons, loving whatever I made, even though my elephants didn't look like elephants, my trees only sometimes looked like trees.

It took me awhile to realize I was lonely for the comfort of another body. When I moaned this discovery to my married students, one of them fixed me up with her single friend. "You won't like him as a boyfriend," she stated flatly, "but he'll be a good companion." Ben Peters had a house hidden among trees on a winding road. He spent his free time teaching in local prisons. Those bars were a comfort to him, a barrier between him and others. And metal bars were far away from the bar stools his father, like mine, had reeled from. Since Ben required a very wide berth from all who knew him, we got along very well. We liked to have dinner together and discuss our lives, and he invited me to sleep over at his house, not for sex, but for pancakes on Sunday morning. We gave each other so much room that we couldn't be the best of friends, yet the directness of our agreement carved a kind of relationship that was new for me.

Ben was the first man I met who had a vasectomy. "I'm fixed," he said one day when we were discussing his numerous bedmates.

"What do you mean, you're fixed?" I sat bolt upright on my living room rug.

"I've had a vasectomy."

"Prove it." I said suspiciously.

"How the hell can I prove it—you think I carry a certificate or something?"

I was being ridiculous. "God, I never met an unmarried man who had a vasectomy."

"I just don't want any problems. Any paternity suits."

If there were a family of people who consciously acted against having children, Ben was a member, and a brother to me. "I do *not* want to be a father," he said vehemently. "I don't want the responsibility. The money. The little kid. The whining. The custody thing." (He presumed the relationship to the mother wouldn't last.) "I can barely give myself what I need."

All he had energy for was himself, and this was not the energy of narcissism that made for victims of his charm strewn in his path. All his personal heat was devoted to firing up a wick that could so easily be extinguished. Every day this man wrote a new encouraging note to himself on his bathroom mirror. He trusted no one, and so he became his own son.

I could not quite build as deep a defense against the world as Ben Peters had done. Something in me kept extending myself to others, even as I withdrew. The phone became a kind of lifeline to me, though it often held a threat in the middle of the night. My father had begun to call me again, and I had allowed it. I thought I might maybe open a little line to my dad. But by this time my father was so brain damaged by alcohol that he could barely keep himself in clean clothes. The incestuous voice rang up in the night, "Hiya Molsie! I'm in Vegas baby. Playin' the slots. Hey, I wake ya up, babe? Got anybody in bed wit'cha? Gettin' any lately? Hey, didja get my Valentine?"

Ted had sent me a naked chocolate Kewpie doll with hard candy nipples. I had thrown the box up in the air with horror, taken the doll and the wrappings and thrown them in the garbage, bagged the garbage and gone to a parking lot with a Dumpster and hurled the doll in, unable even to have it in my own trash can.

"Yeah, Dad," I said.

"Hey, how about that! How about that doll, hey, doll, hey Mol the doll!"

"Well, Dad, I didn't think it was, I didn't think it was . . ." (What was that word Ruta so often used?) "I didn't think it was too *appropriate*." I said her word carefully and coldly. It was 2:47 A.M.

"Whaddya talking about, Mols? I sencha a Valtine, thas all."

"It's the middle of the night, Dad."

"You ain't no fun, Molly, you never were no fun and you ain't got no sensa humor."

"No, I don't."

"Hell with you, Molly. Listen, I'm goin' ta Florida. Back to Treasure Island. I got a little place. Why doncha come down?"

An invitation from my father! Even in this dangerous conversation I felt a soft paw of hope tap at me.

"I could help ya with the plane ticket, Mols."

"Well, gee, Dad, I'll think about it," the reasonable part of me said. "Have you got a number down there?" He gave me half a phone number.

"Hey, Dad, this is only four numbers."

"Yeah, well, four numbers is all I got. I had a stroke, Mol. I dropped my keys. My number's on my keys. But I dropped my keys. I can't pick 'em up. I had a stroke, Mol. I dropped 'em an' I can't pickem up."

"What do you mean you had a stroke?"

"I had a stroke you asshole!"

"Were you in the hospital, Dad?"

"Goddamn right I was in the veterans' hospital. Now I'm out. In Las Vegas. Playing the slots. Hey, Molsie, I didn't pack no socks. Send me some socks, OK?"

"But when are you leaving, Dad? They won't have time to get there." Socks? My father wants me to send him socks? My father who sent me a naked chocolate doll? Am I supposed to be his lover or his mother?

"I'm leavin' Friday. Friday for Treasure Island."

"But it's Wednesday, Dad. By the time I buy socks tomorrow after work I won't be able to get them to you. It's impossible."

"It is? Shit. I need socks, Molsie."

"Aren't you in a hotel, Dad?"

"Sure as shit I'm in a hotel!"

"Well there's a store in the hotel lobby, Dad, you know, one of those clothing shops? They'll have socks. Just go in the store and buy them. You could probably buy them right now, Dad. It's Las Vegas. That store's probably open all night."

"OK, OK, you wanna get off the phone. I'll get the socks, I'll get the socks. I'm never sendin' you no more Valentines."

"Good, Dad, I don't want any more Valentines."

"That was a nice goddamned kewpie doll, Mols."

"It was. It was nice. But not nice for me. I'm your daughter."

Could I be your daughter? Could I come and visit you and be your daughter and not your mother or your lover?

The kind of hope I had was not the good kind of hope in life. It was the kind of hope that is an obstacle. I lay down trembling after jamming the phone in its cradle when Ted hung up. I couldn't sleep, so I got up and made a sign, like Ben Peters's signs in his bathroom, only mine was for my telephone. It said, "DON'T YOU DARE PICK THIS UP. THIS IS WHY YOU HAVE AN ANSWERING MACHINE."

But the telephone was like a string bridge to be thrown over the sudden chasms of my loneliness. On the many nights alone I called Maggie, Lily, all my friends from college, and from graduate school, all over the country I called, running up huge phone bills, even spending hours on the phone with Polly, and sometimes with Gail, who had fled the aging Ed and fallen into the arms of a younger, sexier, harder-living man, Jules.

"Daddy? You talked to Daddy!" Gail squealed long distance.

"Well, he called a couple of times."

"Florida! He said he'd pay for our tickets! Wow, Mol, the beach, the bodies, the bars—it's party time, doll."

"He said he'd pay for *part* of our tickets, Gailie, not *all* of them. We have to come up with the rest."

"Well, it's cool, anyway, I'm getting right out there on Tinker Street and selling my rubbings and candles to those hippie-loving tourists on the road to Woodstock, Molsie. To Florida we go! Beach Blanket Bingo meets Treasure Island! Bring on the pirates!"

"So what I'm going to do is, I'm going to get us tickets, and then Daddy says he'll reimburse us. And when he gives us the money, then you'll take that, OK, and put it with the candle money, and then give it to me for your ticket, all right?"

"Yeah."

"I mean, I have a credit card, and I know you don't have one. . . ."

"Cash, man, I deal exkloosively in cash!"

"And you need to put the ticket on a credit card to reserve it, so I'm doing it, all right?"

"Yeah."

"So when are you free to go?"

"Free? Honey, I'm always free! I'm free as a bird! I'm free as a Peacock!"

"But, like what date, Gail, and well, like how long is it going to take you to get the money together?"

"Coupla weeks, doll. Hey, you know what I'm calling you to everybody here in Woodstock? I'm calling you this to everybody, man, even to the social worker at the fuckin' agency that screws up my goddam fuckin' welfare checks, man, I'm callin'. . . . I'm callin'. . . ." There was not quite a dead silence, since she was gulping, as if to catch her breath. "Little sister," she suddenly crowed. "I'm calling you my little sister! Whaddya think about that! Jules my Louisiana honey, he thinks I'm the older one!"

"That's great, Gail," I said, annoyed as hell.

"Oh, Molly-ooch! I got under your skin, didn't I? Wheee! I love it under your skin!"

"You are not under my skin. You've been introducing me as your little sister since you were five," I said. "So get out on the street with your candles and get some airfare."

She was going to drive down from Woodstock and meet me at my house. Some friend was supposed to drive her. Gail had never gotten a license. And never gotten a job after the candy counter at the Fillmore. And never gone to college. When they went through the welfare rolls and took out "all but the truly needy" my sister was left on. "I had this great shrink, Mol. He wouldda said anything for me. Daphne, my call-girl friend, she knew him. He did the tests and everything. I'm crazy as a loon! The U.S. government is not going to mess with this crazy girl. I'm the truly needy, Mol!"

Two months later a sparkling new red truck with an empty gun rack—was that standard issue?—pulled up outside my house. Gail got out with a huge, rangy, muscular man whose angelic mop of blond curls was caught with a ribbon into a comma of a ponytail.

"Hey, little sister!" she yelled. "We're here! It's me and Jules!"

I leaned across the porch railing to shake his hand. Clean fingernails.

"Hi, Jules!"

"Hey, little sister, I'm glad to meet ya!" he said with a grin.

"Julesie drove all the way from Baton Rouge to Woodstock, Molly. He came up to get me and drive me here in record time," she burbled.

Jules was holding an airplane ticket in one hand. I shook the other. I was going to shake that girl by the shoulders when I got hold of her! She was bringing this goddamn Jules. She had never since we left home seen either of our parents without some male escort. She traveled in a cloud of sexuality with them. Now Jules was going to come with us. The ticket was in his hand.

"I got enough candle money for a whole ticket and I gave it to Julesie, here, he's coming to party! I called up the airline and they fit him right in next to you and me."

"Oh." That was my big response.

When I got her in the bedroom I hissed, "You gave away your money!"

"Don't be such a goody two-shoes, Molly."

"But Dad is only paying for part of yours!" I moaned. "That means I'll have to pay the other part!"

Gail looked around the bedroom. "Hey, nice new sheets. Hah! They don't give you nice new sheets at the Salvation Army where I get mine! Hey, is that a new sundress?"

"Yeah, I got you one, too." I couldn't stand buying the new dress for me without getting her one. I knew they didn't have new dresses at the Salvation Army, either.

"I'm trying it on right now!" Off went her clothes immediately and on went the dress, bare shoulders, red. Mine was the same in cinnamon, only three sizes larger—the cost of giving up smoking. She was a vision in the dress. I was the enlargement.

"Hey thanks, Mol, it's really cute. Don't I look nice, Cher?" Jules had strolled into the bedroom. He picked her up by the waist and twirled her around. "Don't worry, Mol," she said from three feet off the ground, "Daddy'll pay you my part. I'll get him to do it. You know he likes me best!" Her eyes twinkled in mockery.

Our plane was three hours late and Ted had spent it in the bar. He shambled toward us, his left arm hanging loose at his side from the stroke. He was all spiffed up in a white shirt and beige pants and after-shave. "Who's this?" He peered at Jules.

"Hi, Daddy," Gail said. "It's Jules, my new honey from Baton Rouge. We're all here to see ya! You smell like you've been partying, Dad!"

He was snockered.

"You're fat as a schoolteacher!" he said to me. "Listen, girls, I'm tryin' here, but ya gotta . . ." We waited for him to speak again. "Ya gotta un-nerstan my preedicament. My car's in the shop, see? I borrowed a fren's car to get out here. So it's in the shop, see, and I ain't got nothin' done for ya 'cause I been at the shop with the car."

We piled in the borrowed car and wove down the Florida coast. It was July. Even at midnight the heat swung its fist. He parked sideways across the driveway of his bungalow and we went inside. There was probably furniture in there, under the piles of laundry—clean—and empty paper bags from the liquor store. Bags upon bags. The air condi-tioner didn't make a dent in the humidity. The smell of Black Velvet hung over the two bare mattresses on the floor he had gotten for us to sleep on. He hadn't reckoned on Jules. No sheets on the mattresses. The floor was gritty with sand. "I got the laundry done!" he said proudly.

Gail started making up the bed for herself and Jules. I was going to get to sleep next to them. I went into the kitchen for a glass of water and turned on the light.

The counter was slathered in strawberry goo. A broken bottle of Ann Page jam, family size, was stuck on the dirty dishes, and down the yellow cabinets. Not dripping, but pasted on, because it had spilled long ago and solidified. The dirty dishes were piled up on the counter and in the sink. The floor was sticky with jam footprints.

"Oh my God!" I shrieked. I thought of Gram's house, clean as a sac-risty.

"Heh, heh, Molsie." Ted was in the doorway with a big paper bag. "I tol' ya I did not have no time for nuthin' becaus' a the car. Goddamn car. So here." He shoved the bag at me.

"What's the bag for?"

"Throw 'em out!"

"Throw what out?"

"Them dishes, Mol. That's what I do when it gets real bad. I throw out the dirty ones and buy a whole new set!" He started piling the dishes rather neatly in the bag.

"You *throw* them *out*? Regular dishes? Not paper plates?"

"Hate paper plates. Buy cheap sets of dishes. Sometimes I wash 'em. But when it's bad, I ditch 'em. Throw out the cutlery too. Cheap. I just buy them cheap replacements. Heh, heh!" He laughed his thin laugh.

"Hey, Gail, look how your dad does dishes!" Jules hung in the doorway.

"Oh, Teddy," Gail purred, "what are you up to now?" She began picking up dishes and throwing them in another paper bag. Hers broke though. "Wow! You can smash a whole set of dishes!"

Jules clattered the cutlery in against the broken dishes. White, with rosebuds. Then Ted started smashing them. Then Jules.

"Hey, Mol, get in on the fun before we smash 'em all!" Gail squealed. I picked up a dish and threw it in with a thud. "You gotta really throw it, Mol, like this!" Gail grabbed a whole dish with crusted egg on it and whacked it against the other dishes. "Gusto, Mol, you gotta get gusto!"

Car lights swept the driveway. "It's my car!" Ted shouted. Out he went, followed by Gail and Jules. Now the depopulated kitchen was a mess of shards and paper bags. I washed a glass within an inch of its life and dried it on a bathroom towel, then used it to drink some water.

"Molsie!" Ted called from the driveway. I washed a square of the counter and put my glass down. "MOLSIE!" He was waking up the neighborhood.

In the driveway was the buddy who fixed the car, my father's car itself, and the loaner car. The buddy wanted his loaner back, but Ted didn't have all the money.

"I gotta get the car outta hock here, Mols, and I need a hunerd bucks here, 'cause Duane here he needs three hunerd ta fix it and I only got two hunerd ta give him."

"We've got to have a car to get around," Jules said directly to me.

"Fork it over, little sister! You're rich compared to us!" Gail said.

I got my purse, whacking the front door closed and breathing in the air-conditioning and the Black Velvet and the dried jam and the sand and the clean laundry. A line of pain caterpillared across my chest. Then I sneezed.

"Here," I said when I came out again. I gave Duane five $20 bills.

"See, Mols, I got my credit card, but Duane, he don't take no credit, and I'll pay ya back tomorrow."

"Yeah."

Before I fell into a kind of dead sleep on the mattress next to Jules and Gail, I whispered to my sister, "I don't know how long I can stay here."

"Me either."

But it was just me and Ted for breakfast the next morning, since Gail and Jules were already at the beach. And it was me alone for lunch because Ted was at his bar and I wouldn't go there, and Gail and Jules were gone. So was the car. And it was me and Ted for dinner when he remembered to come home because Jules and Gail must have come back while I was out looking at the Gulf of Mexico and left the car in the driveway and gone off again on foot. There was a strip of bars and restaurants you could walk to. Ted and I found them shooting pool.

"So why didn't you stay long enough to make any plans?" I greeted her, whining.

"Hey, Julesie and I didn't want to wake you up! We drove around, man! Pelicans and orange juice! Then we found this place. We love it. We've been here most of the day."

Jules was bringing drinks back from the bar. They had money for cigarettes and money for booze and apparently money for lunch and dinner.

"Well, Daddy, we're glad you're here with your MasterCard!" Gail said. "We've been runnin' up a tab for ya!"

Everybody there knew my father. "Teddy!" the bartender yelled. Several blondes in high-heeled sandals at the bar raised their glasses.

"Jules is a great pool player, Mol, he really is, and we were hustling for money, but we got stiffed. There's some sharks around this fuckin' place." Gail lit a Marlboro. "I can't believe you stopped smoking, Molly!"

"Come on, you kids, come on, Teetotaller Molly, let's get a booth. I'll buy ya dinner on my MasterCard." My father spent dinner describing a hurricane, tree trunk by tree trunk. Gail hung on Jules. She had traded jewelery with a woman on the beach that afternoon and glowed with a carnelian necklace above her red sundress. She tossed her hair, then put a shrimp on her fork and fed Jules. Then he put a shrimp on his fork and fed her. Then she combed his ponytail stub and retied the purple ribbon. "Let the evening begin!" Jules announced. The three of them moved toward the pool tables, leaving me to order dessert.

I had a silky chocolate brownie with ice cream by myself in the booth. Outside the water crashed in the dark below zigzagged strings of lights. Inside the pool balls cracked as somebody opened and the bets were on. "Have you got a newspaper?" I asked the waitress. I read the local paper in the half dark and drank my coffee and let my fork play in the chocolate sauce.

"Hey, Mol, how come you're readin' the friggin' paper, for Chrissake!" Ted yelled from the poolroom. "Jules is great! Ya gotta see Jules!"

I looked over my shoulder to see Jules arch his back in a choreographed movement and place his shot.

After I slipped out of the booth, my sanctuary, I slid up to my father. "Hey, Daddy, didja win anything?" I said coyly.

"I'm breakin' even, Molsie."

"So, have you got my hundred dollars?"

"Fifty, Mols, here's fifty. Give ya the rest tomorrow. Hey, where you goin'? The night's young!"

I was backing out with my $50. "I'm walking home, Ted. See ya, Jules! See ya, Gail!" I was getting out of there before he lost and needed my $50 because he'd never get it out of them. Jules was giving Gail money to buy another round, or was that her money? She was giving him the orange slice from her cocktail.

I dragged my mattress from the living room to a tiny side TV room and squashed it in. I had a novel. I had the TV on to read by. I fell asleep. By the next morning the three of them were crashed and I slipped out for breakfast. I wasn't walking in that kitchen again. But by the time I got back, Jules and Gail and the car were gone again.

Ted had rented a Sunfish, and we were supposed to sail it, except he was drunk and had only one good arm and I kept slipping off the Sunfish and he kept slipping off the Sunfish, and we hadn't even got it out of shallow water yet and the man who rented it kept saying, "I can give you your money back, sir. Really, if you think you'd rather do this another day, I'm authorized to give you back your money."

"We can get our money back, Daddy, the guy says so."

"I'm fine, Mols, I'm fine!" he said as he slipped back into the Gulf of Mexico.

"Really, sir," the man said, "I'm responsible for that boat. I'm afraid I'll have to give your money back."

"All right!" Ted said suddenly, and rather soberly took the bills—his pool winnings—while the man crashed in after the boat.

While Ted went back to the Treasure Island Surfer Bar, I went home to discover the car in the driveway and Gail and Jules in the outdoor shower.

"Hey, Molly! Ya want the car this afternoon?" she asked me over the wooden half-door.

"Well, why don't we all go somewhere together or something?"

"Cool! Hey, Julesie, my little sister probably wants to go to the historical museum or something like that!" Jules was shampooing and gurgling under the showerhead.

I wouldn't have minded. "How about the gardens? We could go out to the gardens they have here," I began to suggest.

"We can't hear you!" my sister shouted. "The water's running." So it was. I hid in my little TV room to let them get dressed. There was a red satin ribbon instead of the purple one. Gail flowed in a long violet dress. "It's for our night on the town!"

"But it's still afternoon, so want to go to the gardens?" I said slowly. Evidently Jules was not the horticultural type.

"Well, Molsie . . ." Gail played for time, but not for long, because my father came in and stumbled for the bathroom and upchucked on the way. Jules rose to the occasion with a towel. "I'm sick," Ted moaned. "I got a bug." Jules guided Ted toward his unmade bed.

"He's sweating and he looks pale," Jules called from the bedroom. My sister stomped in to see him.

"It's because he fell off the Sunfish eight or nine times," I said, pouting, refusing to go in there. Gail breezed out. "Somebody better stay with him. We can't leave the old fart alone."

"Somebody, as in *me?*" I asked.

Gail blanched. "Well," she began, then brightened, "we could take turns!"

"I know what taking turns means. So when does your turn begin?"

"Look, Julesie and me, we'll just take a drive along the water and see the pelicans and stuff, and smoke a joint, and then we'll come back so you can drive to the garden. We won't be gone long. Because tonight's our big night! We're going out on the town!"

"I could go to the garden right now, and then be back for you to go out for the night," I said, edging toward the door.

Jules bustled by. "Going to the drugstore! Come on, Gailie, we gotta get your dad some Maalox!"

"Wait! *I'll* get the Maalox!" I said.

The door was slamming. "We'll be right back!" Gail called.

After I got dressed to go to the gardens I sat there reading Elizabeth Bowen's *Death of the Heart,* listening for the car to drive up. I read about the cottage at the beach and looked up at my father's cottage, the three chairs and the mattresses on the floor. There was the gritty rug with a clean place where my father's vomit had been wiped up. I no longer smelled the Black Velvet or the caked-on food smell from the kitchen. I looked in on Ted, finally. He was snoring. His air conditioner rattled. They'd have to drive up pretty soon.

It was 5:30. The gardens would be closed. I wandered in the bathroom. There was a full bottle of Maalox on the sink. I'd been suckered. I wandered into the kitchen and suddenly looked under the kitchen sink. There was a package of sponges and some Ajax and Fantastik. I didn't bother to change my clothes. I started right in on the jam. I got a knife out and scraped off the worst of it. Then I laid the wet sponges on top of the counter to soak the rest off. I carried the paper bags full of broken dishes out to the neighbor's trash can, hoping I wouldn't be spotted. Ted had no trash cans. Somebody probably took them because he'd never remember to drag them in from the curb. My mother had always done that. Then me. I thought of Polly. *"Gail and I are going to Florida!"* I'd told her. *"Daddy's paying for our tickets!"*

"Yeah, sure," Polly had said meanly.

The tickets! Oh my God, he'd never given me the money! I had a big Ajax stain on my new-for-Florida sleeveless top. I went into the TV room and took it off. I found an old T-shirt of my father's in the pile of laundry and put it on and went back to work. By 7 P.M. I had the kitchen in great shape. The faucets were sparkling. Time for the living room. I found a vacuum cleaner in the closet. Grit Be Gone! I revved up the

Electrolux and was mowing swaths down the living room when something tapped me on the shoulder.

"Turn this goddamned thing off! I've got a bug I tell ya, I'm sick!" It was Ted. I'd woken him up.

"Hi, Dad, look what I did in the kitchen!"

"Molsie, for Chrissake, you're on goddam vacation. What are ya doin' in the fuckin' kitchen with all that jam?"

"There's jam no more! Look what I did!" I took him by his good arm and dragged him to the kitchen. It glowed like the Hope diamond.

"Well now," Ted said. His bad arm hung at his side and his good arm hung around my neck. He looked at me. "Jesus, it's like Gram was here!" I felt the horror and wonder of Gram.

"Clean house, clean mind! That's what she always said!" I chirped.

"I gotta sit down, Mols, I feel like shit on toast."

"Well here, Dad, come on over and sit down."

We each sat in a living room chair.

"God, I'm hungry!" I said. "I've really been working!"

"Yeah, I see you've messed up my favorite T-shirt," my father said. It was streaked with jam and sweat and Fantastik.

"Oh, I thought I picked an old one."

"Well it is old. But I liked it the best anyway."

"Dad, could you give me the money for the tickets?"

"Tickets?"

"The plane tickets."

"Heh, heh, your sister already got it."

"What do you mean she already got it?"

"I only got enough cash for one ticket, Mols."

"But you said you'd pay our way!"

"I can't afford to. It was my car."

"But, Dad, it's not fair!"

"Oh, Molsie, you got a nice job. You can pay your own way."

"That's not the point! You should have given each of us half!"

"It don't work that way, Mols. Heh, heh, that Gail"—he smiled—"that Gail, she got to me right away. She got to me the first night before the car got fixed."

"So that's how they had all this spending money. That scumbag!"

"Watch yer language there."

"Well he is a scumbag!" I was so furious I was blaming Jules instead of Gail. "We were supposed to all be together! You invited us! Everything was supposed to be normal!"

"Normal!" Ted laughed, holding his side. "Shit, my ribs hurt me when I laugh."

"I'm leaving, Dad."

"Well, I don't blame you."

"I'm calling the airport and seeing if I can change my ticket. I'm getting out of here. You've got a clean kitchen and I'm out of here."

"Well, I don't blame you," Ted said again. He'd gotten up to head for the bedroom.

"Dad, don't you want to go out for dinner?"

"Christ no, I'm sick as a dog." He stopped on the way to the bedroom and picked up a Black Velvet bottle. "I got my dinner, honey." Then he disappeared into his room and shut the door.

I listened for cars again, then called the airline and changed my flight, took off Ted's T-shirt and put on my own Ajax-stained top. Oh well, no one would notice in the dark. I walked into the sticky night and took myself to dinner on the beach. Grouper and key lime pie. When I got home, the car was pulling out of the driveway, Jules and Ted in front, Gail in back. "Hey, Molly, we're all goin' out on the town!" Gail screamed out the window.

"Well not me! I'm just coming back from my key lime pie."

My sister waved a joint. "Come on, Mol, don't be a party pooper."

"You're the party pooper," I said as I approached the rear window. "You're the goddamned party pooper."

"Come on, Mol, be nice, we're on vacation!" Gail slurred.

"Yeah, be nice," Jules said from the front seat. "Come on out with us, Molly. We'll buy you a drink!"

Gail opened the car door. "Please, Mol," she said, her eyes nearly crossed from the booze and the dope. "C . . . c . . . " she began, "copped from this guy. Cool guy, Mol." She trailed off, then revived. "Got that Platinum Hash. I mean it's way, way beyond Gold. You'll love this hash, Molly."

I half sat on the back seat, keeping the car door open. "I haven't had stuff like that in ten years! I really don't want any," I said. There in the Florida night in my stained cotton top, I sounded as if I were wearing a tweed suit, a starched blouse, seamed stockings, brogues, and had just had my hair permed in rows of tight gray curls. I was the Nanny from another planet. And in the way of Nannies, I was Vengeance.

"How old are you, Gail?" I interrogated her imperiously.

"Twenty-eight," she said obediently.

"When I was your age I was getting a divorce! I was supporting myself full-time! I was paying taxes!"

"I'm all twisted up in the strap from my bag, Mol. Here, hold my drink while I untwist myself." She shoved a whiskey sour in my hand. "And don't eat my maraschino cherry."

"I'm not going to eat your goddamned cherry! You took all the plane ticket money from Daddy and gave it to Jules!"

"Now just a minute, Molly," Jules said from the front seat. I was scared of Jules. He was the kind of man who slung people over his shoulders for fun.

"And where the fuck have you been!" My voice was a special kind of hissing ice.

"I don't need to make excuses to you!" Gail exclaimed innocently. "You're acting like an asshole!"

"Close the car door, Mol, we're all goin' out on the town now, honey," Ted said placatingly.

"Let's all be friends, now," Jules said.

"Chill out for Chrissake," Gail said. She reached for the whiskey sour, but I held it back. It was gold in the streetlight with its maraschino dot. I held it above my head. Then I threw it in her face, watching it stream in slow motion till it hit her nose and cheeks and neck.

"Jesus Christ I'm going to kill her!" Gail screamed and opened the door on her side.

"Why should I take care of you! You're twenty-eight years old!"

"Hold me back, Julesie! I'm gonna kill her!" She was grabbing at the air, but I was standing on the other side of the car. Then I was moving toward her, as if to *give* her something to grab. Jules was out of the driver's seat and leaping over the hood of the car to hold her. He was pinning her arms and she was struggling to hit me, poking the air and crying now, the tears rolling down her cheeks. Ted was hanging on to the passenger's side front door.

"Shhh!" he called. "My neighbors are gonna hear you!"

"The neighbors!" Gail and I said simultaneously in astonishment. "After all the times you screamed in front of the neighbors," I said to him.

"You've got to be kidding, Teddy!" Gail exploded, then went immediately back to sobbing.

"You better stay away from her," Jules warned. "You don't know how she gets when she's like this." He was holding her from the waist and rocking back and forth with her.

"I'm gonna kill you!" she screamed again at me. He was cradling her loosely. She could have broken from his arms, but she stayed in them. "Hold me back, Julesie! I'm gonna kill this bitch!"

I stood about four feet in front of them, just short of swinging range.

"Get in the house!" Ted was trying to hustle us in, but we weren't moving. Gail was thrashing her arms and Jules was swaying back and forth and I was stuck to my spot by the back of the car. Ted was pinching my arm.

"You lied!" I said. "You took the ticket money and you lied!"

"You went to college!" she said suddenly. "You got married! You have a job!" she accused me.

"You could go to college, too! You could have a job!"

"Fuck you." Jules had let go of her. She was backing out into the street.

"Yer gonna get hit by a car, Gailsie," Ted warned.

Jules was going after her. She turned and ran toward the beach.

Ted tugged on my arm again and I went into the house with him, still clutching the empty plastic cocktail glass with the remains of the sour.

"Don't you want supper, Dad?" I asked him. "Can you order in down here? Do they have a takeout place?"

"I don't want nothing to eat," he said dully, slumping in a chair.

"Wow," I said.

"Wow is right."

"I can't believe you're worried about your neighbors after all these years, Dad."

"People change."

"Polly doesn't think so. She thinks people never change."

"Polly." He spat her name. "I wanna keep my little place here, Mols. I don't want no trouble. Look here, I'll try an' send ya the money."

"No you won't," I said stonily. "I'll get on a plane and you'll get drunk and you'll think that you have better uses for your money than sending it to me. You'll probably even send it to Gail." My voice came out of me like a paper ribbon, flat and tearable.

"You threw that drink right at her!" Ted said, almost admiringly.

"I can't believe I did that."

"You shouldda done it a long time ago."

"I gotta pack, Dad. The cab's coming to get me at ten. My flight's at eleven-thirty."

"Yeah, it's probly good for ya to get out of here."

"Do you think she'll come right back?"

"Nah, they're in a booze hall by now. They ain't coming back right away. I've still got this bug, Molsie. I'm lying down. Don't lock the door when ya go. Those two ain't got keys."

21.

"Surely," wrote my favorite poet, George Herbert, "if each one saw another's heart . . . all would disperse, And live apart." After I looked into the hearts of Ted and Gail, I fled. "All would disperse," George said, the poet who had a Saint's Day all to himself in the Anglican calendar. To live apart was a way of having heaven, a calm place, or at least a way of avoiding hell, a jammed place.

I had to focus when I returned from Treasure Island, yet nothing focused me. I could barely wheel a cart down a supermarket aisle. To survive I invented a rigid routine: rise at 7:30 A.M., make breakfast, be at my desk by 9:30. Go out for lunch at 12 sharp. In those morning hours I pored over my poems, turning the chaos of our lives on Pilgrim Road into the comforting grid of suburbia. *The lawns of June,* I wrote, *flush with the walks and white/driveways of town. . . . smooth, regular as the rules of a fresh white card pulled from the box of a new game. . . .* Those geometric boundaries that might have chafed others felt as good as tight bandages on a broken limb. If I was broken, the lines set the bones, then acted as a cast. Art was not *like* life—it was the way to life. Inside a poem, I could mend.

And in the afternoons I sent my poems out to magazines. Somewhere, there was an editor who would hear me. An adopted literary child, I was determined to find my birth family. I buckled down and dispatched a manuscript of poems to publisher after publisher—and one day read the statistics on the likelihood of getting a first book published, then sank to my knees and wept in the middle of my mint green shag rug. Ben Peters stopped by with an armload of zinnias to find me wetfaced among my groceries and fashion magazines on the floor, poring over the wicked chart in a poets' newsletter.

"You can't let that bother you!" he declared. "You might as well read a horoscope than that crap!" He picked up *Mademoiselle*. "Here, here's our sign, Cancer."

"This is too desperate for words!" I whined.

He read the horoscope and was silent.

"Well, what did it say?"

He silently passed the folded-over glossy page to me. "Read the second sentence," he said.

" 'You could even have a major publication in your field,' " I read aloud.

"Well, that's a lot better than the chart that made you cry!"

It was. It was better. It was the best. Two weeks later I got a notice that I had been runner-up in a poetry book contest. So what. That didn't mean publication. But they had extra money at the press, and they were publishing my book, too! Would I please sign the university press contract and make sure to fill in the title?

After three days of carting the contract around in my purse, I did. I wrote in block letters, the monastic truth according to George Herbert, the priest of a green country parish: *AND LIVE APART*.

iii.

PRUNING

the FAMILY

TREE

22.

In a sweat, I locked my apartment door—then unlocked it, dashed to the bathroom, locked it again, ran to the car, checked for the files, the shorts, the sweaters, the radio, the books, and my manuscript of poems. I had intended to leave at 9 A.M. but now it was 11:30 A.M. I would have to drive without stopping in order to make it before the art colony office closed. *OK, I won't pee,* I thought.

Halfway there at a highway rest stop as the shadows lengthened, I had to call and say I would be late. I wasn't to worry, the person who answered said, the keys to my little stone house would be waiting in my mailbox in the art colony farmhouse. All I had to do was to get there before dinner ended. But it was well after dark by the time I got there, and dinner had long been cleared away. I took a deep whiff of the farmhouse kitchen—a century of apple pie. It smelled like La Grange. There were the keys to my studio, just as they said, plus a map to my little stone house. But the dirt roads were unlit, and I got lost twice before the sign with my house's name loomed up.

Exhausted and hungry, too frightened of the dark and the woods to unload my car, too tired to unpack, too tired even to wash my face, I wept on the unmade bed, hardly noticing that the fieldstone studio smelled of firewood and pine. A sudden fear had dropped down on me: I wasn't a good writer, why had I come here? Why was I so unprepared—

I didn't even notice restaurants on the way, where would I eat? When I switched on the porch light, a swarm of mosquitoes dive-bombed my hair. A layer of dust shone on the bookcase in the light of the lamp with the unbalanced shade. Untalented, unfed, and unhinged: a rustle in the leaves near the porch. "Who is it?" I shouted. Before I could find out I threw myself in the car and drove back to the farmhouse.

It was empty—no, there was a light from one room, and sound from a television. I peered into a tiny TV room. "Brooklyn," said the man with the charming accent in the wing-backed chair, "a show about Brooklyn, where I live when I'm not here, won't you sit down?"

God, I was starving. Did he know a restaurant nearby?

"They will all be closed by now!" he exclaimed. "This is a tiny town! They all close by nine o'clock." It was 10 P.M.

"Well, I guess I'll have to go to bed without dinner."

"No! Impossible!" Somehow he got two syllables out of no—no-ah. He pronounced impossible as impossibile—im poss ee bee lay. Yet his English was fluent and intelligent.

"Oh, well, really, it will be all right."

"No! Impossible!" he repeated. "We must get you some food. We will storm the kitchen. We will break the window and the lock. We will get in there and get you some nice chicken. We had lovely chicken for dinner." When he moved in his chair to gesture, his movements were fluid and easy, though his body had a barrel-chested bulk to it. At one moment he curled house-cat-like in the chair, at another sprang panther-like toward me in hungry gesticulation.

I really was starving, but I didn't want to get caught breaking into the art colony kitchen on the night of my arrival. Then two young women appeared in the doorway.

"Tilla!" they both whispered.

"Anna! Linda! This is a new guest who has not had her dinner, she has arrived late, and this is a disaster! There is no food for her, not even an orange!"

"Hi"—one of them extended her hand—"I'm Anna." She was small and slender, thick hair in a dark, extravagantly cut bob.

"I'm Linda," said the other one, not extending her hand. She, too, was small and slender. Each one was dressed in a T-shirt and black jeans.

"Two of my nieces," the man they called Tilla said. "They are helping me with a program I am doing." He was ushering us from the TV room, through the dining room, to the path outside the kitchen.

"Darlings Linda and Anna, we have to get this guest her dinner. She can't go to bed without eating! You are tiny, Anna, maybe you can wiggle through the kitchen window."

"So what's your name?" Linda asked.

"Molly."

"What an unusual name," Tilla said. "My name is Tilla, Tilla Szabo. My name in Hungary is Attila, like Attila Josef, our great poet, but no one in America knows this name."

"Oh yes, I know the poems of Attila Josef! Are you sure we should be breaking into the kitchen like this . . . ?"

"Are you crazy?" he asked imperiously. "You are hungry. You must eat. This is the most basic human instinct. You deny your instincts?"

"Look, I don't want to cause trouble here . . ."

Though I supposed he was a guest, Tilla seemed to be an authority in charge. "Trouble! You are *without food*. You have driven on the horrible New Englandish roads and you have come here in the night and they have given you only keys."

"And no bed linens or towels." I sulked.

"Do not change the subject from hunger! My body tells me when I am hungry I must eat. That is that. I eat when I am hungry, sleep when I am sleepy, dance when I must dance. This is the way artists must live.

Rules are not for such basic things. And who cares about rules when the body says it needs something! Now, Linda" (he pronounced it Leenda), "you will stand under the kitchen window, and Anna, you will hop on her shoulders and raise up the window.

"Sshhh!" Tilla warned. "Some staffs might be around."

"Staff! Really, I don't think we should be doing this . . ."

"You have no more say in this," he responded.

We were under the kitchen window.

"Hey, Tilla," Linda whispered, "how come you never broke into the kitchen for us?"

"What's so special about her?" Anna challenged, as she climbed onto Linda's shoulders. They were both amazingly agile. I couldn't have gotten someone balanced on my shoulders in a million years.

"Tilla!" another voice whispered from large bushes in front of the house.

"Sshhhh!" he said. I recognized her as she came into the light cast by the window: a famous novelist, dressed exactly like the picture that her publisher printed on book after book, in a shapeless black muumuu with a long necklace, a gigantic piece of handcrafted jewelry, afloat on her bosom.

"What are we doing?" she asked him.

"Helping a guest in need. This is Molly."

"Mariah Moore," I whispered in awe, "I really admire your work."

"No time for congratulations!" Tilla whispered, "Come on, Anna, work at that window!"

"Am I correct?" the amused Mariah Moore asked. "You are breaking into the kitchen of a well-known art colony funded by the National Endowment for the Arts?"

"We are getting a hungry woman something to eat." He said *voman*. "Now," he instructed the world-famous novelist, "hold this." He passed her a loaf of cinnamon raisin bread. Anna was passing the loaves to Linda. I just stood there.

"Uncle Tilla!" Anna exploded from the kitchen. "Everything else is locked! All they've left out on the counter are these loaves of breakfast bread."

"What an unusual dinner I am feeding you then," Tilla announced.

As we toasted our cinnamon raisin bread in the dining room of the farmhouse, Tilla congratulated his nieces on their performance and shrugged off my gratitude. Mariah Moore, who, I learned, usually stayed aloof in her faraway cabin and never came to meals, adored Tilla's story and asked him question after question about Hungary in 1956 when, at age seventeen, he left his home for America. He told about the detention camps, and, when he and his father and mother and three sisters and two brothers finally came to be released from the camp into the West, what he saw:

"Apricots! I saw beautiful apricots. My family had not had such fruits for years and years. All the colors so dull, everything mud, and then we are beyond the fences and there are shops and vendors and here was a man selling apricots. My God! My mother, she loved fruit, and there she was, dragging my tired little sisters by their hands and I said to myself, I'm going to get my mother these apricots! We are free! (And my stubborn father would never think of giving her a thing.) So I took my only possession of value, my pocket watch I had smuggled with me, and I walked up to the vendor of the fruit and I could not believe that no one would stop me. No guards! I talked to the man, because of course I had no money, and arranged to trade my watch for eight apricots and six pieces of American bubble gum—I had often heard of this gum—and thought I had a very good bargain! My mother, she was so happy, and we each ate a fruit, even my father. They were delicious, well worth a pocket watch! There was one piece of bubble gum for each of my sisters and my brothers and me and we chewed and chewed! This was our big bite of freedom."

He gestured, he smiled, he grinned, every emotion he felt passed from his face through his body and into our shining faces as we drank his story and ate his bread. We were at his table, seated in the places he assigned to us, and we were enraptured, as were audiences and critics wherever Tilla could manage to perform.

He was not a novelist or painter or sculptor or composer, the usual crop at an art colony: he was a producer of performances, I learned from Mariah Moore when he left temporarily to usher Anna and Linda back to their nearby motel room, an artist who choreographed updated traditional Hungarian dances, assembling the dancers from his family network, creating the sets and backdrops for the dancing, and editing collages of music for the dancing, from rock and roll to jazz to the Hungarian folk tunes themselves on traditional instruments—then asking famous actors to donate their time to narrate the little stories that formed the background. He was multi-talented, and befriended by many, and poor. He understood how talented he was, Mariah said, and he felt, of course, that everyone should help him. You could not help but succumb to his charm, the novelist acknowledged. Of course, he had not applied to the art colony and been accepted like everyone else, nor had his application been waived, as Mariah's was, because he was super famous. One of his champions on the board had simply called Tilla up and invited him to come for the summer. "In short," Mariah concluded, "he owns this goddamned place."

"Mrs. Moore," Tilla said, reentering the dining room, "I own practically nothing, let alone a whole art colony!"

"You know you own the world, my dear."

"I wish I had owned the world in 1956," he spat.

Encouraged by Mariah, he added further detail to the story of the apricots, then went on to describe how the family first lived in Belgium, then in New York, learning new languages, working in factories . . . Mariah had her hand poised as if she were pressing the record button on an invisible tape recorder while Tilla moved through each story almost bodily, though he sat next to us and did not stir from his chair. Stupefied, caught in the headlights of his excitement and the powerful tractor beams of the novelist's eyes, I could not leave. What energy he exuded, what energy had been required for him to lead his life, so completely attuned to his own needs he seemed, and so fascinating because he overcame, again and again, his circumstances.

Although Tilla and I looked nothing alike—he was tall and sallow-skinned with a shock of thick dark hair, and I, at least a head shorter, was many shades fairer—there was an indefinable similarity between us, a fact confirmed by Mariah Moore. "Good God," she said to me regally, "turn in profile." I obeyed, of course. "Now, Tilla, you turn in profile."

"Mrs. Moore, you are an empress who commands me," he said, turning his whole torso elegantly.

"Hah!" she said. "Both of you now, go to the mirror above the fireplace and turn in profile." There were our noses, exactly alike.

"We could be in the same family!" Tilla exclaimed. "You could be my cousin! Are you Hungarian? Don't you have Hungarian blood?"

By breakfast the next day the capture of the loaves of bread was even more worthy of gossip because mysterious Mrs. Moore had been involved, and, shockingly, she herself appeared at dinner to tell the story. As our adventure was repeated, I found myself swept into their royal circle. The dinners stretched to fill whole evenings with talk and a nighttime swim or an ice cream cone or a movie with the group of artists. Tilla was the organizer. It was an apparently decorous group for an art colony, since both the king and queen were married, Mariah to her fourth husband (though most of her stories involved the infamous first husband, Dr. Moore) and Tilla to a woman whose Hungarian ancestors had come to America generations ago.

"She is not really Hungarian," Tilla announced on the farmhouse porch where the guests gathered to watch the sun plunge below the horizon. "She is American through and through, though she is a wonderful Hungarian dancer. She has inherited all the steps and she has the body for it. But she loves the malls, always she wants *things!* On her birthday I made her a cake with my own hands! A beautiful hazelnut torte. But she would not speak to me. She wanted pearls. Imagine! Where would I get money for them? We are artists!

"Well, she is not an artist, really. She dances, but she prefers the mall. She cooks and bakes and makes holidays with her mother and my mother and her sisters and my sisters and my aunts—they and my uncles are also in this country, and we all dance, all of my family—I feature sometimes my family in my work, Molly." He had turned directly to the two of me. Molly One wanted to write poetry, while Molly Two was ready for a big affair with an important artist I could tell my biographer about when I was a famous elderly poet with a fabulous romantic past. "Don't you have an agent?" I asked him.

"Agents! What an extravagance! I do the deals myself. I'm not going to give some agent his percent. I can get along on very, very little money. It is my pride. See this shirt? It is five years old. Looks like new, right? I do not know when I'm going to get another shirt. I take care of this shirt. It never goes in the washing machine. I wash it by hand. I can't afford to ruin the fibers on your American washing machines."

It actually never occurred to me that washing machines ruined fibers. "I handwash, too," I said meekly.

"I do not need agents or bookkeepers. Nina does this work, and my brothers and sisters. I am the inspiration behind it all, but they do the nuts and bolts. I am busy taking the old dances and making them new with new steps over the old ones, and I am doing the lighting, and I am drawing the designs of the sets for my father to build, and designing the new costumes for my aunt to make and my mother and sisters to embroider, and I am busy finding great new rock musics for us and working with my cousin who plays all the old songs for the dances, and then I am getting the movie stars to volunteer their voices."

"My God, you're making family art!"

"Hah! My family. We fight all the time, I am murdering my father daily, and my aunt is driving me crazy, and my sister is pregnant for the third time at the wrong moment! But of course we are all in this together, this is what we do, but it is all on me, like a wolf in a sack I must carry and never let the wolf out or it will eat me and eat all of us."

Knowing no English and having no education beyond the eighth grade, Tilla had managed to get a high school certificate and to get the musical and ballet training that had led him to the wide network of connections he had. Some of the members of his family still spoke no English at all, though all of the younger ones had American educations. He had taken them on his back, though not completely: They kept slipping off. Some of them wanted to do only traditional dancing, some only rock. Some, like Nina, wanted pearls and malls. And all, at times, had been jealous of Tilla, who now had a Guggenheim fellowship, and was determined to keep every dollar of it to himself.

"I need this support!" he declared in a higher pitch than he usually spoke in. "I am the mainstay! I am the one they all need, and I need to be here at the art colony because I need the silence to make our dances."

Of course the Szabos did not see it his way. He had insisted on, and they had begrudged him, this visit of a whole summer. He had never gone away for summer camp, for college, for graduate school; he had been with them in their village and then in Budapest, as they watched the tanks come down the streets, and as they fled to the border, and as they were interned in camps far, far from summer camp. . . . He had worked heavy construction in Belgium until the permission had come to climb in a cramped bunk on a boat to New York. In the tiny, thin-walled Brooklyn apartment he could hear his sisters coughing and his brothers farting and his parents making love.

Molly One took over. If Mariah could skip meals, I could too. The proofs for my first book of poems had arrived. I shut myself in my studio with takeout food for two days and made massive changes that the University of Missouri Press threatened to charge me for. I was a poet. This was what I was here for. When I surfaced for dinner Tilla welcomed me back to his table from my business trip. By the time I got to dessert, I was Molly Two.

Dessert was terrible: canned fruit. It was an ice cream night for sure, but first came the postprandial sunset-watching ritual. The guests sat silently on the veranda, some puffing on Tilla's proffered Balkan Sobranies. He had a burly but strangely light body. He was thickly graceful in the angles at which he held his head and neck. "Molly!" He suddenly turned that muscular neck toward me. "Why are you out in this night air without a sweater? You will catch cold! Here, here." He began to take off his jacket to give to me.

"I'm OK. I don't really need a sweater tonight. I feel fine." I really did feel fine.

"Nonsense! How can you not feel cold? Of course you need a sweater! You must have one. If you will not take my jacket, and thank you, because I am cold, too, then you must go and get another layer of clothing for yourself." He could not imagine another person might feel different from him.

"Really, I'm fine!"

He stood up in a fury. "I cannot allow you to sit here in the cold! I cannot bear to watch you! Look, you have gooseflesh!"

"I have goose bumps because you're scaring me!"

"You do not know your own body," he stormed, to the bewilderment of the others who sat in the near darkness of the sunset's afterglow. He faced me, red with anger. "Your body says if you are hot or cold! You are not listening to your own body!"

"All right, all right," I groused. He was so sure I was cold, maybe I wasn't in my own body, after all. He was monstrously upset, and my donning a sweater would soothe it. I went inside the farmhouse and borrowed an abandoned sweatshirt off a hook in the coatroom which contained the odds and ends of clothes forgotten by years of guests.

"Tell me that you don't feel much better!" Tilla crowed as I banged the screen door returning to the porch. He slapped a mosquito. Everyone was being eaten alive. None of us would be able to sit there much longer.

"Well, at least I'm protected against mosquitoes," I said.

"It is another advantage of being warmly dressed!" he said in delight. The others were preparing to get in their cars and go to the local ice cream place.

"Want a ride?" I asked everyone in general.

"Actually," Mariah announced, "I could take some people in my car, too." This was so unusual that all the younger writers immediately volunteered to go with her. But those who were left, and this included Tilla, piled into my Toyota, the color of cinnamon raisin toast, and, as Mariah Moore had immediately noted, the color of Tilla's eyes. Mine were blue, however. There were differences between us as well.

"Nice car, is it new?" Tilla marveled from the front seat.

"Yup," I said, feeling honored that he chose to ride with me. I backed out of the gravel driveway, passing the stone-walled garden.

"If you don't mind my asking," Tilla said politely, "how do you afford such a car?"

"I can't—I borrowed to buy it," I said, laughing, as we turned down the hill. The others in the back seat started talking cars.

"But who would lend you this money?" Tilla said, perplexed.

"A bank!"

"But why would a bank lend *you* money for a brand new car?" He was suspicious.

"Well, I filled out the forms," I said at the stop sign at the bottom of the hill. "You know, telling my income from my job, blah, blah."

"You have a job?"

"Of course I have a job! I'm poet-in-residence for my state arts council. I go into schools and teach poetry."

"It is good to have a job like this. It is good to be able to support yourself as you do. Me, it is impossible. If I had a regular job, I could not run the company." He fell silent, then said, "Perhaps I could send my family into schools! We could show everyone dances."

"Hey, maybe you could."

In the back seat sat three stolidly uncommunicative young sculptors, each with a Budweiser can.

"So," Tilla began again slowly, "you are a very smart woman. You have your job, and you have your nice car, and soon you will have your book. Too bad you don't know when to feed yourself dinner and get yourself a sweater."

"I guess that's what I need you for," I said boldly.

"Hah! And I need you to show me how to get jobs in schools for my family, and then we will buy such new cars!"

My car was stopped at a railroad crossing. We were waiting for the train to go by.

"I despise trains. They make me think of Hungary," Tilla mused.

"Speaking of Hungary," one of the dour sculptors suddenly said from the back seat, "I see your wife's coming."

"Yes, my wife, Nina, she is coming to visit this weekend," he confirmed. "And some of my cousins. We are going to do some dances for all of you on Saturday."

The minute we got to the Tasti Freeze I ordered a double chocolate milk shake.

"My God, Molly, you drink that whole thing?"

"Why, aren't I supposed to have a milk shake?"

"Of course! If your body is hungry, then feed it." Now he was telling the three sculptors about his Hungarian village.

"Wasn't that weird?" Mariah asked me, after her carload had arrived. I was standing in the middle of the ice cream stand parking lot feeling stunned at the prospect of Nina. Mariah picked chocolate sprinkles off her muumuu dress and long tangled necklaces.

"What was weird?"

"That business with the sweater!"

"It's hard to figure him out," I trailed off cautiously.

"But not hard to figure you out, darling," she said. "You're in love with him."

I laughed uncomfortably. "He's married," I began.

"Oh for Christ's sake!" she sneered.

"Mrs. Moore," Tilla called to the famous novelist, "I am telling these people that you have five children! They are not believing me, so you will be telling them also this is true, will you? We have six children in my family also," he said to the sculptors, "three girls and three men."

"Oh heavens yes, it is absolutely true," Mariah gurgled.

"I salute you, Mrs. Moore, how you must concentrate! To write novels with five children in the house—at least all the children in my family were taught to dance."

"Hah! I didn't write novels while my kids were little, heavens no, I wrote short stories. I only wrote novels later on when they all started school. I had them one right after the other, in the succession of my husbands, and no regrets."

Tilla threw his arm around her. "I admire you, Mrs. Moore! How you

wrote even short stories with your babies. My sisters' babies are screaming right this minute. If I close my eyes I can hear them screaming all the
way from Brooklyn! Hear them?" Tilla made wah-wah baby sounds, and
we watched his whole body reshape into an infant's. His typically graceful gestures were suddenly spastic, and he cried crocodile tears. "All
three of my sisters have babies now," he said as he finished his tiny parking lot performance. "Thank God my brothers' and cousins' kids are
more grown up."

"So everyone has children but you and Nina," Mrs. Moore said.

"Oh yes, Nina would like to have a child, I think, but I do not! My
sisters and brothers have enough children for me. How can I dance and
run the company and take responsibility for one more child, even my
own? And the screaming, Mrs. Moore, I cannot take it!"

"But what about when you are too old to dance and need your sons
and daughters to dance for you?" she asked.

"I am too old for good dancing right now, Mrs. Moore, forty-two
years old, but not too old to direct our performances."

"But who will carry on your work?" she persisted.

"Ah, I will have the pleasure of choosing among all the children of
my sisters and my brother and my cousins. Right now there are fifteen
of them! And probably more to come."

I drove my passengers back to the art colony, dropping them off at
their cottages, and returned to the farmhouse, where I met Mrs. Moore
dumping her last passenger. We chatted on the gravel road. "Well, that
marriage is going down the toilet," she said to me as I absently kicked
mulch back over the roots of the hollyhocks by the gardening shed, a
miniature shuttered yellow clapboard cottage.

"You think so?"

"My God, she wants children, he doesn't. She wants a regular house,
he doesn't. She wants a middle-class life. He doesn't. All he wants is

ephemeral fame and fortune and, my God, she's an American, how long will she be able to take that family? He's yours for the asking, darling."

"All I want to do is write my poems."

"Keep lying, Molly. Why don't you just enjoy yourself?" she said as she opened her car door. "He's nice for a fling. He's sexy, no? Especially since he doesn't have sex with his wife."

"Whoa! What do you mean he doesn't have sex with his wife?"

"That's what he told me, *entre nous*, they haven't had sex in three years."

"I can't believe it! He's oozing sex." I actually shocked myself by saying this. I hadn't admitted it to myself before.

"Well, darling, that's what he confided in me, so enjoy yourself!" she said as she closed the car door. "But watch out," she called as she drove past the trellised steps, "he's a handful!"

When the Szabo cousins and Tilla and Nina performed, all the jealous guests crowded into the barn to judge them, but the dances, so rambunctious, yet traditional, were sharply formed, and stunning. We clapped till our hands hurt. We wrung our wrists to relieve them of clapping so long. Mariah clambered to her feet yelling, "Bravo!"

"My God, Tilla," I said, breathlessly hugging him in his sweat-drenched costume, "that's the sexiest thing I ever saw!"

During the weekend of Nina's visit, I watched Tilla forbid her to gamble—there was a card game—forbid her to smoke, forbid her to drink, and tell a story of how he, in a fit of temper, threw a lemon chiffon pie at the wall, just missing her. I saw the stony fury in Nina's high-cheekboned face and I knew that Mariah Moore, as novelists often so presciently are about the behavior of others, was completely right about their marriage. I thought, *My God, I'd never let him forbid those things to me. I'd never let him throw a pie at ME.*

All Nina wanted, she told Mariah, was a nice house with a swing set in the back yard, and two sets of dishes, one for everyday and a gold leaf one for company.

"You'll wait a lifetime for that gold leaf," Mariah sneered.

After Nina left, the weekend shrank to an island our river of mutual admiration flowed past. Like double reflecting currents we cast light after angle of light on Tilla's dances and my poems. I could articulate what he put bodily into his art. My descriptions of what he did delighted him—he taped them and transcribed them into his foundation applications; and his encouragement of my poetry thrilled me—yes, of course I should move to New York and read my delicate metaphors that were like dances themselves in front of an audience.

By now we were having picnic lunches in a meadow near his studio. Breakfast, lunch, dinner, and all evening, every evening.

How would I justify to myself sleeping with this married man?

"It's over, Molly," Mariah Moore said as she removed a piece of tobacco from her tongue. "His marriage is kaput. Have no qualms."

"But you have no qualms about *anything*, Mariah!" I said.

"Darling, you don't know what qualms are."

I hated her condescension to me, but was fascinated by the blasé wisdom she exhaled. "You are far too inexperienced to understand qualms, my dear. Qualms require mistakes in life, and you are too young to have made serious mistakes. Though perhaps just now you are about to."

"I thought you told me to grab him! First you tell me his marriage is kaput and I should go after him, and now you tell me I'm going to make the mistake of my life!"

"I'm telling you adulthood is ambiguity, Molly." She cast her infamous cold eye on me. I wriggled to escape that unblinkered gaze.

"I want my life to be about good decisions."

"I never made a good decision until I reached menopause. Hormones made all my decisions all my life."

"*Hormones!* I can't listen to this, Mariah. You're giving me a sore throat."

She took no offense, but fished in her giant canvas bag for a throat lozenge. "Here, darling, try to take care of yourself," she said. "I've got to get back to my novel. I've left two characters at it in bed for three days now. The poor things are exhausted and I've at least got to get them to the bathroom."

I held out until my last evening at the art colony. Tilla and I stood in my stone house, the books, the papers, the clothes piled haphazardly in their boxes and suitcases.

"You must pack this," Tilla whispered, giving me a sheaf of drawings. "These are the notations for the steps, and drawings of the sets for my new work, *Peacock Walk.*" It was a performance piece for me. The sketches of the costumes displayed outrageous peacock-feathered contraptions.

"Oh my God, oh my God," I repeated stupidly. "Oh, Tilla . . . these are beautiful! I am so . . ." I said lamely, ". . . honored!"

"You are a good friend to me, Molly, you help me say what I need to say about my dances, you understand how I need to be away from my family, just as you need to be away from yours, to grow." Slowly, in fragments, the story of my family had emerged in our conversations, sandwiched in tightly among Tilla's stories, mostly in response to questions by Mariah. "This is how I thank you."

Of course, I had a thank-you for him as well. I had written a poem about the dancing and about his imitation of a baby as we ate ice cream in the parking lot the night he announced Nina was coming. After I read him the poem, he reached for me in the way that we had not reached for one another, although we had occasionally taken one another's hand, or sat shoulder to shoulder.

"Let's take off our clothes," he said then.

After we did, we lay on the naked little pallet that served as a bed in my stone house, and Tilla Szabo told me I was beautiful. "But how can I be beautiful to you? I'm not a dancer—I sit with my chubby little belly on my lap as I type my poems for hours. . . ."

"But you are beautiful because you are not a dancer. You are my soft, lovely poet. I can look at muscles all day long, Molly. What I want to look at it is you."

I didn't believe him, but I accepted it, like a plant so deprived of water that the soil actually repels the moisture at first, the watering having to soften the mineraled crust before the moisture can seep, creeping down to the roots where my need for this admiration was so profound. Once I had seen him probe the pistil of a wildflower, and now he pored over me with his eyes and hands, as if I were his specimen, the object of all his gaze, as he was of mine. His clean barrel chest, almost without hair, its pink nipples planted in pectoral muscles which were almost rectangular, his beginning of a belly, his hooded penis against his thigh, he lay like an Odalisque, calm and luxurious, lifting an expressive arm toward me as I reached toward him, hungry, yet removed, looking to see what was before me. He touched my breasts firmly, as if he were a culinary maestro, testing fruit in awe at the market. "Beautiful," he whispered. He didn't seem to be lying. He had a kind of surrender in his eyes. "Lie back for me," he suggested, and held my chin in his hand as he kissed me. "Loosen your tongue," he instructed. "There. . . ." There we were, kissing so long our tongues didn't know whose mouth they belonged in. We crushed together, and then we finally parted.

I took his penis in my hand. "Oh God, don't touch me so! I feel I will come too soon," he said, and put his finger unerringly on my clitoris sparing me the necessity to teach him about my body. After all, as he had told me, he knew my body better than I did.

———

When I returned to the arts council, I applied for every grant in *The Guide to Foundations*, taught the children, ran up long distance phone bills so expensive I had to put them on my credit cards, and received Tilla on the interspersed days his family was performing within striking distance. I was having an affair with a married man.

"Try not to bore me with your flimsy ethics, Molly," Mariah said on the phone from her Broome Street loft. "This is a major move in your life. And, I might add, a major move in Nina Szabo's life, whoever she is and whatever she decides to do."

"But it's wrong, I'm doing something wrong, Mariah."

"See a therapist."

"I don't have a therapist right now." Ruta had moved her practice to New York, and I had struck out on my own.

"Get one."

"I will soon, I'm moving to New York in a few months."

"You are! Jesus Christ, how did this happen? You never tell the best news first!"

"I got the Chevrolet Grant, I've got the money to move—now I just have to get a job."

"I've got some leads, darling, maybe I can help you get a job. But I can't help you with your morals, Molly. I'm completely neutral there. I don't want to be your mother any more than I can help it, and I sure as hell won't be your therapist. The minute you get to New York, you must get some help. New York is going to crush you if you don't watch out, that is, if you don't get someone to watch out for you. And believe me, our darling boy Tilla Szabo is *not* going to watch out for you in that way. The only place he's going to take care of you is in bed. Not insignificant, Miss Poet, but not sufficient, either."

It always surprised me that Mariah took an interest in me. And Tilla's interest surprised me. I was clumsy. I couldn't dance or tell witty stories full of famous people's names. I was neither a social nor a physical acrobat. I wasn't even sure I could write. Sometimes my poems looked like bright parakeets to me, flying and communicative. Other times they looked like guano.

"You are a smart woman in the world. You are a sexy woman in bed. That's a good kind of dancing. And that's all I care about," Tilla said summarily on the phone.

"Don't you think I should learn to speak Hungarian?" I said, daunted by the prospect.

"There's enough Hungarian in my life," he said, to my relief. "If you meet my family sometime, I will teach you to say thank you in Hungarian to my mother and you will keep your eyes lowered when my father talks to you and that will be enough. What I need to learn I can learn from you in English."

So I sold the cinnamon Toyota I'd bought with Polly's down payment for my new life alone, resigned from the arts council, and tramped the streets of Manhattan looking at one dingy sublet after another until the little white studio with the parquet floors and the disreputable elevator that looked like an empty unclean fishbowl appeared, and I agreed to a rent three times what my new clerical job with an arts agency would pay for. My astronomical new rent left nothing for food, clothes, transportation, or my overdue phone bills, let alone the moving expenses I incurred and the psychotherapy I was contemplating. All this happened while Tilla was on tour in South America with part of the troupe. Nina had stayed home to help the accountant straighten out the everlasting mess of the Szabo Dancers' books.

I'd given away half my possessions, to Polly's surprise. After all, I was the sentimental one who wanted to keep everything from La Grange. My move took a lot of explaining to Polly, who thought I had a good deal where I was, and it never occurred to me to lie. I even told her about Nina. Skeptical and disgusted, my mother had her own problems. She had been diagnosed with diabetes and the chocolate-covered cherries that accompanied the novels and cigarettes she cherished were out of her life. She hated her food. The roof at La Grange needed fixing. She would wait till I visited to do that. Visited? How on earth was I going to afford that? I would have to think of something. I stood exhilarated in my new apartment in New York with my grant spent and every credit card at its limit, my heart a helium balloon. My new phone rang. It was Ruta, who was willing to take me on again. The phone rang again: Maggie, back from her tour with her new string quartet. A third time: Tilla from Bogota. Nina had left the Brooklyn apartment and no one knew where she was. The last call came from the arts agency I was to be a typist for. I was fired. The agency was suffering cutbacks.

I was the luckiest woman on earth. I had New York and my old friend for company. I was rid of a job I would have hated. And Tilla was coming back for his forty-third birthday, two weeks away. My thirty-fourth birthday was six weeks away. My bills flew overhead like a flock of exciting migrating shoreline birds, flashing the silver of their wings against the sky. All was possible. Everything was poetry.

23.

A sonnet is the size of a plump made bed, and a blank page is a room. A sonnet is a garden bed, bordered by a paper lawn. It is where consciousness sleeps, and the sleeping beauty of the unconscious wakes. *Wake up and make that bed!* I said to myself. *And while you're at it, make yourself up. Make up a self.* I'd begun a group of sonnets about love and desire. *Dreams, brains, fur/ and guts,* I wrote, *what we are,* then teased the idea some more:

> *That's my bargain, the Pax*
> *Peacock, with the world. Look hard, life's soft. Life's cache*
> *is flesh, flesh, and flesh.*

The world was my body. Not only my body with Tilla—Tilla and an amaryllis bulb, Tilla and grapes, wet in a bowl—but my body on its own. I gloried in sex, the secret of life that all adults knew. If I'd dared to move to New York, could I dare use this life-force to fill the lungs of a type of poem most people thought was dead? I sensed the words breathing under the concrete. *She lays each beautifully mooned index finger/in the furrow on the right and on the left/sides of her clitoris and lets them linger/in their swollen cribs. . . .*

But I wrote my poems only on Saturday mornings. Each of the weekday mornings I crammed onto the Second Avenue bus that crawled through the rush hour downtown to Friends Seminary, a Quaker day school. Now I was a full-time English teacher and worried about gum on the chairs and whether sixty twelve-year-olds could spell. When I lucked into my job as a last-minute replacement, I was told that teachers always teach the grade of their own turning point. I taught seventh grade, the same year I became a mother to Gail and a caretaker to Ted.

At 8:29 A.M. in the old Meeting House on Fifteenth Street I climbed in beside my adolescent charges who wiggled back and forth on the nineteenth-century benches, paint-thickened by the annual coats of gray that shielded the wood from their scuffs.

At 8:30 A.M. the Meeting House fell silent by unanimous agreement. Several hundred children, ages ten through thirteen, settled into a stillness deep enough to hear the traffic outside and to feel the light, or the damp, or the heat, and whatever feelings had been racing through us since we woke. For ten minutes the shifts and creaks of the benches, the whispers, the illicit page turning shaped the noiselessness into a children's peace, achieved through children's wills. With it, a dignity that lay disguised in each of us assumed an outline. Then the ten minutes were up and we all shook hands and the voluble morning announcements began. By the time we left for our classes we were an ordinary mass of bodies flooding the stairwells, though a rind of the extraordinary remained—we had after all, for one whole sixth of an hour, entered a silence cool as a hand on each of our foreheads.

Up in Room 303 it was poetry-writing day, though first we were working on *The Catcher in the Rye*. A few of the fifteen kids lay on the floor, composing their Holden Caulfield New York Travelogues, others worked at tables, pasting up their Holden Caulfield Scrapbooks, digging for the best quotes to use as captions, while a couple of boys stretched out on the fifteen-foot stuffed corduroy worm that was usually slung across the bookcase. They were still reading the novel. Up front at the desks, a group of four discussed the book.

"You mean he's telling the whole story from a *mental hospital!*" Wild-haired Hazel Zimmer was shocked.

Smooth little Fionula Frye exclaimed, "You mean he's *crazy?*"

Niles Baldassarian unwound his long legs from his desk and said in a voice so slow an anxious person would be tempted to supply the words for him, "My . . . dad says . . ." All the kids except Hazel had known Niles since kindergarten, so a familiarity soft as flannel swathed the room as he continued, ". . . says people in nut houses are . . ." It wasn't exactly that he paused between every word, it was that his voice seemed to unwind from a spool larger than most people's, ". . . saner than we are."

"I think he's sane," Hazel pronounced from behind her special blue glasses. She was trying them as a filter for more efficient reading. Frizzy haired and lanky, Hazel was the newest member of this group, a refugee from a less understanding uptown school. They'd taught her to take co-pious notes, and she looked up from them expectantly. Her block print—she'd failed to master script—pushed all the way to the left and right sides of the page without a concept of margins.

"I think he's weird," Philip Wu muttered, doing his vocabulary home-work under his book. He wore a huge man's wristwatch.

"I don't. I love Holden," Fionula said. She had a perfect oval face, as if she had been drawn in a beginning art class, and straight, shining brown hair. She wore a turtleneck with Scotty dogs on it, and she was smart as a whip.

"So, Molly," Niles said, "do you think . . . Salinger is a genius?"

"Well, I don't know," I said to Niles. "What do you think? Is Salinger a genius?"

"Sure."

"Are all geniuses crazy?" Fionula asked seriously.

"What is crazy?" I asked, just as seriously.

Niles said without pauses, "Having nothing inside you."

It stopped us all dead. The four of us stared at him while my eleven other students buzzed in the background.

"Being empty," he said, brisk as a math teacher.

"Crazy is being empty?" Hazel cocked her head.

"He's talking about the Quaker thing," Philip said.

"What Quaker thing?" she asked.

"About that of God in every human!" Fionula announced triumphantly. "About the light that's inside everyone, that George Fox said." The early Quaker George Fox maintained that there was "that of God" in every person, a phrase all the students who had been there for a while knew, whether they were Quaker or not.

"If everyone . . . has God . . . inside them," Niles went on, "then no God inside you means . . . no center in you. No center . . . is . . . crazy."

We all understood him instantly.

"I'm writing this down," Hazel declared, smearing the sweat and ink from overgripping her pen across the wood of the table, "in my Vocabulary Section under C. Crazy is no center."

"Actually, according to Niles," Fionula corrected, "Holden is crazy because he has no God within."

"He's . . . crazy," Niles noted.

"We all feel crazy sometimes," I said.

"Hey, let's write poems about . . . crazy things," Niles said.

"But I thought poems had centers," Fionula said, "so how can we make a crazy poem?"

I was stumped.

"We could have a crazy subject," Philip said to help me out, "like dreams."

We loved the dream idea. I began to corral the other students from their projects, but they balked. They'd just gotten into their work, and didn't want to stop for the new assignment. How much I had underesti-

mated their concentration, almost failing to recall my own agonies in
school, continually barred from one thing because it was time for something else. I let them go on while the four of us up front turned to our
dream poems.

Scrawling a line length on the board, and a number of total lines—
a grid to follow if they needed one—I admonished, "And don't say *it was
just a dream*, you guys! Really get inside that dream and uncover it."

Everyone was writing in relative quiet except Philip. I stole toward
him.

"The only dreams I have are about my dad," he said, looking at his
wristwatch.

"Oh, is that your dad's watch?" I said.

"Yeah."

"So write about your dad," I said stupidly, then remembered with a
burn of regret that his parents were estranged. Philip never saw his father. But when he looked up in despair, I knew what I could say to him.
"In dreams he's *part* of you, Philip. It's wonderful that you dream of him.
That way you get to see him every night."

"Does that make me crazy?"

"No," I said firmly, "that makes you sane."

"But that's not the assignment," he worried.

"No, it isn't for everybody else. But for you the assignment is to write
the sane poem."

As the poem writing continued, the cutting, pasting, reading, and
writing at the back of the room was breaking up. They were getting
tired. I zoomed from student to student whispering, "OK, everyone, it's
time to put the projects away." When they began to clatter scissors and
glue tubes, I hissed, "Hey! You got to do your work—let them do theirs!"
Then they crept in exaggerated stealth toward their lockers, mocking my
instructions. The period, too, was creeping to its end. Soon I had to ask
Hazel, Fionula, Philip, and Niles to finish their poems over the weekend.

The extraordinary was passing into the ordinary. That was the way of growth—a miracle would merge into the day and somehow become it, though the day was already itself.

On these things I could depend: Every day I went to a place where there were ten minutes of benign nothingness that might be construed as God. Every day I learned how to live from children who were not the flesh of my flesh. Every day that less harm was done, somehow more good amassed. Every night I spoke on the phone with my lover whose wife had finally reappeared with divorce papers. Saturday night and Sunday morning we had sex. Every weekend I wrote a sonnet, and now I had fifty-two of them, like a deck of fortune-telling cards, and with Tilla's encouragement I was sending them out to fancier literary magazines than I had dared before. A windy freedom blew through the big midtown buildings my bus passed on the way to school each morning, skyscrapers full of the publishers where I suddenly felt free to send my new collection of poems.

Weeks went by. The Holden Caulfield Scrapbooks were finished, and corrected, and handed back. The school trip loomed up, then sank away into a sleepy memory only the yearbook would wake, months later. We started *Of Mice and Men*. We cooked up a poetry reading and gave our own assembly. We finished *Of Mice and Men*, desolate over how they shot the dog and then shot Lenny. We were fools for Steinbeck. For the test I coaxed them into writing about foreshadowing, how the dog's death foreshadowed Lenny's death. Structure, structure, that's what writing was about. And that's what days were about, too.

The tempo beneath a line, the rhythm a sentence uncoils . . . The structures I had learned to secure with words I began to make in lived time. The hours of the school day passed like a Book of Hours, matins through vespers. Like evensong, I attended poetry readings, sometimes with Maggie. "There's Howard Moss, the poetry editor of *The New Yorker*." She jabbed me in the ribs as we sat upstairs at Books & Co. Maggie knew everybody. "The social spider web"—she made a vampire face, quavered her voice, and flapped her fingers—"has unseen uses." This was what Juilliard had taught her.

With Ruta's help, I'd devised a little rule to get me through the aftermaths of these readings. If I met and talked to one new person, then my job was done. I could relax, no matter how many other people there were to meet. While Maggie added new names to her purple notebook, I introduced myself only to Howard Moss, the close-shaven man in the sweater vest.

"Oh yes, I saw your poem in *Boulevard*," he mused. "Now why didn't you send that poem to me?"

But I did! I didn't say to him. I just looked blank.

"But you will send me something next time?" He cocked his head to one side of his bow tie.

"Oh yes!" I replied, resisting the urge to curtsy, then marched home to correct papers and go to bed. Evensong was over.

No one was supposed to be put through to the dingy faculty sanctum sanctorum except friends or family of teachers, so one day when I ran to answer the ring before it interrupted the Study Hall I was supervising, I barked facetiously, "Fiends Cemetery Faculty Room."

A cultivated voice emanated from the receiver. "May I speak with Molly Peacock?"

Instead of saying, *This is she,* to the unfamiliar voice, I demanded, "How did you get connected here?"

"I said it was very, very important that I speak to Miss Peacock." The voice sharpened. "Is she there?"

"Oh," I said, deflated, "that's me."

The voice belonged to an editor from one of the publishers in the skyscrapers, and he quietly asked me if anyone else had taken my book.

"No, no one has," I answered, feeling embarrassed by what seemed my failure. Yet he engaged me in a long conversation about possible titles and the schedule and when I might finish the manuscript. My voice got surer and the editor's reedy voice relaxed. Still, I wondered if my book had in fact been *accepted*.

"But," I interrupted him, "are you actually going to publish my book?"

"Why else would we be having this conversation?" he asked, astonished.

"Well, I . . ."

"You just want to be sure?" He laughed. "You can be absolutely sure!"

My book was going to be published by a man in a tall, tall building. It felt as though he had reached down from that building to curl his finger around the god in me—the god the Quakers insisted was in everyone. The acceptance made the holiness of my new life sensuously palpable, and the next weekend the title came to me: *Raw Heaven*.

24.

"Everything's taken care of, Molly," Gram said. "There's not gonna be no funeral, and no announcement or nothing. They cremated your dad right from the hospital after he had his stroke. Everything's all cleaned up. Your uncle's here and your grandfather and everything's shipshape."

Gram and Grandpa's apartment was spotless, as was their gleaming Ford I had parked my rental next to. I stood just inside the door, with a view into the living room. On the mahogany cabinet that contained the television set were thirty or so well-dusted china dogs. Gram had never allowed a real animal in her house. In her spotless kitchen a spice cake with thick frosting stood at attention on its risered plate next to Gram, who never sat down. Over her camel slacks and sweater was a starched blue-flowered apron.

"Oh, Molly, why did you come?" she said. "I told Gail not to come and she stayed home. Everything's been taken care of, honey."

"Hiya, Molsie," my grandfather said, hanging in the doorway.

His favorite son, my father's brother Uncle Dave sat at the polished mahogany dining room table, his face cheery above his beer. Like a stage set with x's on the floor to mark exactly where each piece of furniture must be for the actors' blocking, the dining-living room waited for a voice. As I opened my mouth, nothing came out, because I suddenly had an image of my father's head popping through the floor. Then another Ted head, then another, popping through the floorboards, through the wall-to-wall carpet, making a mess. Being there made me want to make a mess, too. Like a real dog pissing on the carpet, my father had fouled their lives. "It was the war," Grandpa was saying to me about World War II. "Your father was never the same when he come home from the Navy."

Long, long before the war he'd been dirty Teddy. Their first child, named Edward, had died. The pure dead Edward got replaced by the next Edward, nicknamed Ted, who messed up. The only thing he liked in school was woodshop. He'd made the wooden cabinet that held a collection of china dolls with china skirts in the corner near the TV.

Now there were Ted's heads, twenty or more of them, a collection, just like the dogs on the TV and the dolls in the cabinet, all popping up through the carpet. Oh, Daddy!

Once I threw my arms around him and he held me tight. Our black dog Mitzi had been sitting at my feet, watching me do the dishes, as she always did, when I messed up. I dropped a dinner plate that flukishly hit her on the eyebrow. The impact popped her eye right out of its socket. "You blinded her! You blinded my dog!" Gail screamed while I threw myself in my father's arms, because Polly had scooped up Mitzi in a towel and was holding her while Gail stood yelling.

"We gotta get to the vet," my dad, the vet, commanded.

"But it's so far!" Polly despaired.

"I know where a close vet is," I whispered into his neck. "I saw it on my bike."

Trusting my advice, Ted piled us into the car with Mitzi, her eyeball plopped on her snout, and followed my directions to the veterinarian, who snapped the eye back into its socket with no harm done. Now Ted's heads, like multiple dogs' eyes, popped impossibly up from the floor. As each one sprang, I mentally hammered it down. I was popping my Pop. But he wouldn't stay in his socket. He was messy. And dogged. He kept coming back.

Gram had taken off her apron. She meant business. I excused myself to the bathroom and witnessed, from my toilet perch, the gleaming fixtures, the scrubbed tile, the spotless glass shelf with its jar of cotton swabs.

Back at the dining room table papers had appeared.

"I want you to look at everything, Molly. It's all cleaned up. All taken care of," Gram said. "Want a Three Musketeers?" She pointed to a bowl of miniature candy bars, but stopped my hand before I reached. Then she selected three miniature Musketeers for me, and put them carefully in my outstretched palm.

Imagine a mother who would not let you take anything for yourself, even a candy bar. Polly and Ted's house, before they got the store, was pleasantly messy, full of food and delicious leftovers. Nobody ever made to clean up a plate, everybody allowed to eat what they wanted, mashed potatoes to feed a navy, take what you want, gravy in big bowl, self serve—Ted must have loved it.

Now the heads were gone, pounded back into the floor and walls. But before I could concentrate on the papers, an image of an egg loomed. It was all prepared for dyeing: a hole pricked by a pin in its top, its white and yolk blown into a bowl and discarded. An ancient hand had swabbed it out with a Q-Tip.

Oh, Ted, the mess to be swabbed. The badness within them become bad in you.

Squatting before us was a short stack of documents: birth and death certificates, two marriage certificates and two sets of divorce decrees, an insurance policy with my sister as beneficiary, and no policy for me. He had told me he was cashing mine in years before. He needed the money, but he would try to replace it. He had not. There was not a single piece of paper with my name on it. I was empty as an egg.

"Now there was other money, Molly, but that was transferred to your uncle and me," Gram said. "Me and your grandfather. Your father couldn't take care of his own affairs, you know. He couldn't do nothing. He never could. Now let's get the rest squared away before dinner," she said, rising from the table to lead me to the basement where all his clothes hung neatly on a clothesline.

"What a job!" she said. "But now it's all done."

A pain began to excoriate my blown-out shell.

"I don't want anything, Gram."

"Nothing! You've got to take something, Mols, it's not right."

"I do not want one thing." Under the clothes stood a box of war mementoes.

"Even a photograph?"

"No." I was bitumen, fragile, and prepared for dyeing. I would have to dye myself in every color, design myself, be the poet of my shell, gleaming in my emptiness.

"I'm not saving this for you, Molly. Once you go, it's gone."

"Fine, don't save it. Maybe Gail wants it."

"Gail has what she wants. She already took it a few months ago when she visited."

When she visited? How did she know she was supposed to come? Who told her? I thought. Once again I was left out of some mysterious circle of communication among them. "OK, Gram," I said. "Throw it out."

We trooped upstairs for roast beef and I ate my dinner, everything so homey and tasty on the patterned plates. I took my spice cake neatly foiled in a special package back to my motel room and left the next morning, having slept with the television on, so Ted's head couldn't pop up through the floor.

After I opened my apartment door, I walked directly to my kitchen and stood in front of the oven in my coat. Then I opened the oven door and almost lay my head on it, contemplating turning on the gas. But the oven door was greasy with drippings. So I rose to remove my coat and get a towel. Ceremoniously, I lay the towel on the fat-sprayed door. Then I lay my head on it, looking into the oven. The towel was soft and the oven was dark as a womb, messy, oily, and used for creation.

Now there would be no more Ted, no more phone calls. He couldn't do a thing to me now, not one thing more. I cried a little, in preparation for anger. The Peacock line was going to have to go on through Uncle Dave's kids, not Ted's—unless Gail had a baby. If anything with Peacock in it was going on through me, it would be a name attached to a poem. If anything passed through my womb, it would be art, not life. Fury allowed me to get up and throw the towel in the hamper, close the oven door, and eat the squashed spice cake I'd stuffed in my suitcase.

25.

"Oh my God, Tilla," I yelled from the cold, unfinished bathroom of his Williamsburg loft, sitting on a paint-specked toilet seat, looking at the bare pipes sunk through a hole in the floor where you could see his neighbor, a painter, down in her bathroom until she sealed Tilla's peephole, "there's a tear in this diaphragm! Jesus, I wonder how long it's been here." It was an old, neglected one, the rubber stiffening and yellowing from the freshwater pink it had been when new. I kept it in his bathroom just in case I unexpectedly found myself at his place unprepared, as I did on this Sunday morning.

"No kidding, Tilla, look—this diaphragm is absolutely no good," I said, wandering out into the loft where I rarely came. I hated taking the train to this place that Tilla acquired after his separation from Nina. It was huge and bare, and on Sundays, unheated: a long dance studio with a wall of mirrors and random heaps of sound equipment. The living area was cozier, but completely dark, built in a windowless square.

Sundays were the only time that the studio was empty of the Szabo family who retired for a day of rest in their apartments in Brooklyn or in their houses in New Jersey. The breakup with Nina had broken up part of the family art, too. Now some of them weren't dancing, but working in offices and buying houses of their own. The family itself had not ruptured though: On Sunday evenings every Szabo convened at Tilla's mother's for goulash.

But on Sunday mornings Tilla Szabo and I made love, as we had been making love for five years. "I would love you if you were four hundred pounds." He kissed my neck, saying, "I love your breasts, I love your ass! I love this!" kissing my elbow, "I love that!" kissing my knees. "I love when you do this—" I kissed his neck—"and when you do that!" kissing his navel, and so we began our own dance in bed.

Tilla took his hand to guide the small of my back, and we caught each other's eyes in the locking look of those who must watch each other's every move because the dance depends on it. It was the gaze of hungry love. It was both movement and food and it never, never failed month after month, year after year. Like our art, our sexual delight burst with an energy that would not quell. It never even really ebbed and flowed. Constant and steady, like our creative impulses, was the sex of our courtship.

Courtship, the mating dance before children. If we were birds we would have been bobbing our heads and flapping our wings, eternally caught in the preparation to nest. We caught ourselves in time, or time held us in a moment that lasted years. Since courtship has rules, we followed them: We did not live together. We were not committed to each other's families. We met during the week to go to performances or openings or readings by friends. We spoke every night on the phone. We were devoted to our sacred Saturday afternoons and Sunday mornings together which we never gave up no matter what. And in the summers we continued courting at various art colonies. The boundaries of courting, like proscenium arches, frame the special stasis that never bores, because in its realm is art. But children do not observe the conventions of art. Frames are broken by their burgeoning. As a matter of fact, when we are pregnant we say we are expecting, but it is the unexpected we try to prepare for.

What keeps them together? people wondered about us. What, his family wondered, gives him pleasure in this woman who keeps so to herself? What, my friends wondered, gives her pleasure in this man who orders her around "for her own good," claiming to know her better than she knows herself? If Tilla and I were continents and our love was a globe, then the floor of the ocean which bonded us was the bottom necessity we felt: to control surprise. The political upheavals of his early life and the alcoholic upheavals of mine formed our ocean floor. Our deep, unspoken pact kept the world as it was, unchanged. Alone together we could be volatile because we had held both time and place in safe abeyance. We ourselves could be the winds of change. But we howled in a frame where our howling could do no harm.

And the frame itself did me good. It was Tilla-size, gigantic and baroque. But as imperious as he could be with human beings, he was modest toward his art—and respectful of mine. When *Raw Heaven* got its review in the *New York Times*, Tilla dragged me to Xerox copies, then wrote the mailing labels, and clapped at my readings. When I groaned about judging 300 poetry manuscripts for the National Endowment for the Arts—how would I teach and write and shop for groceries and get to the dry cleaners?—he coaxed me on. "It will be so good for you, darling. First you make your poems. Then they are so rightly admired. Now you will make culture itself!" I rolled my eyes. "Of course it is hard and takes time," he said calmly, "but you will have the energy because your talent will give it to you. Capitalize on it now," he advised, quietly as a banker in the gilded hall of art, "say yes to everything." Though he wrapped his body in persimmon silk, his voice wore tweed, soft, authorial.

Come on, I said to myself, *it's only once. No thirty-eight-year-old woman gets pregnant doing it unprotected only once.*

"I know my body," Tilla said to me as we lowered ourselves onto his futon bed in the corner of the living area of the loft. I hadn't put the diaphragm in. It was hopelessly wrecked. Usually we made love at my place in Manhattan, but I had stayed in Williamsburg with Tilla because we had come from a family birthday party and were scheduled to go to brunch in Manhattan with Mariah and one of her ex-husbands who had turned out to be a set-designer friend of Tilla's. "God, do we have time? We're supposed to meet them at twelve-thirty and we've got to drive all the way in."

"We always have time to make love."

"I'm not so sure about this, Mr. Treasure."

"I know my body, Molly, I will withdraw from you and ejaculate on your stomach."

"Yeah," I said, kissing him, my turtleneck halfway up and my pants halfway down—it was too cold to make love with all our clothes off. "But what about those little drops in the beginning? That's *sperm* you know."

"I can control those little drops."

"No man can control those little drops. Men aren't made to control those little drops. They taught me that in high school." Tilla, who eschewed facts, once convinced a whole dinner table of the scientific basis of his grandmother's recipe for insomnia until a *Science Times* article suggested otherwise, and even then he disputed the reportage. But perhaps he knew a secret older than the medical establishment.

Come on, I said to myself again, *it's only once.*

"I am a dancer, Molly, I know my body, and I can control those little drops," he said. "Relax your jaw, Molly, your lips are so hard!"

I let him in, I *invited* him in, I *gave* in, not just to him, but to something very much deeper: a desire to give in. My father was dead. The wall could come down.

We took off all our clothes and climbed under the covers so we could really make love. Then we hopped out again, Tilla to bring the electric heater closer and me to call Mariah to say we would be late. Back under the heap of blankets between the flannel sheets we gave up our vigilance because no one was there to kill us. We were no longer in Hungary or on Pilgrim Road, but free. And in our freedom I opened my legs and he opened the lips of my vagina with his fingers and entered my vagina with the fingers of one hand, and circled my clitoris with the fingers of his other. My jaw relaxed. I could kiss him now. My nipples hardened. When my clitoris was the size of a hazelnut I had my orgasm, coming with him holding me, my eyes open and his eyes watching me, and then I felt the naked entering of his penis inside me without a barrier, that trusted wall now with a chink in it, like the chink in the wall the lovers Pyramis and Thisbe would whisper into, planning their escape. And I watched his eyes open and shut, open and shut with his thrusts, then the twist of his face and the clamping shut of his eyelids as he came, lying exhausted in me with his sweet, turnip-y smell. He was my darling. And I his.

After I became pregnant that morning, we met Mariah and husband number four for brunch.

26.

When my gynecologist's nurse called and told me the test was positive, I suddenly couldn't remember what positive meant. "Does this mean I'm not pregnant or I am pregnant?" I asked.

"Oh, congratulations!" she said. "You *are* pregnant!" I turned cold with despair at the same time as a warmth infused me, like a feeder stream into a reservoir.

Down, down, down I sat in my wing-backed chair while my little pet parrot flew to my side and pulled on my earring, then tore the rubber away from the telephone cord. I had thought I'd bought a male, but one day an egg lay on the bottom of her cage, and there she sat. Of course it wasn't going to hatch, but I let the bird nest there, contrary to the vet's advice. It was her nature to sit, I thought. And finally she abandoned the egg. I wasn't going to get a male parrot and start raising exotic birds in a studio apartment—I had enough guano to clean up. The parrot played, the tulips bobbed in the wooden box I'd planted them in, the paper-weights glowed on my desk, the very small expensive Turkish rug under my feet purred its red and blue. I sat in a trance, absorbing the phone call, letting my eyes stroll the apartment I was in the process of buying. We were going co-op. I loved this padded place, the sunlight in my real kitchen, my overstuffed closets, the foldout couch I slept in and had insomnia in ever since my father died. Cookie the parrot chattered on, and a pleasing, gossipy chatter began in my body.

My body was humming like a workshop, complete with elves. I could become pregnant, after all! Shocked as I was, it felt good to discover that I *worked*. Then a wave of exhaustion. I wasn't up to it. I felt old—the oldness that is a form of hopelessness.

But in moments I was energized again by my new state, feeling a raw kind of hope.

"What? On a Wednesday?" Tilla said to my request that he come right over.

"It's an emergency. There's nothing wrong, but it's still an emergency." Tilla hated emergencies. His young life had nearly been destroyed by them, and now they made him hysterical. I so completely dumbfounded him that he immediately got in his car and faced his hated rush hour traffic to come to me. When he arrived, I was still sitting in the chair, smoothing the head feathers of Cookie the parrot, who took her usual swipe at him, then settled down on my shoulder until I removed her, squawking, to her cage.

"We have to sit on the couch, so we can be next to each other," I said, "because you'll never guess what's happened."

"You got a MacArthur Grant!"

"No."

"The Ninety-second Street Y called you for a reading!"

"No, no," I said. "Listen, Tilla, I'm pregnant."

"Oh my God!" His eyes twinkled. "Oh my God, we're pregnant!" He threw his arms around me, taking to the thought right away. Look what we had done! It was sweet. It was a darling bud.

We cooed on the couch. "Are you sure? The test was sure?" he asked.

"Positive."

"How strange," he marveled, "I love this idea! I am a father—not just a father to the troupe, but a real father!"

And now both of our marathon imaginations were at work. How would we do it? We were overwhelmed. How could we figure it out? What would we do? We didn't know, we didn't know, but we hugged each other and I cried, and he kissed me, and I kissed him, and we decided to tell no one until . . .

Until we decided what we would do. Within the hour, and within the powerful fantasy of our baby and our parenthood, grew the twin idea that we could stop it.

"Let's go have dinner," Tilla said. It was the first time he'd ever suggested going out. Tilla cooked at home, either his or someone else's. I was the one who ate out, but by now it was far too late to cook, and we were hungry.

We sat in a little Hungarian restaurant with net curtains on Second Avenue eating noodles. "My mother will really like this, if we go through with it," he said.

"Oh my God, my mother!" I said.

Not only would there be Szabos above me, below me, and to the left and right, but Polly. Polly doing her duty and hightailing it back to Buffalo ASAP. Polly and the Szabos. Sentinels of Szabos. Advice from Szabos. Criticism from Szabos. Szabos dressing the baby, Szabos changing the baby, Szabos holding the baby until it stopped crying. I would be surrounded by both our families. And by a baby who would need me night and day. And Gail. Polly and Gail and the Szabos.

We could not live in my studio apartment. We could not really live in the loft, which was like a crash pad. A huge amount of money, money I didn't have, would have to be poured into the loft. Or we would have to rent a new place. Someplace far, far out into a borough that we could afford. Scratch that. That *I* could afford. Tilla had no money except for grants for costumes and space and he was proud to live on nothing.

Or I could live alone. Alone with the baby. Stay in my little place and have the baby by myself and not marry Tilla or even live with him. A kind of despair set in.

That was my mother's fantasy. "If only you didn't have to have a husband," she used to say, "in order to have children. That's the way I would have done it, if I could have." Polly loved the idea of being a single mother. She daydreamed of a de-Dadded heaven of motherhood without Ted.

But it was not my fantasy. I knew how impossible single motherhood would be for me. First, I would have to find a new job. I could not work with children all day long and come home exhausted to my child. There are teachers who do this with equanimity, but I would not be one of them. The demands of the children at school depleted me utterly. How could I offer my child the dregs of me? How would I write? Even now I had trouble writing all I needed to, and that was with summers off. A new job, whatever that was, could not be teaching. What would it be? In an office somewhere. With my child at home.

I would not jeopardize my child with the pipe dream that I could do this alone. I couldn't do it alone. Everything I did in my life I did with the stops pulled out. My personality was not going to change. I barely had life for one under control. I could not add another without help, without a father. There had to be two partners. But Tilla and I were not partners in the equal, parental sense. We led two lives, and these lives already cost me: though he came to stay every weekend, not once had Tilla offered to pay for groceries, nor did he bring a gift of a bottle of wine or a pound of coffee.

"A toast," Tilla was whispering, beaming, at the restaurant, holding up his wine. I held up my wine, then thought, *If you are having this baby, don't drink the wine.* I compromised with a spoonful.

"Stop worrying, little mother," he said to me. "We will find our way." So I gave up on reason, and fell back into the pregnant state, not putting

mind over matter anymore. It was lovely not to put mind over matter—
I had so rarely had the experience. Vigilance was everything, until now.
Now I was pregnant and sleepy. I left my papers uncorrected, and Tilla
and I shared a rare weeknight sleepover. After all, things were different
now. Now I was an animal, living a life according to my physical needs.

The next day I taught in a daydream state, made an extra appointment with Ruta for the following Monday and went home to discover
my mailbox jammed—I'd forgotten to open yesterday's mail! In the stack
of correspondence was a letter postmarked from Canada. Though it was
from Mike Groden, whom I hadn't heard from in nineteen years, I put it
with the rest of the mail. Curiously, I was devoid of curiosity. In this hy-
perawareness of the feelings of my body, and a deep pleasure that something was growing inside me, heightened by Tilla's approval and by the
fact that I had told no one except Ruta, I felt a skin growing, a skin of
protection about my baby and me, a thick, but permeable blood-infused
wall about us. It was as if *I* were in a womb, and in my womb-within-a-
womb grew a tiny cotyledon, a speck of a human plant.

I, who had no skin, and who had worked so hard for borders, was
suddenly supplied them by biology. All my body wanted was to have this
baby. How hard it was to get my mind to think, *think! You've got to, Molly,*
I told myself. *I can't, I'm too sleepy.* Nature had installed me in a metaphorical rocking chair. I need do nothing but be. I scratched my parrot's head
and stared out the window. It was like summers at La Grange, lying on
the lawn of Ruth's garden in the old apple orchard for hours, drifting, in
a state of waiting that was mildly expectant. When an idea came, I turned
from the mental window to greet it with the calm, warm statement: *Hello,
I've been expecting you.* I was expecting. The sense of pleasant fullness was
unlike any other satisfaction.

Think! I told myself, then thought, *You can think Monday, honey, when you have the appointment with Ruta. You can think it through then, honey-pie.* Honey-pie. I wasn't calling myself a jerk. I wasn't flogging myself for having made a mistake. For the next three days, I told myself, *Just be.*

When Tilla came on Saturday afternoon, I had not written my poem. I had read last Sunday's Book Review and lounged around watering my plants. Then we walked the five blocks to the Frick which seemed like twenty. I stopped in the conservatory to rest. Tilla was solicitous and attending and adoring. We looked at the Vermeer we liked and walked home, stopping to shop for dinner. Tilla cooked while I played Billie Holiday. We ate and never bothered cleaning up the table, but just pulled out my convertible couch and got into bed to talk.

Tilla told me the story of his friend, an acrobat, who locked his child in a closet because the boy was making too much noise.

"I'm telling you," he said, "if my son was annoying me and I could not work . . . I will not kid you, Molly . . . If my work does not come first, I'm not myself."

"So what are you saying?" I asked. "Wouldn't you just *imagine* doing what your friend did and yell at the kid instead?"

"I'm not in my right mind if I do not do my work. That's all I have to say."

"What if you had a daughter? Would she come first?"

"No difference!" he declared. "But you are carrying a son for me, Molly, I know this in my heart."

"Jesus Christ."

"Why are you swearing? It is the truth. Such a truth I feel and I know."

"For God's sake, Tilla, the *truth* here is fifty-fifty. Actually, fifty-one–forty-nine."

"This is not sexism, Molly, this is instinct, and what I feel in my body."

Now I had bodily feelings to match Tilla's own. The sexism I tried to avoid by my rigorous rules, rules that Tilla, consumed by his art, abided by conveniently, would never be avoided when we were a family, even if we were a family who lived in two places. He was already full of folk advice for me. All his shoulds and should nots multiplied, as if his advice itself were pregnant. Wear a sweater. Put those light socks away. Wear these heavy socks. He was taking things out of my drawers and my closets. Don't wear those tight pants! Too binding! Molly! Listen to me!

Borders were hacked away. If I had not been safe inside the womb of pregnancy, I would have fought. But I nodded. Somehow I knew that the hormones protecting me would not always surge so strategically. I also knew that Tilla's story about the acrobat was an allegory I had to heed. *I might abuse this child*, the story said.

Decisions to abort children do not come from a hatred of children, but from the opposite: the desire to want them. My wish to be a good mother competed with the despair of coping with Tilla as a father, a father who was already imagining the fetus as a threat to his life. All my images of a baby as a succubus were gone in the reality of biology. I replaced them with the soft, helpless need of a real infant. Yet I might damage an infant too, not by physical abuse, but by simply falling apart. I imagined myself weakened, dissolved in tears, the baby wailing, my boss screaming, poems unwritten, the bills unpaid, my fierce tears frightening my baby, and then screaming at the baby myself, unable to get hold of myself, then getting hold somehow, but the damage to the tiny thing done, the psychological damage. And I myself dying inside from the struggle to support and love while needing support and love in return.

I could not be a mother alone. I despaired of being a mother alone. I despaired of being a mother at all. *Do you really want to be a mother?* I asked myself, clearheaded for the first time in three days. *No. Well. I don't know.* Whatever the real answer was, it wasn't a resounding yes. I was carrying, if not an unwanted child, a less than desired child. And now Tilla was telling me he could reject this "son" he was sure of having.

"Let's watch TV," I said.

Usually it was I who made Sunday breakfast, but it was Tilla who was up. I was in my fog again.

"I am hungry for Hungarian soul food this afternoon. My body says eat food for the soul. Let's go out to my mother's early, so we can have some of every dish she is making right in the kitchen before the others come."

Who said we were going to Brooklyn? *No one*, I answered to myself. *But now you're pregnant, you're a Szabo. You're going to Brooklyn whether you like it or not. It's not so bad*, I said to myself. *Everyone out there is awfully nice. You can bring your papers and correct them with the TV movie Mr. Szabo will watch. It's just this once.* Once! No, it was the beginning of forever. Of wifedom. Of a highly sophisticated metaphorical kind of purdah lite. Of having to fight for every single inch or having a will-less life.

I went to the bathroom.

"I'm sick," I said when I came out. "Oh," I lied, "I hope I can go to Brooklyn. I hope I'm not too sick."

"Take off your clothes! Put on your pajamas! Get back in bed!"

Great ideas.

"I will take charge of this day," Tilla said. "I will make lunch for you, and the rest will go in the refrigerator and you can eat that for dinner. You will stay here. You mustn't travel. I will go to Brooklyn later on myself, and after rehearsal tomorrow I will come here."

He got busy. Out to the supermarket. Into the kitchen. Over to me.

"Put those papers down! You cannot give energy to papers. Rest!" he commanded. He was exhausted and imperious. And afraid. All this activity was cover. And soon he threw the cover off.

"I'll have to get a different job, you know, Tilla." I hesitated, then began again. "I can't teach children and have a child, too. I just couldn't be good enough to the child. I'll have to look for a different job."

"I have no money, Molly. I cannot help with money."

"Well, do you think you could get a part-time job?"

"How can I do that!" he exploded. "What about the troupe? I am *their* father! I am first in their minds."

"Well, if I work full-time, the baby needs someone at home until I get back from work." I was taking the plunge. I was saying that I would work in an office and that I would support Tilla and the baby, and that I would be the chief breadwinner and the mother and play the role of chattel that Tilla still could order around. Tilla would not be a sexist when it came to having me support him. Somehow, I knew, he felt I *should* support him. He deserved it.

"And I would be househusband, you mean?"

"Well, yes, you would hold the fort till I got home." (And handed you my paycheck since you didn't believe I could handle my money well.)

"I would be good at that!" he declared. "I am good at staying home! I could direct the troupe and have the baby by my side . . . until you came home."

"I'm going to have a full-time job and a baby and support you and somehow make poems," I said. A panic was setting in, but it was a low, interior panic. It was not loud.

"Molly," Tilla said, holding my hand. "I can be househusband, stay-ing home, but I cannot be Mother."

"Well, you'd have to be a part-time mother. Just till I got home."

"I cannot, Molly. The baby will cry, my little son will need me. And I will dance. And I will meet with the music mixers. And the performers will be needing my direction. And I will not answer my son's cries. I cannot be Mother."

This time I heard him. He was honest and clear. He would not do it. He could not surrender to it.

"Go get some soul food," I said, "and call me tomorrow night, but you don't have to come over. After school I'm going to see Ruta. Then I'm just coming home and going to sleep. I know you have a late rehearsal tomorrow. We can talk tomorrow night on the phone." My voice was firm and calm and mothering.

"All right," he said, and left me to the rest of my Sunday. I immediately called Maggie, who was living in Queens, having sublet her West Side apartment to make ends meet until her string quartet got established. By the time I spent the afternoon talking things through with Maggie, I wasn't feeling pregnant at all. I took a nap, paid some bills, and got ready to meet her for dinner. In the midst of paying the bills I saw Mike Groden's unopened letter again, and stuck it under the paperweight that held down a pile of other things I had no idea what to do about. But when I got to Bangkok Thai, Maggie wasn't there. In my hunger to keep on talking, I'd mixed up our arrangement. It was the wrong night.

27.

"I'm a murderer."

"Do you really believe you'll be a murderer if you have an abortion?" Ruta asked from her chair just behind my head. I was encased in yet another kind of womb, the sunlit therapy room, which was also her living room with its glass table and Persian carpet and Dutch landscape painting and her own watercolors hung on the creamy walls—a far cry from the operating room I was contemplating.

"Actually no." By now I knew I didn't have to carry the world on my back, no matter what anyone said. "But," I said to her, "I'd be putting an end to something."

"Maybe you'd be saving something."

"Me, you mean?"

"Possibly."

"Or the baby itself, saving it from this situation."

"Yes."

"Or Tilla."

"Yes."

"Look, Ruta, people don't usually think of abortions as saving people."

"What matters is what you think," she said.

"Can I support the three of us financially," I started to cry, "spiritually, physically, emotionally, socially? I can't do it!" After I sobbed for a while, the release of the weeping let me feel pregnant again, both vulnerable and fierce. "But," I began again, "I can't, I can't see a way to do it that won't destroy me, and destroy all of us. There has to be *two*, there has to be a *father*. I can't do this alone. I need help. Not just helpers, real help, like from a husband."

I struggled against my bodily contentment. "I like being pregnant. I like walking around thinking, *I'm pregnant*. I love knowing that my body works. It works! I can have a baby!"

"You could have another baby, then, couldn't you?" Ruta said.

"Yes, I could, couldn't I? I could do five thousand tons of exercise and get really strong and try it again." I stopped and lay there silent, then continued, "I'm sad to lose this feeling." Then I sobbed again.

"Can you tell me why you're crying?"

"Because." I sat up and blew my nose on a tissue from her continuous source of Kleenexes, then lay back down and reached over my head for her hand. "Because I'm sad, I'm sad for me all alone and I'm sad for me with a baby."

I lay there, simply breathing, and finally said, "I'm sad because I'm going to do this. I'm going to have an abortion."

I arrived at the same Thai restaurant for the second night, this time with swollen eyes no makeup could hide. There was Maggie, uncharacteristically on time and waiting for me.

"You sounded so terrible I knew I had to be on time," she said, her ruddy face pale with concern. She took her long flat fingers and pulled back her hair. "Oh, Molly, I'm so sorry you have to endure this."

We talked for a while about my decision, which had been hers nearly twenty years before. I watched a sympathy in her face play behind an almost-frown, her responses monosyllabic. This was still a trial for her.

"I know Tilla will go along with it," I said aloud. "And he won't even have to pay for it, I found out in school today. The insurance pays." I knew, of course, that I would have written the check in any case.

"Oh, Molly." Maggie reached out her hand and touched my sleeve. Her face stirred up then clouded, like sediment disturbing a pond. The waitress came back to our table again and again to see what we decided to order. We numbed our states by ordering shrimp in coconut sauce and vegetables in a ginger sauce and salad and chicken satay, and normalcy crept in.

"You know they have shrines in Japan for unborn fetuses," Maggie said as we waited for our food. She had played in Japan the previous year. "The temples there are piled with little dolls that look like babies. Women dress them up as babies. The culture gives them a way to mourn publicly for what they've lost."

I took comfort in the idea of those shrines, in open mourning for what cannot be. Tears for the choice you do not make. The road you do not take. The bed you make you will not lie in. A shrine for regret. A shrine for what must be grieved for.

No one grieved harder than Tilla, who wept in the hallway outside my room in Roosevelt Hospital. Whatever he was, he was honest about fatherhood. He did not deceive me or himself about his inability to take it on. And he wept as openly as I have ever seen a man weep, and felt as severely this loss, this impossible situation that we had acknowledged to be impossible. We had not lied to ourselves or to one another. We had called together for the appointment. He had driven me to the hospital and would wait for me, then drive me home.

The abortion was an outpatient procedure, a matter of a few hours. We waited in the lemon-walled room that was my home for the after-noon. Tears slid down Tilla's cheeks, while I, who am so easily moved to tears, sat frozen instead into one position, yet alert as an animal, sniffing for danger.

When the attendants came with a gurney, I got on. They wheeled me to an operating room, and there was my gynecologist, Sarah. I did not say "No! No, stop this! Let me get off this cart!" or yell for Tilla, or for God. I had had to sign papers to the effect that I was sure about doing this. And I was. I was going, by my action, to free myself and Tilla, to enter the new path of our lives, since of course our lives would never be the same.

The anesthesiologist in her green gown gave me something which kept me vaguely conscious throughout the suction procedure. I was partly awake as the gurney was wheeled into the operating room, and an image of a fox in a trap grew into my drugged fog, and I wondered if I could chew off my own leg to be released from the trap. Just before the anesthesia did another level of its work, I saw myself lean to my ankle with a set of canine teeth, pointed, ready for the shock of my own blood as I sank them into the flesh of a leg that could never again carry me away from danger. Then the anesthesia did the deepest level of its work, and the procedure began. As the doctors and nurses joked above me, the operating room seemed like a grease pit in a car dealership, the medical personnel insular and softly jocular, like mechanics working on a car on a lift, joking and teasing one another. I suppose I could have resented being worked on like a car . . . as they expertly turned a screw, as they fished out a ripped hose and replaced it, fixing, fixing . . . but I felt I was being repaired, returned to an original state.

Then the garage was gone and the fox in its trap was back. Now the procedure was nearing completion, the anesthesia changing levels again, and I was again the fox, poised over my leg, though the teeth in my mouth were human now, and human hands were opening the trap, holding it so wide I needn't even scrape my shaven, human, female leg.

After I woke up fully in the recovery room, wondering what that terrible bleating was—it was a woman, crying then howling, down the aisle—I was wheeled back to the lemon-walled room where Tilla waited. While I rested in bed, he held my hand and the sun rays grew oblique. High in a hospital in an electric city, again I was too exhausted and stricken to cry.

That evening I walked to the elevator by myself, Tilla at my elbow, and we went down to the street. It was Easter week. Death and resurrection were not lost on us. Tilla drove me home, parked, walked me quietly to my building. The leaves were freshly out on the ginkgoes. We rode the elevator up to my place, clean, as I had insisted on leaving it for my return, although he had felt it vastly unnecessary, complaining loudly that we would be late. Late for our abortion. But we had been on time, and now I was bleeding, but not as profusely as I thought. I had left the sofa bed out and all made up and fluffed. I had bought myself flowers since I didn't think anyone would send them. Who sends flowers for an abortion? Yet I knew I would need to look at them. I carefully took off my clothes and put on my nightgown. Then I led Tilla, mildly protesting, to the door. Now he could go back to his life. And I would keep my life as I had built it, with one more aspect, a kind of wholeness of thought.

When I turned the locks and was alone, I released my parrot from her cage and she sat on my shoulder as I fell asleep, waking wildly at the unexpected buzz of the doorbell. It was a delivery, but I hadn't ordered anything.

"Flowers! Flowers!" the man shouted hoarsely through the intercom. It was a basket of magenta hyacinths, from Maggie. There was someone, of course, who knew why flowers should be sent. They nodded on their swollen stems as I guided Cookie back to her perch, then lay in bed and watched TV. It was school vacation. I didn't have to get up the next day, Good Friday, on which it rained in torrents.

People held their umbrellas against the wind as rain sheets ploughed the streets. I sat at my desk looking out at the wind-whipped locust in the courtyard, talking softly to Tilla on the phone. I was fine, I whispered, I was fine. We were strangers with a bond, a bond of refusal. A little green cotyledon of a fantasy was gone. *It was a fetus, Molly. Cut the crap. It couldn't have lived outside you,* a sturdy no-nonsense voice inside me said. *All right, all right.* I sighed. My adult soul, new and green, grew as a weed amid fragments of glass, and set bud in the Good Friday rain.

Where did I put the grief that I'd becalmed? I swaddled it and laid it in a wicker boat and floated it among the bulrushes. I grew it into flowers I harvested and wheelbarrowed to a shrine. I clutched a rattle of grief seeds until time pried my fingers from it one by one.

28.

"I'm broken," I declared to Ruta, lying on her beige couch. "It's as if I've been in an accident and need surgery after surgery to get fixed, and I know I'll never really be fixed. And each operation is so *painful*."

The only action I felt able to take was to become careful. I moved through my life hardly daring to put weight on my bones, carefully keeping up all my correspondence, grading papers meticulously. A substitute parent from 8:30 to 3, I engrossed the kids with a massive video book review project, complete with equipment, props, and volunteer cameraman. My English classroom, now combined with a Center for Learning-Disabled Students, was a hive. Hives thrive, I rhymed to myself as I watched the students I'd taught in middle school now at age seventeen. I had all grades now that I was available for anyone with a writing or reading or study skills problem. Like many of my students, I felt unable to do what other people seemed to be able to do. Yet a kind of creative energy kept me going.

"I'm in a mental wheelchair," I said to Ruta every Friday. "I look normal, but I'm not."

Saturdays I wrote the poems of mourning for my loss. It was no use hiding it, my life was the subject of my poems. Other poets could write about walks in the woods, but I could only write about my abortion. Ordinary rhyme schemes weren't enough. I needed to scheme so hard to get the words out that I rhymed the inner half of the line with the end of it. Then the only way to stop the rhythm was not to rhyme the very end at all, leaving me falling.

> *I can't do this alone, yet I am so alone*
> *no one, not even this child inside me, even*
> *the me I was, can feel the wild cold buzz*
> *that presses me into this place, bleakness*
> *that will break me, except I cannot be*
> *broken merely by wilderness, I can only*
> *be lost.*

The more that happened to me, the more honest I got. And the bolder I got, the higher my expectations became—my poems were going to lead somewhere. I shouldered the idea without thinking. I was like a woman balancing a jar on my head; the balance came to me effortlessly, unlike having a child.

"Expectations" was the subject of the faculty meetings, high standards. The teenagers I taught often fell "below expectation." They were terrorized by having to give their best, which was not "The Best." My own best had been a No. My best was *not* to be expecting.

Going down the school stairwell I stumbled awkwardly into Jesse Fried, who held out his arm to catch me. "Whoa!" he said, as if to a twelve-year-old. A tennis fanatic with floppy dark hair and a curiously bulky body, Dr. Jesse the pediatrician came to the school three times a week to conduct his research with a group of my learning-disabled students. Five years before, the first time I laid eyes on him, he was in the school courtyard in the rain yelling, "Mush! Mush!" to my little bereft student Hazel and her pal Niles. He had them running laps around the courtyard, and he had been running, too. The three of them were drenched. I thought of Hazel's dad and Niles's mom having to pick the two kids up and wring them out at the end of the day.

"I'm in trouble, Molly," Jesse said as he helped me right my footing. I let my hand stay on his damp tweed back. Like my students, I had a crush on Dr. Jesse.

"I'm in trouble with Emma." Jesse was divorced from his first wife, and had been seeing Emma, an art historian at Sotheby's, for years. He was in his mid-fifties. She was forty. "You can still do it," Jesse mocked Emma's mother in falsetto, "you can still dump Jesse and find a nice young, normal doctor who wants a family!" Jesse didn't want a family, though he spent his life among them, appearing to do a better job at parenting than parents because, of course, he was not these children's dad. He and I were adult shepherds, playmates, and comprehenders. But we left our students to their mothers and fathers after all. I taught, he doctored, and we went home and closed a shade on them, although both of us could spend half our evenings on the phone with parents, and certainly every Sunday evening as these frantic families faced another school week. Jesse spent every non-Emma, non-tennis waking moment with them, because when he wasn't actually with them he was writing and lecturing about them, and running his practice.

"I have *no room* for my own children," he said to me exasperatedly, "I do not want my own children. *That* particular kind of narcissism I don't have. My neuroses lie elsewhere." Like mine, Jesse's interest in children was reflective: In watching them, he watched himself, and took the insights about them into himself, and brought the insights of his experience out to them, and connected, or reconnected, to deep emotions, usually unspoken—except sometimes with kids. He gave a few swings with an imaginary tennis racket, whirling around on the stairs and grunting, arms tangled in the fringe of his ancient cashmere scarf.

"Other people's children"—he swung again—"that's what I need, *other* people's children, not my own!" He swung again. "Oh, Emma, I pray you hold out against your momma!" he said loudly, his voice boomerang-ing off the stairwell walls.

Then the metal door to the stairwell opened with a whoosh of rank air, and kids from the gym barreled past us, pinning him to the railing and me to the wall, though Jesse kept talking. "There's enough of them, yes, you"—he pointed to the tall, wild-haired Hazel, now a junior, as she surged past—"there's enough of you!" Then he raised his eye-brows and lowered his voice. "And there's enough of their anxious, self-aggrandizing parents, too." Hazel, however, had only one parent, a slouching, bewildered architect who became mom *and* dad after Hazel's mother died.

Hazel slammed the big metal door on the floor above. She was going to my room.

"Dr. Fried has had his childhood," Jesse went on in the third person, his imaginary backhand forcing me to leap down several stairs, "and he doesn't want to relive it in a child of his own. And he doesn't need to make a narcissistic mark by siring kid after kid in his image. He has the life he wants."

The life he wants. The life I want. The sentence snapped my atten-tion like a stick. If we were to go on like this, I'd end up telling him I'd had an abortion and I'd cry and that would be the next piece of staff gos-sip to be passed around like precious jewels. I said, conspiratorially, pulling on his scarf, "We look normal, Jesse, but we're not," and fled up to my room without the cup of coffee I'd been on my way to get.

The room was flayed when I opened the door. The assembly had been dismissed early, and the unsupervised students had run wild. Niles and Fionula whipped one end of the corduroy earthworm pillow out the window. Hazel was growling, "The worm's gonna get you!" Philip and the others raced among the overturned desks. It wasn't my room at all times; I shared this turquoise palace with other teachers, hogging the bulletin board for my kids and the cabinets for my supplies. The school's idea of communal space destroyed everyone's nesting instincts, and was easily trashed. It was last period Monday afternoon.

"What's the word for what this room should be?" I screamed over the screaming.

Philip sat down.

"Do you remember that word?" I screeched, asking them the same question I would have posed when they were twelve. The others began to sit down, but not fast enough. "How about making these desks into their circle and pulling the worm back from the window, you guys. Let's get going."

"It's not *our* fault!" Hazel declared. "It was like this when we got here!"

"I know that, doll, but we've got to pull it back together."

"Go get the eighth-graders! It's their fault!"

"Come on, let's do it," I said, straightening the desks. They all began to move as I gave instructions, calling each of them by name and giving each a task. We had twenty minutes left by the time we cleaned up, and it was vocabulary prep day.

"You say this room is a sanctuary, and it is not!" Hazel declared. "It gets wrecked all the time."

"Well, nobody said a sanctuary is inviolate, you just have to rebuild it when it's wrecked. What's inviolate?"

We had to look it up.

"OK, time for Vocab Charades," I said with a brightness I didn't feel. It was a game we'd invented to kill the boredom of the vocabulary lists at the end of their long day. I'd hand-lettered the words on cards I picked out of a box for each student to act out or to draw on the board. I agonized over whether the kids themselves should pick them, then commandeered the box so I could adjust each word to each student's memory and skills.

"I'm first!" It was Hazel.

"OK, Hazel: RECUMBENT." She scrambled under the computer

table and lay down. I handed MAGNANIMOUS to Fionula who began drawing a huge hand reaching down to a tiny one on the board and PSYCHOSOMATIC to Niles. He brought it to the corner of the room where we had a butterfly chair and sat down to muse. By the time all the other kids had done two or three words, he would be ready with a killer performance.

"Great, Good, Wonderful, Excellent!" I clapped, walking around the room supervising each student separately. Niles enlisted Philip to be the doctor in a mini-play called "The Psychosomatic Problem," and at 3:12 P.M. they performed to our thundering applause. Then it was 3:15 P.M. and the drop of the minute hand signaled chaos again, the students scrambling to their lockers, me shouting to remember the assignment for tomorrow which I was reinforcing on the board, knowing I should have done it earlier and none but Philip and Fionula was reading it. Then I fled to the teachers' room for tea.

When I made my way back after the good-bye rush, I discovered Hazel still under the computer table, curled in a nearly fetal position.

"What's the matter?" I asked. Alarmed, I scrambled down on all fours next to her.

"I have a test!" she moaned.

"Thank God it's only a test! I thought you'd fainted under there!"

"It's not only a test!" she whined. "It's a history test for Clemson!"

I got up, realizing I had chalk dust all over my black pants. "Poop," I whispered.

"Pooooop! I've got to study sooo much," she wailed.

"Well, you can't study under there, Hazel, so you've got to get up and go home. Your Dad waits for you whenever you have a big test."

"Not today."

"Well, you're old enough to study on your own." This wasn't entirely true. She had a set of subtle learning disabilities that constantly threw her off. Her sense of sequence fell apart under pressure. And a history test is all about what happened when. Almost ethereally bright, Hazel could easily grasp the reasons for a social movement, but never get the order of events. She'd been sabotaged by sequence as a small child, when her mother's sudden stroke unglued life's order.

"I hate our empty apartment!" Body bunched up in a ball, head sticking out from under the table, Hazel whimpered on the verge of tears.

A pain flashed across my chest. It was the heart pain I got at awful moments. I thought of her on the phone the week before. She had locked herself in the bathroom with the telephone, screaming at her dad to leave her alone, her father helplessly pounding on the door in frustration. It was probably a big old bathroom in a prewar building. The pounding had a deep bass wood sound to it.

Hazel hadn't gotten an extension for a history project that was due, so she'd locked herself in the bathroom, overwhelmed. "I'm afraid of him!" she'd yelped. A zag of fear ripped through me, till I remembered. *He's only a poor shnook with a dead wife, Molly. He's not a monster. He's not Ted. He's not going to harm her. He's yelling from frustration, as anyone would.* I knew this benighted father, who hadn't a clue about Hazel's Tampax or sport bras. He was fumbling now, but he'd be all right. I'd watched him watch his daughter in dumbfounded adoration, and I was taking his side. I had crossed over. There's a line you're only supposed to cross when you become a parent, but I had traversed it, without having a child.

"OK, honeypie, do you have a Kleenex?" I had asked her on the phone.

Yes, she had a Kleenex.

"Now get the Kleenex and blow your nose, and get out your memory, because I'm going to give you Mrs. Clemson's phone number, and you're going to try to remember her number even though that's hard for you, and when we hang up you're going to call her and ask for an extension, and then you're going to call me back and tell me what she said."

"I'M ON THE PHONE," she screamed, "ON THE PHONE WITH MOLLY!"

"Shit," I heard Hazel's father say.

"Come on, Hazel, I'm going to give you Clemson's number."

"I can't!" she sniffled. "I can't call her."

"It's going to be awful, Hazel, you're going to hate it. She might be nasty and she might be decent, I honestly don't know, sweetheart, but this is what you've got to do."

"Can't you call her?" I was waiting for that. Of course I could, but I had crossed the line. I stood on the parents' side now, with all the adults who knew they must stand by and watch as teenagers performed so painfully imperfectly those tasks so easy for adults to do.

"You have to do it, honey, even though it's hard. I'm going to stay right by the phone so you can call me back." I had to wait on my side of the line, knowing that I couldn't recross it. After a certain point, watching from the sideline is all a grown-up can do.

"HAZEL!" Her father was still yelling.

"Tell him you'll be right out."

"I'm talking to Molly!" she said. "Molly says to tell you I'll be right out!"

"You've got five minutes to open that door, Hazel!"

"Listen, Hazelpie, call Clemson and call me back. You've only got five minutes."

And so she did. Clemson was decent and gave her the extension. By 9 P.M. I was watching *Mystery!* in bed, alone, all alone in a monk-like blackness that was rich as soil.

"It's a test for that witch!" Hazel moaned, bringing me back to Room 303.

"Come on, Hazel, Mrs. Clemson isn't that bad—after all, she gave you your extension."

"She's still a goddamn witch."

Arianna Clemson was frugally fair with her students, the kind of veteran teacher who rarely gave exceptions because *if I do it for one, I'll have to do it for everybody.* The juniors learned their American history, and they all learned it well, most with a grudging respect for her white-haired rules. Arianna had recognized that Hazel needed exceptions, though, and she granted them economically.

"Come on, Hazel, Hazel," I repeated her name softly, "you know Clemson isn't a witch."

"I hate my name! Why did my mother name me this?"

"Listen, I once knew a magnificent Hazel who raised Morgan horses. She had springy wiry hair like yours. This Hazel was the coolest thing in four counties and all the kids your age died to work for her."

"Fuck her."

"Just a minute here, madam, let's not get out of bounds."

"Fuck her, fuck her, fuck her!"

"Well, that certainly is a lot of fucking, Hazie. Aren't you tired, dollface?"

"Don't call me dollface. Fuck you!"

I crawled down to face her. "Hazel is a name I have loved all my life, and because I love that name I'm tolerating you, even though you are a junior in high school and acting like you are ten. But one more fuck and you have to leave."

"Fuck you!"

Instead, I put on my coat, piled my papers into my backpack, and left the room.

"OK, I'm going, I'm going!" she said, and followed me out into the hall.

"I'm gonna fail this test!" she yelped, butting up against the lockers.

"I'll bet you released time on two vocab lists that you can't get a zero on your history test."

"Fucking history," she began.

"Ah, ah, ah! Do not take one more step until you apologize." Why was I asking her to apologize? I myself had thwarted history, the imperative of generations.

"All right, I'm sorry, OK?" She looked plaintively pre-Raphaelite, her fair skin and red hair haloed above her violet parka.

"OK," I said, tempted to lift a wisp out of her face, but refraining. "Now go home!"

"I'll walk you to the subway." She pouted.

We tromped along Sixteenth Street. Though I felt gray from exhaustion, my feet surprised me by moving back and forth in the rhythm of walking.

"Where are you going?" Hazel asked. "Are you going home?"

"No, tonight I have a class for kids who have trouble in school."

"Really?" she said. Her eyes opened wide.

"Yes, and one of my best friends is speaking, so I'm really looking forward to it."

"Is your friend married?"

"Yup."

"Aren't you ever gonna get married, Molly?" Hazel quizzed me. Her father had a serious girlfriend now.

"I doubt it. I did that, a long time ago. It's not for me."

"But don't you want kids?"

We had stopped at the corner to wait for the WALK sign. I turned toward her but was speechless. The No inside me felt pink and tender as a blister. Yet I refused to be irritated with her. "Well," I teased, "not every kid can be as wonderful as you!"

"Oh, Molly, you know what I mean."

"Well, what I mean is, having you guys in school is good enough for me."

"But you don't want kids of your own?" She was as unyielding as a new shoe.

"Well, it's not exactly that. It's that I want . . . something else," I said, nearly on the verge of tears.

"Oh! Because you're a poet!" It appeared to Hazel that poetry was legitimately preclusive to children.

"It's because I want . . . a journey. A journey that's different from being a mother." I watched her face, open as a small plate. "But I'm glad to have kids around me, Hazel, even when they're a pain in the tush like you." She smiled, then seemed pensive for the rest of our walk to the station, eyeing me as I fumbled in my coat pocket for a clean tissue. My allergies had instantly acted up.

"Good luck with the history studying," I honked as she hopped down the stairs.

The grimy NYU seminar room smelled of the fungus that had infested the ventilation system. The guest this week for my graduate course in learning disabilities was none other than Lily Allisman, the youngest superintendent of schools in the state. She was brilliant on the subject of legislation for the learning disabled, and looked brilliant, too, in a lavender shantung blouse and amethyst earrings below her short dark hair and excited brown eyes. As Lily's bony shoulders moved inside the blouse, it shimmered, and the earrings flashed at the sides of her angular face. But the blouse barely covered the famous ass, now perhaps even more famous because of its increase in width. She fielded questions from the posturing graduate students and from visiting teachers and the graduate faculty member who'd invited her. Efficient and funny, she wisealecked with the interlocutors as she gave knowing answers. Maggie and I had been wrong to pooh-pooh her practical choice of education school. It was just the first step toward becoming the social mover we always thought she'd be, though in a realm we hadn't imagined.

"I'm taking you out to dinner," she said as we put on our coats after the seminar. "Let's go to Cafe Loup." That was the restaurant where the three of us, all still friends, had our reunions, though tonight it would be us two.

"You don't have to take me!"

"Expense account, sweetie pie."

We strolled through the crowds on Eighth Street, gawking in the store windows at the T-shirts.

"Who do you think buys those things?" Lily asked, pointing to one that sported a cartoon blonde, shouting from the bubble over her head, *Oh no, I forgot to have children!*

"Gruesomely inappropriate." I shuddered, then smiled.

"It is funny, but, I mean, can you imagine owning one?"

"God no."

"But they're in every window. *Somebody* must be buying them." Yet of all the T-shirts parading on Eighth Street, this one was not in evidence.

"I'm going to keep on looking," Lily said. "I want to find the brave girl who's going to wear one." *How about the plain old brave girl by your side?* I was too aggrieved to ask.

We turned up Sixth Avenue, sticking to the crowd so Lily could continue her search, our bags banging against our hips, our conversation veering as we missed colliding with other pedestrians.

"Alex is graduating from college this year, and he's off to the West Coast. Now it's just me and Tom all cozy and nice," Lily shouted in my ear. Her sister had died and Lily and her husband, Tom the carpenter, had taken in their nephew. "I love the kid, but God I'll be glad to see him out of the . . ." Lily stopped. A horde of teenage boys swarmed past us.

"There it is!" she whispered, pointing to the T-shirt on a scrawny torso below bleached-blond dreadlocks. The boy sneered in surprise.

"Hah! Now I know who wears them," she said sourly, "the ones without the biological clocks." She grabbed my shoulder in sudden sympathy, rocking me against her book bag.

"We're ticking, we're ticking," I mocked, "like the alligator in *Peter Pan.*" The alligator had swallowed its clock. As I was doing.

Finally we turned onto quiet Thirteenth Street. Why had we steered so long through the noise and crowds?

"So, as I was saying before we were assaulted by that shirt, it will be just Tom and me, all nice and cozy the way we like it."

"That's great for you," I whimpered. "Tilla and I are a mess."

On the weekend I crabbed and whined, my voice a dripping stalagmite onto the rock of Tilla. He would not change, he insisted. I, the materialist, should change. Like Nina, I wanted too many luxuries. "You're buying extraordinary things," he stormed when I appeared with striped shopping bags with new blouses. "I cannot even pay for ordinary things!"

"Can't you ever pay a few bills?" I nagged. We were a mess, I repeated, we were going to break up, I repeated, is that what he wanted? For once he didn't quote me Popeye. He didn't say, "I yam what I yam, Molly Oil." Instead he used a line he also seemed to have memorized. "Yes, Molly Oil," he said formally, "maybe someone can give us some advice." Immediately I produced the number of a counselor that Ruta had given me.

Our couples therapist, Eloise, had a generous face that hung above her shapeless clothes like a pumpkin over a sheet on Halloween. The word *mourning* was never uttered, not by Eloise, or Tilla, or me. Yet it was grief that had driven me to relentless activity and continual harping at Tilla's anorexic wallet. The grief had found its way to expression through the subtle cracks of blaming. Tilla was to blame. If only he had been more solvent, more stable, willing to sacrifice himself . . . but of course, he was only himself. And I, too, was only who I was, curiously becoming more complete as the refusal sunk in. We were in mourning for a loss we chose. We elected to have an abortion, but that did not stop our pain or make our choice a mistake. We were not wrong, we were sad.

Eloise tried to chase away what ailed us with a question. We had decided against having a baby, she reminded us. We had done that *together*. Could we do things together for the rest of our lives? Of course we wanted to answer yes. I wanted what I promised myself, a stable relationship, no matter what. "If this doesn't work with you, I cannot imagine being with anyone else," Tilla said, as clearly as he had said he could not be a father. He could only be a lover, he was telling me.

The tiny church cozied up to the tall apartment buildings on its Upper East Side block. On our way to the Frick again, Tilla and I stopped to read a little hand-lettered sign that announced "English Tea." "It's like Barbara Pym!" I exclaimed. "Let's go in." Several ladies in periwinkle rayon stood behind the tea urns in the rectory. The Anglican church had come to Manhattan, unbeknownst to me, the church that had made my beloved George Herbert a minor saint, and the church year Barbara Pym timed her novels to. "Let's get out of here!" Tilla groused, but I had already accepted my tea in a rose-trimmed cup and was fooling with the tongs to get the sugar cube in. With a newly cultivated patience, he remained at my side.

Occasionally Tilla himself performed at a huge church on Long Island with his family, leaving me to luxuriate alone on a Sunday morning.

A month later on one of these occasions I gussied up and went alone in the pouring rain back to the cottage-like church, its tiny narthex stuffed with umbrellas. From the back row I could see the oddball congregation of humans and dogs. A large collie guarded the baptismal font, and a West Highland terrier sat a few pews ahead of me. At communion an apricot poodle headed for the rail with its mistress. The priest delivered the host to the woman and a pat to the dog. It was a divine and doggy place, reeking of incense and wet fur.

Though every morning I sat in Quaker meeting with my charges for the school year, the drab meeting house smelling of their sneakers had no mystery in it, or humor. Often when the stillness was right, I got my God feeling with the kids rustling as I would have rustled during the sermon at the La Grange Baptist Church, Ruth silencing me with a pineapple Life Saver—just as I allowed the kids to pass TicTacs in the morning. But the Eucharist with a poodle gave me a God feeling with humor and delight.

In my head I invented a liturgy. Instead of *Kyrie eleison,* I said, *Take comfort,* and instead of *Christe eleison,* I said, *Take heart.*

"I'm broken," I continually chanted to Ruta. "I'm in pieces." I explained to her that I felt like a cardboard children's puzzle-map, the pieces all near each other, almost in the right place, but *not exactly* in place.

"Well, at least you have all your pieces," she joked.

I yelped, "You're not listening to me!" Shifting out of my prone position on the beige couch, I twisted around to look at her. "Each piece is . . . slightly turned. They don't fit snugly the way puzzle pieces are supposed to."

"So you've got all your parts, but something is off."

"Yes." It was a pleasure to have her agree with me as I thought of the mental wheelchair zooming from school to workshop to seminar to therapy to writing to school . . . then Tilla on weekends.

"I have to put the brake on this wheelchair," I ventured. "I'm adding and adding and adding to what I can bear." I sighed. "Sorry to have rhymed those sentences, it's an occupational hazard."

The mass was like a sonnet, formal and full of emotion. Because of its repetition, I found myself saying things I didn't believe. I didn't believe I wasn't worthy! Years with Ruta led me away from that. In opposition, I silently insisted in the prayers that I *was* worthy, altering the ritual as I altered verse forms, the complex repetition a comfort of layers, just as making a complex poem was. *Take heart, honeypie,* I told myself, as if I were Hazel. I was trying to make a new book of poems, but this one wasn't coming out as easily as the first two. I struggled harder to say things more directly, and the poems were getting rejected harder, too. *There must be room in love for hate* . . . I wrote in the last poem. *Presume that love has room/for all other emotions, and resume, resume.* I meant it. I was going to resume with Tilla, to mend. My manuscript was really making the rounds. It took months and months almost to be accepted, then many more months for it almost to be accepted again. With each rejection I changed the title. Now my beleaguered new editor who'd succeeded in her fight to take the book was threatening to make the final decision herself.

"No, no!" I squirmed. "I'll give you a title next week!"

"Take Heart," I said to the overworked young woman on the phone.

"Oh thanks, I really have been having a tough day. Now what did you decide for a title?"

"*Take Heart,* that's the title," I repeated.

29.

"It's burning, it's burning every time we have sex," I whispered.

"Stay still," Sarah the gynecologist said.

Oh, God, it's psychosomatic, I thought. The therapies hadn't worked. *I must hate Tilla,* I thought, *and I'm unconsciously using my burning innards to let myself know!*

Nearly two years after the abortion my vagina had begun to burn painfully every time Tilla and I made love. I hotfooted it to Sarah and lay on the table, my feet in stirrups.

"This is allergy," she pronounced. *Oh God, I was allergic to Tilla!* I panicked. "You've got a terrific allergic reaction here to the diaphragm jelly."

"The jelly?"

"Yes, Miss Molly poet, the jelly. How long have you been using a diaphragm, anyway?"

"Fifteen, sixteen years," I calculated.

"Well, it builds up. A lot of women get allergies to spermicidal jellies. Try the cream. Sometimes a switch will work."

Of course. I had slathered a sperm-killing agent on a miniature rubber flying saucer for a score and a half years and had thought nothing of

the damage it could do, and here I was, excoriated now each time I inserted it. I shopped for creams.

Cream worked for another half year, then the burning began
again.

"Well," my doctor clucked, her black curls bobbing between my legs,
"I guess the cream bothers you, too."

"*Bothers* me? It *pinions* me to the bed in pain!"

"Well, you can't go on like this."

"No, I can't. What next?"

"Pills. IUD. How old are you?"

"Forty-one."

"Pills, IUD, condoms or vasectomy for your partner, or tubal ligation
for you. That's it. Them's the choices."

"I hate these choices. I hated taking pills. IUD's scare the hell out of
me—I'm afraid of all the terrible stories I've heard about them. Forget
condoms, he'll never use them consistently."

"Vasectomy?"

"I can't imagine this guy having a vasectomy, but I'll check it out. In
the meantime, write me a prescription for pills." When I was dressed
and in her office face-to-face I added, "And tell me about tubal ligations." SoHo lay beyond the huge loft windows of her office. I looked
out at the light on the red brick buildings as she said, "Easy . . .

"Easy as pie. We make an incision in your belly button and go in with
a thin scope and clamp a silicone clip just like a staple on each of your
fallopian tubes."

"A clip?"

"Yes, it just sort of dissolves over the years."

"Dissolves? But then how does it work? I thought these things were
supposed to be ninety-nine-percent sure."

"They are. So don't count on getting it reversed. The clamp dissolves long after the fallopian tube is so damaged by being shut up that it just sort of shrivels up. No egg is going to make the leap."

"Well, I'll think about all this. But first I'll start on the pills."

Birth control pills, at age forty-one, gave me the same sexually deadened feeling I'd had when I was in my early twenties. And now they were far more dangerous for me. Tilla was outraged at the prospect of condoms—and nervous. "Even if we use them, Molly, they are not one-hundred-percent effective, and I cannot repeat that abortion. I cannot go through it again, darling."

"*You* can't go through it! I felt *crippled* by it."

"So take the pills, Molly."

"Take the pills, take the pills—I wish there was something you could do, Tilla."

"Oh my God in heaven, Molly, oh Jesus the holy shepherd, Mary, and Joseph, Molly this I cannot risk. What if something slips? I will be castrated! I cannot risk this!"

"Just a try, Mr. Treasure. Just thought I'd broach the idea."

"Oh, my lovely girl, you cannot ask this of me. It is not possible!"

"Well, it was just a try."

Over the last twenty years, as I'd inserted the diaphragms, as I'd tensed at a calendar trying to predict when my period would come and panicked if it failed to arrive on time and smiled in deep satisfaction when it did, I had thought, *Why not have it all over?*

You'll have to wait, I told myself year after year for two decades. *Having your tubes tied is a radical act. And I am not a radical. I am a nice, ordinary girl, and I might change my mind. Who am I to cut off my choices?* But was a tubal ligation so lamebrained? Could I make a wise refusal of motherhood?

Time after time over those two decades I had said to myself, *I wish this were over.* Then slowly what I had said to myself changed. For the past few years I said, *I can't wait till I can make it be over.* I never said the word *sterilized* to myself. It made me think of kitchen counters Chloroxed to a terrible whiteness. Sterile. It was everything I was not. I flowed with the juice of my ideas and desires. Fertility meant *being alive.* Sterility meant the whiteness that was death. Could you have a tubal ligation and remain sensuously alive?

Things grew because of me: My fragile students became strong, my friends laughed in an orbit of empathy. My writing grew, and love grew there, love for Tilla and love for patterns, for structures and organizations. I had published three books and I'd become president of the Poetry Society of America. I hadn't been president of anything except my sixth-grade class when my friends were the other officers, and it felt just as thrilling when the director and I schemed like schoolgirls about putting poetry everywhere. We dreamed about changing the face of New York, not with architecture, but mental structures, plastering poems all over the subways and buses. But, like Tilla, the little Poetry Society didn't have a dime. The part-time accountant couldn't even cash her paycheck. Then we wrote grants and took businessmen to lunch and asked them to write checks. And the checks came in, and more people, lured by the wildness of our dream, came to put in their money and time. Now *Poetry in Motion* was going to happen. We were in league with New York City Transit and millions of subway riders were going to be reading Elizabeth Bishop and Walt Whitman on the way to work. The idea was bearing fruit. New York was my orchard. And I made a fertile ground for my aging mother, too—me, the one who could make Polly chuckle—and for my sister, whom I was speaking to again, the one only I could calm down.

But I did not want to bear. To bear up. To bear up under. To forbear. At earlier times in rage and terror, I refused to have children. But the refusal in fear and anger was not the same as what I came to think of now as the paradox of "the Saving No." The Saving No is the decision to be child free, made free of panic. And now I was going to make such a decision. I asked myself, *Will I be a complete human being if I do not have children?* And my answer was yes. And since my answer was yes, I asked myself, *Will I be a complete* woman *without having borne a child?* And my answer had become yes.

"You're only forty-one years old!" Mariah exclaimed to me over our broiled fish dinner. She was on another diet. She had just come from her Overeaters Anonymous meeting to this quiet, unchic little seafood place. Scorning Tilla, who was not at all turning out as she predicted, she said in disgust, "He's lying down and taking it, he's lying down and taking life, something I never thought I'd see."

"Nonsense!" I said to the woman who had taught me to say *nonsense!* "He's struggling just like everybody else."

"Yes, but he's lost a little bit of his shine, dear, you have to admit that." Mariah had stopped wearing her black muumuus and enormous necklaces. Now she was wearing an ivory silk shirt and pale pants and enormous earrings. She had lost a considerable amount of weight. She had dumped—been dumped by? (I'd never know because certainly she'd never tell me)—the last husband and replaced him with Derek Sjovall, her prize-winning biochemical engineer. He was building her a house in Stonington, Connecticut. Together they would have seven children and three grandchildren. The house would easily sleep twenty. Tilla and I had spent a disastrous weekend with them in the Brobdingnagian rental next to the contemporary blond castle they were building. We'd missed the return train and had to spend an additional uncomfortable day with them, pretending to love cooking our whole flounder according to Derek's step-by-step instructions. Mariah had more or less stopped writing novels, becoming obsessed with architecture.

"After all, five novels are enough, don't you think?" she asked me as she tore at her rusty salad. It seemed to be a serious question.

"No," I said. She looked horrified. I could see how vulnerable she was in her ivory silk. "Well, I mean, how many novels are ever enough? You're not actually stopping writing, are you?"

"At the moment, at the moment, my dear, I am writing life, not a book."

"Speaking of life, I have a real life problem," I began.

"Advice! Oh, goody, I'm going to get to give advice—my favorite!" Mariah burbled. The crow's feet around her eyes had deepened. The laugh lines from her nose to her lips were as deeply indented as before she had the celebrated collagen treatments she wrote about in several women's magazines. Thrown over the back of her chair was a sheared beaver coat, softer than a baby blanket, compliments of international biochemical engineering. Who was she? Who had she ever been to me? Why were we friends? And why was I going to ask her advice about something I could barely speak about to myself?

"I'm thinking about getting a tubal ligation," I said abruptly. Mariah was about to send back her fish: too much butter! She motioned to the waitress with a wristful of bracelets banging.

"You're not!" she said to me, then turned to the waitress and gave detailed cooking instructions to be relayed to a chef who, I speculated, looking around the restaurant that needed a paint job and all the plants replaced, was just a tired cook wanting to go home.

I wanted to go home, too. Why was I telling her this?

"Oh, Molly," she said, genuinely concerned, "what if you break up with Tilla? What if you meet someone else and want to have a baby? You're only forty-one years old, darling."

"I know this is hard to understand, but, Mariah, in a way I've been waiting to do this for years and years."

The look of incomprehension on her face was such an obstacle to me I couldn't go further in explaining. The waitress returned with Mariah's plate; the now-overbroiled fish lay curled on its side like a black banana.

"Thank you." Mariah sighed sarcastically. "Thank you so, so, so very much for my dinner." The waitress lowered her eyes and moved to the next table. Mariah started dissecting the fish.

"Why do you think I would break up with Tilla?" I asked her. "I'm making this decision because I'm *not* breaking up with him. We've got to do something. I can't take these pills and I'm allergic to every spermicidal product on the market."

"Every one, you've tried every single one?"

"It's not like there are a hundred brands out there. There's four for the diaphragm, two kinds in two brands. And now there's none."

"And I don't suppose Mr. Virility is going to get a vasectomy, he also being absolutely sure as you are that you two are going to be together forever?"

"What do you think?" I asked in response to her. I took another scoop of warm butter and slathered it on a piece of bread. Mariah's diets affected me this way.

I watched her eyes watch me eat the thickly buttered bread.

"Don't make this decision so hastily, Molly. There's a lot of regret built into this. What does your doctor say?"

"She says she'll be giving me another ten years of great sex."

"It's your life—and your life could change."

"I'm going to do this, Mariah, I'm going to make this decision finally. I'm completely committed to Tilla."

"Just keep talking about it, talk the whole thing out. You can't take this back, you know."

"I know," I said softly. She was making me hesitate.

"You're only forty-one. People have babies till they're forty-five, forty-seven, don't cut yourself off."

"I hear you," I finally said.

Why had I insisted on asking her? For support I talked to Maggie and Lily, neither of whom had had to make my decision.

"I'd do it if I were you," they'd said at exactly the same time in Cafe Loup the night we were slurping mussels.

"Would you?" I'd said eagerly. "Really?"

"Damn right I would," Lily had declared. "Between my tipped uterus and Tom's low sperm count, we're a naturally sterilized couple, but I would do it, doll, I'm sure."

"It's a good thing you didn't want kids, or you'd be spending the Allisman fortune on in vitro fertilization," Maggie conjectured. "Great mussels," she added, wiping her mouth.

"Mussels to give me muscles for my big decision," I said.

Maggie laughed. "Well, you're a grown-up, now, Molly P. Whitewater rafting through the rivers of the Big Choice. I'm glad I'm not joining you." Maggie's partner, George, had had a vasectomy.

"What did you do before the vasectomy?" Lily asked.

"I made him wear condoms and I had my IUD."

"*Both?*" Both Lily and I said.

"You know I'm a birth control freak. If I ever, ever had to go . . . Oh, you guys, thank God you were both there in college," Maggie said, "because I was such a numbskull. I never want to repeat that, ever." She poured the Sauvignon Blanc. "So I tortured every man I was with. If they wanted to fuck me, they had to let me roll one on. Every time. AIDS test or no AIDS test. That wasn't the issue. The issue was babies."

"You're tough, Maggie Mack," I whispered, awestruck. I tried to imagine a condom on my clitoris.

"It's a good thing old George came along," Lily said, "to solve the problem."

Strangely, it didn't feel like a problem to me anymore. It felt like an opening, like loosening the knotted handles of a string bag. I had an image of oranges rolling from that bag into a big, deep blue bowl, then looked at my friends and suggested that we all share the orange tart.

As Mariah made me hesitate, I realized that I'd brought the subject up because I'd wanted an opponent. I was ready for one.

"I know you don't understand this," I said to her determinedly, "but having the tubal ligation will permanently settle something I have to resolve. It's come to a crisis and I have to make a decision about motherhood," I said quietly.

"You're sermonizing, Molly." She grimaced.

"I'm deciding that having children won't define who I am," I said with uncharacteristic explicitness. I was on the right path.

Mariah, however, trod a path very different from mine, and as a matter of fact, would live an entirely separate life from mine in the future. Another dinner or two, a compulsory appearance at her Stonington wedding—a tiny snapshot of Tilla and me in the back of *Harper's Bazaar* to commemorate nearly the last occasion of our crossing Mariah's and Derek's paths—then a tête-à-tête on a one-degree-below-zero winter Sunday afternoon at Minty Myths, home of the no-cal ice cream sundae, would finish us off.

Slurping our lo-cal hot chocolates to warm up before our no-cal hot butterscotch sundaes, Mariah told me how disgusted she was with another friend of hers for not divorcing her no-good husband. I understood this to be a thinly veiled parable for me, spoken from the altitude of her new superior marriage, wealth, and career turnaround as an architectural writer. I walked home deciding not to call her again; after all, it was usually I who called, in one of my efforts at seamless life. It took many months of my not calling to cause her to leave a brief message on my answering machine one day, but I decided not to return it, and neither of us contacted one another again.

But I did call Eloise, so that Tilla and I might check with a professional before this momentous act. "In the end, it is your decision," she said with a mild flap of her arm, her loose sleeve swinging. She and Tilla looked at me kindly, as did Ruta, and my gynecologist, and my other friends.

Yes it was. And it was not Tilla's decision, though he reaped its benefits. It was completely mine.

"When George volunteered to have his vasectomy," Maggie said as we sat on a bench at the Central Park Zoo, "I felt so released." It was a mild winter day, and we luxuriated with our heavy coats open. "It's like some grubby hand finally let go of me, Mol," she continued.

"I almost can't conceive of the amount of energy it took for you to insist on double protection every single time with every single man you were with," I said, still in awe at the intensity of her determination.

"I didn't even feel it as a burden, Mol, until now, afterward. Now I'm on my own, all detached and happy—except I'm attached to George, and my sisters, and my cello, and my friends." She beamed at me with loopy clarity. George Sinopolous was the reason we were sitting on this particular bench near the Upper East Side town house apartment Maggie now lived in, on the other side of the park from the ratty West Side one bedroom she used to have to sublet for extra cash when she went on the road. A music-loving businessman, he met Maggie when she'd played at a fundraising salon for Lincoln Center, and then had backed a special tour for her string quartet. Her first nonmusician lover, George was older than Maggie, and long-divorced from his first wife. They'd had no children.

"Wow, he volunteered to get a vasectomy and you're not even married!" I said, impressed.

"Yep."

We sat with our eyes closed, our faces tipped to the weak sun. Maggie's voice hung quietly in the air near my ear as I absorbed the sunlight in the dark relief of having closed my eyes.

"He loves my story of the day I wanted children for exactly twenty-four hours," she went on. "He says he's using it as his own."

"What day?" I said lazily.

"You know, the day I woke from the dream of the beautiful little girl!"

"Yes?" I wasn't sure I remembered.

"Remember, Molly? I was her mother in the dream, taking care of her, seeing she made the right choices. I woke up utterly bereft, thinking, *My God, I've made the wrong choices in my life. I should have had a child and it's too late*, and I rushed to Dr. Fish to tell him all along I'd wrecked my life and not known it."

"Then you found out the little girl was you." I supplied the answer. I had remembered, after all. Beyond us the seals splashed.

"She was me," Maggie said quietly, "the me I wanted to take care of."

"And now you can," I said.

"Now I do," she said.

Hardly anyone was paying the entrance fee at the zoo. Midweek, and no weekend fathers stood in line to mollify their kids. A few nannies wheeled strollers by.

"I haven't told my mother."

Maggie laughed her coral bells laugh. "Oh God, are you planning to?"

Although the statements of my parents that I should have children only if I wanted to contributed, in part, to this decision, I could not tell Polly, risking her condemnation, or her disappointment, or her interference. I had had a long, complex separation from her. This was my decision, just as my artistic decisions were mine. I couldn't *guarantee* that Polly would be behind me, but I let her know in many ways, at many times, that I did not intend to have children. "It's not for me," I said clearly whenever the subject came up, though it rarely did. I did not know how to explain the paradox of emptiness and fullness I felt, even though I saw it in her own life, the solitary life she luxuriated in, and might not easily have given up for grandchildren.

A woman who does not have children, whether she chooses not to have them or simply ends up not having them, is always defined by a kind of minus. Whether she calls herself child*less* or child*free*, motherhood is so entrenched in the definition of female that not mothering comes to be seen as not fully female. The move a woman has to make is from feeling negatively empty to openly empty.

The defining of a self is not the same as the defining of a role. I felt fully female, completely identified with my sex. And I felt capacious, roomy, open, and ready to be who I was and take on the tasks that would fall to me. That capacity came from a feeling of *ready emptiness*. It was being full of what I did not want that *in*capacitated me, afraid of getting pregnant, afraid of never having good sex.

I made my decision because of my examples, Flo, Hazel, the post-child world of my Grandma Ruth, because of Maggie's parallel life, and Lily's desire to be loved wholly by one man without interruption, and because of Marianne Moore, and Elizabeth Bishop, and Edna St. Vincent Millay, and Emily Dickinson herself, all poets who were not mothers. And I made my choice because the medical technology was there, and, in a beginning form, the ideology was there: It was a developing ideology that said one could be a woman *and* a mother, that "and" separating, maybe for the first time in history, femaleness from childbearing. It was an unusual decision, I thought, but it was *all right* if I was sure. My mother had made it all right through the living of the compromises of her life. My good friends had made it all right through their confidence in me. Tilla made it all right because of the feeling that he was with me—as with me as he was capable, which I knew was not fully with me of course, but he did not lie about that. Our therapist had made it all right by confirming that the decision was mine. And Ruta had been making it all right all along, since she had helped me to come to know who I was.

In the gynecologist's waiting room with its fascinating wall sculptures by people I knew, Tilla and I sat. When we entered Sarah's office, I asked her just how many of these tubal ligations she had performed.

"Molly!" Tilla was horrified. He considered this a breach of politeness.

"Lots," she said. "Don't worry. I have all the experience I need to do a good job."

She was going to do a good job. A permanent job. I was going to say no forever. I was going to interfere with my body, as I had interfered before with the abortion. And Tilla, as before, was going to witness. He was passing me the consent form to sign, and I was signing it, and he was going to drive me to the outpatient unit of the hospital the following week, and he was going to wait in the waiting room, and drive me home, and put me to bed, and my biologically reproductive life would be over. And the emptiness that is fullness would begin.

A different hospital this time, crowded and more confusing. Tilla had to wait floors away and I lost track of him. In a surgical gown on a gurney I was wheeled and left, wheeled and left, by attendants so preoccupied I couldn't believe that they would correctly identify what procedure I needed. Wheeled first into an elevator for an upper floor, then wheeled into an elevator for a lower floor—then to a little green room. I heard my doctor's voice somewhere. I'd had a general anesthetic. Had I known how deeply it would disorient me, I would have objected. The shadow of an early panic hovered over me, not like an angel's wings spread, but the spread, tipped wings of a raptor. You still might be meat for someone's else's hunger. "It's th' law a th' jungle, Molsie," my father would say to me when I looked disappointed or alarmed, "the law a th' jungle," and laugh and turn away.

In the operating room, confused about our plans, I imagined Tilla driving in his ancient car up First Avenue. Where was he going? I panicked, then settled down at the sight of Sarah, her curls neatly packed under a green surgical cap, joking again that here was ten good years of sex— why ten? Delivering me through to menopause, I suppose. And the anesthetic deepened and I was out.

I did not see her make the small incision in my navel, a navel so deep that if I do not dry it carefully in humid weather, it gets an irritating infection. There was my stomach with its escutcheon of hair—a stripe down the middle of it from my navel to my pubic hair, a line that had embarrassed me into one-piece bathing suits. My mother had this stripe. It was like a stripe of independence connecting me to another line of women with escutcheons. The curious word comes from medieval heraldry and means the shield shape of a coat of arms. In preventing myself from becoming a mother I felt attached to this independent heritage, one in a long line of women claiming themselves, saying yes to something important inside themselves through a refusal, the saving no. The escutcheon fastened me through time, geography, and centuries to all women who understood that they were women without being mothers.

I did not see the scope Sarah used, or the clamps she fitted so nicely and later was so proud of since she had done a perfect job. I did not hear her joke with the others in the operating room which I know she must have done. Here was possibility literally, physically being cut off and I, unconscious, deep under blackwater, lay forming a link to all those born of themselves, possibility becoming possible through its severing. Paradox bloomed out of paradox like the rings from the stone of consciousness thrown into the still pool of the anesthetic emanating larger and larger rings and I was waking.

The recovery room was cramped, crowded, and confusing, and I was in pain I had not anticipated. Of course, why not hurt? I had had surgery. My whole life had been a matter of surgeries, fixing and forming and restoring. I was a kind of renovation project, after all. Two enormous hands pushed me down on my cart and a contralto voice I attached to the hands but to nothing else said, "You're not ready yet. You've got another hour. Your cranberry juice is on the way."

Cranberry juice? I suddenly screamed, "Tilla!" just as if I were waking in a war movie hospital, calling out the name of my lost love. I yelled it louder. After a third time, the hands came back with the glass of juice.

"You are *not* ready yet, lady," said the contralto voice.

So I put my head down. I was not ready *yet*, the voice had said. *Yet.* Soon I would be who I am.

Groggy and woozy and wobbly and shaky and weak-kneed and weak. Tilla had gripped my arm when I came into the waiting room and steered me out, bouncing me home in the car. It was awful. The tubal ligation was much more physically painful than I had expected. I'd never had full anesthesia and did not expect to feel so enervated, and subject to a curious glitch in my sense of smell. Suddenly, I would sniff a smell not in the room, a distinctive odor of rubber, as if I were inside an industrial balloon and had stuck my nose up to its inner wall. A whiff of the birth canal I arranged for myself. For that's what I had done, given birth to an identity.

30.

"Yes," I said to the caller, I would look at a sunny one-bedroom apartment at the same price as my mortgage on Wednesday morning. Wednesdays had been the days of my appointments with Ruta, but now I did not have to get up appallingly early to see her before school because I had graduated from therapy. I considered myself a complete woman now. So why would I need a therapist? Ruta had accepted my decision graciously.

Then I decided to rent a bigger apartment and sublet the one I owned. At last I'd have a real bedroom and no bars on the windows. And live downtown. I could walk to my job! The morning I was to look at the apartment, Tilla and I had breakfast in a Polish restaurant on Second Avenue. "It has finally happened," he moaned dramatically over his pancake. "The real Szabo troupe is no more. There is not one single member of my family left in the troupe. They are all strangers, they are all clamoring to get paid their astronomical salaries, and none of them would know a true Hungarian step if they stepped on it by mistake! Girls, these dumb American girls they should be doing the jitterbugs!"

Tilla looked at the waitress and began playing the Hungarian spotting game. "She is not a Pole, even though this is a Polish restaurant. She is Czech. I can tell. I will ask her." He spoke to her in Polish, though, and she answered in Polish that he was right, she was indeed Czech. Tilla munched pancakes and distracted himself by determining the ethnicities of the other waitresses and the cooks behind the counter. Finally when they were all tagged and verified through our waitress (he made only two mistakes), and when his pancakes were finished, he looked up at me and said again, "It has finally happened."

"You mean something *more* has finally happened?"

"I closed up shop."

"What do you mean, you closed up shop?" I said suspiciously.

He sighed.

He signaled for a coffee refill. "Decaf, darling," he said to the waitress. To me he said, "I have canceled the spring season."

"Are you kidding? Canceled it? The whole thing?"

"I who have never canceled a performance in my life, I have done this."

I stared in the disbelief that accompanies change you hear will happen but never truly expect. He had lost the last bit of public funding he had. All his family had deserted him for air-conditioned offices, brass-railed restaurants, and distant malls. His cheeks were a mass of popped blood vessels from screaming at the new girls.

"I have told them all to go home," he said. "I cannot pay them, these little jitterbuggers. Two of them are suing me. Let them sue. I have nothing. I am wiped out from Nina's lawsuit, and even she, I am satisfied to say, got very, very little from me." Bulging his eyes like a frog, crouching his body in the chair, and angling his arms on the Formica table, he exclaimed, "I am a frog! On the highway about to be squashed!" He went limp, then into the death spasm of the amphibian. By now he had an audience in the restaurant. Two people actually clapped.

OK, you're a frog, I should have said, so hop away. Instead I said, "Oh, Tilla! What will you do?"

"I can do nothing," he said, assuming human form and slouching in

his chair like his father in front of the TV. "I am broke. I have given notice at the loft. I will have to leave. I will go to live again with my mother
and father. In their basement. I will have to live in their basement like a
toad."

Spare me the toad imitation, I should have said. Instead I said,
"In their *basement?*" I was horrified. I did not see his parents' carpeted, stuc-
coed, well-lit half basement with actual full-size windows. I saw instead
my parents' basement in Buffalo from long ago, the coal bin, the furnace,
the cobwebby darkness, and the screaming from the kitchen overhead.

Oh, monster, what shall I do to cure you? To take away your talons and scales?
Surely you are under a spell and my real father is buried beneath you, waiting to be re-
leased so he can love me.

"Oh my God, your appointment!" Tilla shrieked. "It is ten o'clock!"

"It's only a few blocks away. We won't be that late," I said, not mind-
ing being a few minutes late. But for Tilla timing was everything.

"Come on, come on, pay the check, darling, let's get going, let's get
out of here, my God, they are waiting, let's go!"

I paid our bill. It went without saying that I paid our bill.

A late light snow had covered the East Village early that morning and
now was melting in brilliant sun. The apartment had a southern expo-
sure. We walked with the agent into a blast of sunlight, the hardwood
floors gleaming, the white walls the cleanest slates of our lives.

I'll take it, I should have said. Instead I said to the agent impulsively,
"We'll take it, my husband and I will take it." I did not trip over the word
husband or the word *we.* Tilla did not look at me in surprise. He looked at
me *expectantly.* Then he smiled.

"I don't know," Tilla said, still smiling, pacing out the number of square
feet. "I'm not sure it will be big enough for us." He looked at the agent.

"I will have to build walls, you see, because I need privacy for my office. Is there a limit on the number of telephone lines the building will allow?"

Telephone lines?

The agent assured him he could have as many lines as he wished.

"Well, darling, we will not have much room left for our living room, but who needs a living room? I will take this for my office space." The apartment had an L-shaped dining-living room. The space he gestured to was the large part of the L, the living room with the big window. "Then we will build the wall here." He pointed to a place where the wall would effectively block out the sun from the rest of the space. "That will leave us a good cooking and eating area, and of course, a very nice bedroom!"

But the bedroom would have to be divided, too. I was determined to have a place to write.

"All right, all right, darling, we can build a wall right here, with a study for you like this." This wall, too, would preserve the light for our bedroom but leave my study in darkness.

The rental agent was handing Tilla the papers. "Oh no, don't hand them to me, sir!" He leapt away like a burly antelope. "My wife"—he smiled at me both shyly and wickedly—"my wife takes care of all our business."

I took the papers and told the agent when I could have the rest of the money in a certified check and also told him that the lease would be in both of our names. Less than an hour had passed since I sold myself into bondage, me, the complete woman.

"You knew what he was like when you moved in together. You've known him for years!" Maggie was right, of course.

I had packed. Tilla had packed. I had paid the movers. I had put Tilla's name on my checking account, and we paid for the walls, and for the phones, but we could not pay the next month's rent. Running out of money, I took a loan. This I did not tell Polly when I gave her the new phone number. We were trying it, I said. After ten years, why not try it?

I was going to save him the way I could not save . . . But Tilla really wasn't my dad (it was only I who cast him so, though he took the role). I was saving him from the circumstances of an artist's life; he wasn't struggling with an addiction like alcoholism.

"I know I've known him for years," I said to Maggie, my head back on the couch in her apartment, listening to the program she was preparing, "but it's not the same."

"Oh, Mol, he's not changed very much," she said, brushing her forehead with her sleeve, leaving a swath of mascara above her blue eye. She was exasperated and mildly reproachful. We were both sweating. The late afternoon sun was pouring through her windows, and she had been practicing for hours. It was after school. Way after school. Time to go home. But I couldn't go home. Home was where the walls were built giving me no sun. Home was where Tilla had forbidden me from entering the kitchen because he needed his own special food for breakfast, lunch, and dinner and I couldn't cook it and so he would. He had taken over. It was only fair, he explained. If I went out and made the money, then he should cook.

Increasingly I made my living from private poetry students. My adult students didn't want to come to the little dark corner I had to give them, and they became hard to schedule. There was Tilla, greeting them unshaven in his bathrobe, a spoon in his hand. I was living with a housewife with a beard who, like other depressed housewives, couldn't seem to cope with the housework.

"How about the laundry?" I growled at him when I finally got home.

"The laundry? Yes. Someday I will do the laundry. But not today. Today did not feel like laundry day to me."

"But the sheets are overflowing the hamper!"

"You and your hamper! You are hampering me! I am trying to rebuild my troupe! I have nowhere to dance! I have nowhere to work!" His face was reddening.

"All I do is work! I teach at Friends, I teach private students, and now I teach a graduate course!"

"Work is good for you, darling. You have an excellent reputation as a poet, so you are asked to do these courses."

"Tilla, all I do is work to pay your rent!"

Let me do this for you, and do that as well, let me do and do and do—and when I am so tired won't you care for me?

"It is your rent, darling, it is the exact same rent you always pay, so do not tell me that I am costing you a cent. I cost you nothing. Look at your friend Lily. She has the live-in Tom who makes the beds for her and puts the roof over her head for which she pays!"

"But Tom actually makes the beds, Tilla. You won't even wash the clothes."

"Don't be ridiculous! Bed-making, laundry, these are minor things! The big fact is that I save you money because by yourself you are always eating out, and I cook for you. What do you want for dinner, by the way? Well, don't spend time thinking about it. I have already ordered the groceries."

I had not sublet the studio I owned, but had kept it, empty but for a couple of chairs, to meet my adult students in, and eventually to share with someone else who needed extra space. Now I was paying both rents. I might as well have written out a check to Tilla when he was still in Brooklyn and paid for the loft. It would have been a better deal for both of us, but instead, I became a husband.

"It was an accident!" he repeated before he grew silent.

"It was no accident, you asshole! You haven't got the nerve to tell me that there was no motivation for you to break that vase! I don't care if the table slipped—if your object had been on that table you would have caught it!"

I had crashed, of course, as well as the vase. I had broken. When I went to the bathroom and looked at my face, it was apoplectically red. I never in my life had seen this look in my eyes, contorted, squalling, accusing, infantile. I'd called him an asshole. All my life I'd tried not to say the awful things my parents said to one another, and now I was doing it.

Throughout our argument—*"You're potbellied!"* I spat at him.

"Your spine is crooked and you look like an old woman. Where is your babushka? I can't believe you're going uptown to Maggie's looking like you do!" he spat back—my poor, dislocated parrot shrieked. Tilla and my pet did not get along. Cookie had started to bite. She attacked him whenever he opened the door to her cage.

It was like our house on Pilgrim Road. Polly was at the store. Gail was out at cheerleading practice. And I was home. Home and helpless against my poor father, the boy who was astonished to see he had grown into a monster. *Surely you are under a spell and my real father is buried beneath you, waiting to be released so he can love me.*

Oh, Mother, what cry can I utter to call you home to make the monster stop? Ruta was at the store, I mean, in her office, far uptown. Everything was on an even keel, wasn't it? I was, finally, who I was, wasn't I? Three steps forward, two steps back. I got dressed and put the cover on the parrot's cage to calm it down. It had not stopped shrieking, even though I had.

"I'm going to have to leave him," I said softly, as if I had been asked to pray aloud. Above us hung Maggie's candelabra with twenty candle stubs, all lit. It swayed in a mild breeze from the ceiling fan, and lit the room in uneven swaths. The mantel, full of white carnations, was reflected in a mirror above the sideboard with its white pitcher.

"Well, yes"—she nodded, her own head bobbing, flower-like—"you might have to . . . you probably will have to."

"I'll have to face living alone," I said dully.

Maggie looked at me aghast. "Living alone isn't a plague, you know. We've both enjoyed living alone."

"I know that, but . . ."

"I was satisfied, I was *contented* to be alone," she continued. "Stayed up till three in the morning reading what I wanted when I wanted, wonderful friends, darling, sweet men to date and be with, but I didn't want to marry them."

"But now you're very comfy, Maggie!" I protested.

"Now I play my cello and I keep George at bay," she joked.

Her black cats, Fleur and Soames, crawled into our laps.

"He asked me to marry him again." She chuckled.

"Will you?"

"God, no, no, no! It ruins everything! I'm determined to do this my own wrongheaded way." She'd never finished her B.A., never finished at Juilliard, wouldn't get an academic job, wouldn't marry.

"Why does he want to get married? Has he suddenly changed his mind about a family? Does he want to adopt children now?"

"No, no." She scowled. "He's the one who volunteered to get the vasectomy, remember? He's in the middle of his life, buzzing around the world making deals and having me. And I have my cello and him."

The apartment was dark, except for the light over Tilla's desk, when I returned. Tilla loomed in the doorway of the bedroom, sobbing. "It was not my fault, Molly! I swear to you it was not my fault at all! It was an accident!"

"I don't think the way we fight is such an accident," I said saucily.

"No! NO! It is not our fighting, it is the little bird!"

The parrot's cage was empty. The cover was draped over a chair. The window was open.

"I only wanted to make friends with it! I thought that since you were gone, I would try, I would really try to make friends with the bird that is also you, even though you are peacock and not parrot."

A train with an unexpected switch of track ahead, I had to move my huge mechanical body, angling dangerously to the detour track. My landscape flew by me.

"I took off the cover," Tilla said, "and I opened the cage door, and the thing flew out so fast I did not know what happened. And the window, it was opened only this far! Honestly, just this little bit!" He had turned his own body into the body of the parrot, narrowing toward the window. He was acting and dancing the reconstructed scene.

It was the kind of window that opened horizontally. Even if it were open at its full angle, it would have been hard for the parrot to fly through, and the opening was now at about two inches. Had he narrowed the opening after the bird flew out?

In what direction did she fly? It had happened hours before. In the dark—birds don't see in the dark. I fled downstairs and Tilla followed me. I paced the streets and called, not energetically, but through a strange mobilized kind of exhaustion. I moved lugubriously, as if I weighed 400 pounds in 90 percent humidity. Buildings, more buildings, and, in the park, trees full of predators. She would be eaten. Or, she would get hungry and fly to someone's shoulder and be adopted. Or fly to someone's windowsill. Or stay in the trees and starve. Or she had flown into something and crashed and died, or was hurt, and then would die.

Tilla paced the streets after me, saying again what he had done, in exact detail. It was an accident, he insisted.

I should have fought him harder to get the ugly, expensive, sun-blocking window screens he adamantly refused to cooperate in buying or installing. I should have clipped the bird's wings rather than carefully closing all the windows when I allowed her to fly around on her own. Every bird owner knows you should keep them clipped and never let them fly. But I couldn't. I loved that animal who flew to my shoulder. I lived with feathers and bird shit to be with her, she who landed on bowls of berries and flung them at walls, who ate the heads off sixteen tulips I'd carefully grown, who posted a vigil in the night when I was sick, who severed the telephone cord, who cocked her head to get her neck scratched. She clucked. She kissed. She grabbed food from my mouth. We were great pets to one another. *And she had flown away.*

She was as gone as the beautiful vase my student had given me was broken. Tilla had let her out. Tilla had broken the vase. Now two shimmering things were destroyed and, and still, strangely, I did not completely blame him in the way that I still blamed Ted. I had felt until then that I had to save Tilla, the way I could not save Ted. For the first time in a decade it occurred to me that Ted and Tilla began with the same sound.

Then the hopelessness of finding the bird became hopelessness itself.

As I had moved in slow painful gigantean maneuvers to save her, even as I knew I could not, guilt and panic seemed to calcify into my joints, and I walked in a state of crusted exhaustion.

The subway to the Upper West Side seemed to take all next afternoon. "I've suddenly gotten ten years older," I said to Ruta, for I had finally made an appointment with her. I could hardly consider myself graduated from therapy now. "I'm aging. I'm stiff," I whispered. "That's why I'm back." Having fought against depression all my life with the weapon of sheer activity, I could only conclude that I had gotten old when I lay that weapon, the only one in my arsenal, down on the ground of despair.

"It's the end," Maggie said, as she helped me try to get an enormous plastic bag over the brass bird cage a few weeks later. Now all I had left of Cookie was the poem I'd written about first seeing her: *a chartreuse candy kiss/nibbling on my sundress.*

"How can you go on with someone who's killed your pet?"

"Well, he didn't exactly kill it," I said defensively. "It was an accident."

Maggie was speechless. She opened her eyes wide and looked as if what I'd said was a wilted salad someone expected *her*, a woman who ate her greens impeccably fresh, to consume. I handed her the packing tape. We were taking the cage up to my old apartment. Of course I could have taken the cage uptown myself. That is, when I was myself. A heavy numbness had fallen over me. I heard my voice on the answering machine lumbering slow and far away. My clothes were dirty. I put on any old thing.

31.

From our quiet barge, motoring the Welsh canals at a pace slower than walking, through locks so easy a child could spin the wheels to open them, Maggie and George and Tilla and I were mesmerized by what we first mistook for white blooms on the distant hills. Then the flowers moved, and we realized the hills were polka-dotted with grazing sheep. Back home Maggie herself borrowed sheep from a farmer to crop the meadow at her parents' house. The meadow edged a fanciful garden she and her sisters had dug. So the sheep echoed her grandmother's Welsh childhood, which the four of us had come to investigate. We had fallen into the pages of an antique diary, complete with misty autumn days and, oddly for Wales, sunny days—two American women artists and their flamboyant European husband-equivalents.

George was paying our way, inspired by Maggie's wish to take care of us in our obvious need, and I was very moved.

"We are beyond our station," Tilla whispered to me after one of our little meals in the galley of the barge. We were folding up the blue-and-white-striped tablecloth Maggie had brought in her suitcase in case there were no domestic amenities on board. She was right. After we cleared the table, we hooked it back on the wall, and the galley retransformed into our bedroom. "When you are beyond your station," he insisted, "it is only imbalance and unhappiness."

"Don't be ridiculous," I said.

It was time to play one of the many fantasy parlor games the four of us loved to exhaustion. Maggie invented the topic: Who Would You Want to Be If You Were Born the Opposite Sex? and then decided that the man she would want to be was George. "You're the most valorous human being I've ever met," she declared while the leonine George beamed. Would I choose Tilla? Sullen and jealous of her, I passed my turn. The men, after naming news reporters and dead queens, decided they would spice up the game by assuming the identities of famous prostitutes, then Maggie and I got busy assuring them that they wouldn't like their lives at all. "You are right, Molly and Maggie, darlings," Tilla said at last. "I often have thought that is no way to live a life."

By our third day together Tilla had become, irrepressibly, the choreographer of our boat, our dance master, the leader of our troupe. And thus he pitted himself against George Sinopolous, the Greek businessman, complaining at George's decisions, ordering him about, whispering to me how badly everything was done. He could not share the driving of the boat with Maggie's rich boyfriend. He simply didn't know how.

On we floated, down the waterways, sleeping in our too-small bunks, too near one another to make love. On we ate, little candies we found at every stop, George with his easy angular body, Maggie nearly as tall, her eyes peering from her face held on the straight stem of her cellist's spine, and me shorter, Tilla burlier, all of us tanned at the end of the summer.

One day at the helm, with Tilla standing by helping to dock, George calculated their ages, announcing that the difference would make Tilla the age of his son, if George had had a child at sixteen. We were tying up at a tiny, busy canal village whose entire population seemed to be gathering for the Grandfather-Grandchild Fishing Contest. At this Tilla flew into a rage.

"George the father," he spat, "you are *mere*, you are merely a wealthy Athenian! You think you can conquer New York on your family money? I, Tilla, was selling my camera over a barbed-wire fence in Eastern Europe so I could conquer New York!" As if on stage Tilla shouted at the top of his lungs from the deck of the barge. The grandfathers in their jackets and the grandchildren in their sweaters gazed in wonder and horror at the man who was either wrecking or starring in their annual fete. Tilla leapt off the barge and sprinted down the towpath through the hundred sun-splotched faces, leaving me to face my oldest friend, which I did, stammering apologies, tempted to turn against Tilla and stay with her—he would be back, he would have to—but the tension was too much for me, and I ran after him.

There in the local pub he insisted that I rent us a car and fly us back to New York, no matter what the cost. But I soothed and fed him, paid the bill and hated him, walking back with him on the towpath in the dark to the barge where by then Maggie and George had gone to sleep. We crept into our bunk where I hated him even more, the prodigy who had become my prodigal, my prodigal who had become a wastrel.

Forbearance on all our parts allowed us to endure the rest of the trip, and in spite of myself, the pleasure of being driven down the canals with nothing to see but trees gnarled as if for the homes of gnomes, and sheep curled in poses for etchings, and busy black and white dogs going about their herding business, and nothing important to say to Maggie, indulging in gossip and idle wordplay, went to the quick of me.

Tilla was shy and truculent but obedient. George was gracious. Maggie's intrepid energy filled me with the resurgence of a life I was not aware had ebbed so completely away. Because trust and respect were too eroded to be counted on, it was politeness we leaned against. After we finally found Maggie's grandmother's town and even the gray stone house she had lived in, we finished the trip in a mannerly exhaustion.

There in the mail on the return home was the notice that I had gotten a grant I had applied for and been turned down for again and again over a period of eighteen years. Sometimes fate really does wait for the right moment. Now I had a way to pay my bank loan, and a lever. My money, tied with the tiny piece of the fabric of decency left over from our trip, was the lever I used when I asked Tilla to leave our apartment, when we drew up a legal agreement that let me buy him out of the lease, with some help to build a new troupe, and when he insisted we should never see or speak to one another again. And as a measure of the adroitness of our final dance, we have not.

iv.

PARADISE,

PIECE

by **PIECE**

32.

"My God, Lily, look at your derriere!" Maggie shrieked as Lily banged the door to Maggie's parents' screened-in porch.

"I did it!" Lily announced. "I had my ass done!"

"*Removed* is more like it." Maggie half sneered. She took a dim view of face lifts, tummy tucks, and certainly ass sculpting. "Molly," she demanded, "get out of that chair and get over here and ob*serve* this pair of cheeks!"

"Don't even ask me how much it cost, I'm refusing ever to say."

"You look fantastic," I said loyally. In theory I'd imagined the three of us aging into wise, wrinkled women, but here was practice. Her disfiguring buttocks had been shaved into the negligible derriere of a well-exercised, media-wise local politician. Lily Allisman was running for her city council.

"Whatever they write about this ass, it's going to be a helluva lot better than what they said about the old one! No more jokes about my 'seat' on the council. Give me a hug, you two!"

Nearly three decades after we first came here with our poison rings, the three of us toasted each other with iced tea. Maggie's father was in the hospital again, her frail mother lay upstairs in bed, and it was Maggie's turn to hold the fort—three of the four sisters shared the parent-sitting schedule. The last sister had entered an alcoholic treatment center. A troop of bees crawled up the beachhead of the honeysuckle by the porch railing.

"Make sure that door's latched!" she shouted.

Beyond the bees, beyond the honeysuckle, the Jacob's sheep mowed the late June lawn. Deep inside summer, safe inside the shade of the porch, we sank into the ragged cushions of the wicker chairs. Maggie had thrown a white tablecloth over the old square table. We put down our glasses.

"I can't believe we all got free today!" Maggie said. Innumerable phone calls and reschedulings had navigated us to that porch, all our schedules coinciding for a mere two hours.

"A free couple of hours on a summer afternoon, sitting on my new rear end," Lily said dreamily.

"I'm free all right," I said nervously.

"You certainly are, madam," said Lily.

"Tilla-free, and childfree," I said.

"*Childfree*"—Maggie made a face—"sounds like *fat-free.*"

"I sort of like it," I said.

"I'm sticking to my standard statement," Lily declared. "I tell people I don't have the Call for children."

"That's great, Lily. *You* can sound like a nun," I said, pouting. "Ordinary people have to have a *word* for what they mean, not a religious tag line."

"Well, you don't have to be so prickly about it!"

I was being prickly and didn't deny it. "Oh, Lily, I'm out here alone in the world armed only with a tubal ligation," I began, but she interrupted me.

"Poor Mol, you're really having a hard time. I'm sorry, doll."

"You're the only person who can call me doll and get away with it."

Lily, who notoriously hated dolls, called all her intimates "doll." During her mother's illnesses, little girl Lil had quarantined her plastic babies in their carriage, laid a blanket over the top, and announced to her family that her dolls had measles and couldn't play. Then one by one she engineered worse diseases, until each of them dropped dead.

"Does Gail still have her Marilyn doll?" Maggie interrupted. My sister had carted the nearly wigless platinum blonde through many changes of address.

"I'll have to ask her." Slowly through the decade I spent with Tilla, Gail and I had begun speaking again. It started with the box of china dogs I received in the mail not long after Gram and Grandpa Peacock died. They hadn't wanted any funerals, and my uncle had agreed. Neither Gail nor I had seen them after our father died, and I had long since suspended my dutiful holiday cards, never receiving any from them. Gram and Grandpa seemed to have been swallowed into our uncle's family, merged with their favorite son and favorite grandchildren. Instead of their funerals, within months of one another, there were phone calls from my uncle's family. Did Gail and I want mementos? Clearly any inheritance would not be coming to us. Half dumbstruck, half guilty, I asked for the china dogs and the cabinet my dad had made in high school; then I rustled around and called Ed, Gail's old boyfriend, for her number. We were only getting the dogs, I explained to her after I broke the news, since nobody knew where the cabinet was.

"I want the boxer!" she yelped into the telephone. "And the spaniel, and the terrier, and the Doberman pinscher! You get the collie, Molly. It rhymes with you. You're the poet!" Apparently we weren't going to mention the fact that we hadn't spoken for nearly two years.

"Is she still with Jules?" Lily asked.

"Oh God, no, she's with somebody else now. My mother loves this guy because he bought Gail a toaster oven. But she's delusional, Lily. She actually called me and told me she was going to medical school!"

"She's just so jealous of you she can't stand it," Maggie said. "You're running the Poetry Society and your poems are in *The New Republic* making your mother proud. Gail has to lie to keep up."

Maggie made sense of course. The iced tea pitcher sweated, the bees bombed the bushes, and the talk shifted to our work. Maggie agonized over changing publicists, Lily outlined her opposition, and I rattled on about the Poetry Society. "We're transforming it, Lil," I said, "just like your ass."

"Invasive body surgery is a social statement of an entirely different order," Maggie pontificated.

"Oh, shut up!" Lily grinned. The sense of sheer release from what had plagued her was as palpable as its absence. "Speaking of invasive surgery," she turned to me and said, "you're not really having second thoughts about the tubal ligation now that the Hungarian is gone, are you? Tell the truth," she badgered. "You're talking to the woman who first introduced you to birth control pills." Typically Lily, she was going to get my emotional life packaged up to make perfect sense.

"I'm . . . I'm at sea," I found myself saying. "I'm out here in a little boat and I've left one shore and I can't see the other shore yet."

Maggie leaned forward and Lily cocked her head.

"I finished something, I *really, really* finished something, not only with Tilla, but with the whole children thing, and I'm . . . going on, but I don't really know what that . . ." I hesitated.

"Means?" Lily supplied.

"Is?" Maggie offered.

"Well, what shape my life will have. I'm kind of scared, and I'm kind of thrilled." It was as if I spoke from that little boat, floating, my voice an echo from water, even to myself. "I'm rowing, but I really can't see what's in front of me." It was an image of mourning I described. I had abandoned what would no longer define me, yet felt abandoned myself.

"Now you need courage," Lily began, then swatted at a slow bee flown in through the tear in the screen, ushering it with a newspaper to the porch door, "to lead," she continued romantically, "your ambiguous life."

"Oh, shut up!" Maggie parroted Lily. "You have plenty of courage, chickadee," she said to me as she heaved out of her chair and padded upstairs to her mother, cursing all her sisters for leaving her alone. The shadows elongated on the lawn.

"My favorite time of day," I said. "Long shadows remind me of La Grange."

"What a magic place it was," Lily rhapsodized.

"It's terrible to have it gone!" Maggie yelled from the stairs.

The year before Polly had sold it to the neighbors. She needed the money to retire on, and the place went. The death of the house had its own smell to me, a dry, burnt odor, so far from the sweet dampness of the place I'd loved. I missed it purely, from the lilac that had got its seasons reversed and bloomed in November to the rain barrel at the side of the store. Now all the furniture was in the basement of Polly's apartment in Buffalo, stacked there by Howie and Flo and me—Polly had conveniently thrown her back out on the day we moved it. Now the La Grange smell was transferred to her basement.

But by a hideous accident I drove past the house en route to a poetry reading in Rochester. The neighbors had it half torn down. I almost squeezed my eyes shut and sped on but found myself stopping, grabbing the camera from the car seat, and running out to the site. It was a site now, not a house. The roof had caved in and the front had collapsed onto the hydrangeas. You could see the beige flowered paper of the living room wall exposed to the air. La Grange had a squashed, sunken look, like a pumpkin face when too many candles have been lit in it. It was a fluke that I had a camera with me, and that I'd arrived in time to make a death mask in snapshots. Later I almost tortured Polly with the pictures but instead kept them for nearly three months in the inner pocket of the Friends Seminary book bag I always carried.

Now I shoved them impulsively at Lily. She flipped through and offered me a Gram-like platitude, "Well, that house had a nice life for itself in your family and now it's going on its way."

"But it's dead and done," I flashed, "so, let me miss it, Lily. And I miss Tilla, too," I added, "even though he was a tyrant."

"You've got plenty to miss, there, doll," she said, wry and unoffended, standing up to smooth her pants over her new hips.

Maggie stood in the doorway, ready to usher Lily out to her car.

Before she headed out, while we all hugged good-bye, I was still unaware that someone had secretly accompanied me on a parallel journey for the last twenty years. Stung with solitude, I wasn't as alone as I'd thought when I dragged back to Maggie's porch and prepared to sit with her mother while Maggie visited her sister in the treatment center.

"I can't stand it," she moaned, shoving a scrunchee around her gathered hair, "running from the hospital to the treatment center to my mother upstairs. Here"—she fished a scrap of paper from her pocket—"here's what pills to get down her, if you can."

"I don't know what Gail is doing now, alcohol or drugs or both," I said wistfully.

"Molly," my friend admonished me, "it's Gail who's got to decide what to do with her life, not you."

Not me. I was all alone and responsible for no one. No matter what the weather, or what I wore, or how I did my hair, every day I felt that I had the shortest haircut of my life and was wearing a blouse without sleeves. My skin prickled at every breeze.

33.

Two hands holding two pencils in mirror images of one another—an M. C. Escher drawing—poked out from the envelope with Mike Groden's return address. Years before, nearly a week after the abortion, on a Friday night when Cookie and I had shared a pound of asparagus for our dinner, I'd finally opened that card. It was packed with his fast, small scrawl—the cramped handwriting I remembered from high school and college. Even before I read it, I recognized and enjoyed the complexity of the drawing and the symbolism of the opposite hands. He reintroduced himself matter-of-factly: In college, he'd left math and become a literature major, got declared 4F because of his eyesight, went to Princeton for his Ph.D., then to Canada where he became a professor. The card was neutral and informative. He had let many friendships lapse, he said, and was sorry he did that. Now he was picking them up again, if the other people were willing. He did not say what prompted the urgency to renew these friendships, but I thought I knew what it was. *He's been sick, really sick, with cancer,* his—what was she, his girlfriend?—had said to me at the dinner after a poetry reading where I had suddenly heard his name spoken after nineteen years.

"I think I know someone you know," the thin, scarfed, and suited assistant professor had purred, "Michael Groden."

"My old boyfriend!" I blurted out. "I remember the smell of his shirts!

We went to all the high school proms, and I slow-danced with my nose pushed into his collarbone."

She informed me that he'd become a prominent James Joyce scholar. And that he had cancer. *What kind? How was he? Where was he?*

"In Canada," she said coyly. A ripple of possession in her tone let me know that she was his girlfriend now, but I pushed my address at her anyway, almost beseeching her to give it to him, even though she had not wanted to. The brassy note in my voice must have bullied her, because she wrote out the name of his university on the dessert card. I was going to contact him, afraid he was sick. But he beat me to it—not that sick, I guessed.

He was coming to New York, he'd said in the note.

Lunch with an old boyfriend had been a surefire path to a blowup with Tilla, but I had carefully explained that Mike was dying. Tilla knew perfectly well that you couldn't catch cancer, but he despised being around sick people and refused, as I knew he would, to come to lunch with us. We met at Caffe Bianco, with its white tables and chairs out in the sun of Second Avenue, and Mike Groden, now a thin, stringy-muscular man in the way that runners are—a marathon runner, it turned out—began a purposeful search for the deepest shade he could find and suggested we sit there. I was embarrassed because I had chosen the place for its sunlight. Of course someone with, well, it must be skin cancer—what kind? the kind you die from?—would not want to sit in the sun, however mild. How unthinking of me. After our very soft hellos, and settling in at a cramped table in the only shade, a terrible awkwardness fell on us, like another form of unwanted light.

Mike didn't look like he was dying—not that I was sure I knew what a young person dying of cancer looked like—he just looked nervous. He had always been a nervous sort of person, quick to get flustered, as if he were giving an oral report in a possibly hostile classroom. But there was only me. We picked at our salads and focaccia and later dove into our gelati without ever mentioning our mature bodies: his that had been so ill, mine that had just endured its abortion—or, for that matter, our young bodies that had given us so much pleasure.

"I guess Tilla—is that how his name is pronounced?—is a pretty serious relationship," Mike Groden had ventured.

"It's really serious all right. But we don't live together. We have a . . . a serious weekend relationship."

"Lots of academics have those kind of relationships."

"And you? Are you in a relationship with someone?" I had asked him back.

"Well yes, I'm . . . ah . . . I'm dating someone." He paused. "Um, seriously."

So if he was dating someone seriously, was he also seriously dying or what? I didn't ask.

The shade had shifted, and then we were in the sun again. When the waiter cleared our table and we had relaxed enough to realize that of course there were tables *inside* the restaurant we could move to, we moved, easily finding a comfortable spot, a table with elbow room and fresh place settings and filtered light from a skylight above. We started over, able to smile at our exasperated waiter, ordering two cappuccinos. While we waited for our coffees, we told each other about our accomplishments: We had both published books, he had edited all the James Joyce facsimile manuscripts and gotten early tenure. We had stuck to our guns. We had not been derailed into jobs we hated. We had chosen what we wanted and steered our courses toward it.

"God, how did your father feel when you left math and became an English major!" I exclaimed.

"Not so great, it wasn't so great, he couldn't understand it, but just after I graduated from college he died."

"Oh God, really? Oh, I'm sorry," I said goofily. I never knew what to say when people died. "My father died, too."

"Was that hard for you?" he asked.

"Well, it was complicated when he died, it took a lot of psychotherapy even to start to understand it all."

"Oh, are you in therapy too?" he asked with delight. "This is great," he murmured, lowering his voice to a barely audible pitch, "can I, can I call you when, ah, when something comes up in therapy that you, ah, that you, um, might know about? Like my family?"

"Oh sure!" I smiled. "I love conversations like that."

We both needed to understand the things that had happened to us, that had formed who we turned out to be. We never mentioned sex. We didn't veer down the sensuous memory path of each other, nor did we mention our breakup in college. And certainly we did not talk about his cancer or my abortion. But we had thrown two important rappelling ropes to one another in our determined scaling of the face of who we were: we had made it out of Buffalo! and we hungered to understand what formed us.

With wicked pleasure and laughter, we talked about the people we hated in high school and by the end of lunch I had almost forgotten Mike was supposed to be so sick.

But I woke the next morning full of questions. Why had we catalogued all our honors and awards to one another and never spoken about our tender early lives? To think Mike was dying (was he dying?) and I never mentioned the comfort of our sexuality to him! And all this, from our lovemaking so long ago in the cold New Hampshire motel to the Caffe Bianco, I crammed into a double sonnet and sent it to him with a letter remembering even more.

No, no, he was *not* dying, he wrote to me immediately. Yes, he had had melanoma, but now he had been symptom free for more than five years. Now he was thinking and feeling so much more fully and in such good physical shape that I didn't have to worry about him. He was teaching and writing and lying on a couch twice a week, and running marathons, running for his life.

Slowly life unfolds, if you have time to live it. By the spring after Tilla and I broke up, Mike and I had had several years to develop an adult friendship. Once or twice a year, often when Mike came in to run the marathon, we had lunch or dinner, carefully avoiding romance, or, if romance came up, one of us got soft-eyed while the other pretended not to see. Mike knew everything about Tilla and Polly and Ted and Gail and Ruta and Maggie and Lily. I knew all about his job, his family, the girl-friend who eventually dumped him. In perhaps two phone calls and two get-togethers every year, we made a kind of secret contact, not a sexual secret, a psychological one. Because we were not involved in each other's lives, we were intimately neutral, and inquisitive in the way that knowing someone a long time can make you feel you have the right to ask nosy questions and get honest answers.

I sat in my silk blouse transfixed by the sensuous acrobats of Cirque du Soleil, and Mike Groden sneezed. And I oohed and ahhhed at the colors and the leaps, and Mike Groden sneezed. He sneezed in line for tickets, and he sneezed as he read his program. As we walked to the restaurant along Battery Park with its spring flowers, he coughed. He coughed when he asked for our table. He sneezed through our pasta dinners. He went through his own packet, then my wad of tissues. He worked his way through a stack of napkins the pitying waitress had given him. Then he produced a gift for me, a book about Buffalo high school yearbooks—how specialized could you get? Clearly he had searched for such a book. I hadn't felt such depth of concentration in a gift since I was in high school when he gave me a long thin scroll of a Chinese painting, with a peacock in it, of course, the first sort of painting like that I'd seen.

Evidently relieved not to be sneezing for a moment, Mike Groden dug into his mile-high chocolate extravaganza cake. He went at it with such gusto that he got chocolate on his nose. On the empty chair next to me lay the soiled beige book bag from which he had produced my gift along with a rain slicker so old I couldn't imagine what color it had been. When he finished his cake, he looked up at me from his unironed, button-down shirt. He could have worn that shirt in high school.

Somewhere behind the contact lenses and the five o'clock shadow, underneath the enervated responses of a man who had a cold, was the boy I took a bubble bath with almost exactly a quarter of a century before. He had called and wanted to know how I was. I was nervous, that's how I was, though that only occurred to me when I had changed my clothes top to bottom four times before taking the subway way downtown to meet him. Why I had finally settled on the bluish-greenish silk blouse I understood only when I thought of the Chinese scroll: The blouse was the color of its border.

Borders. We were full of them. Canadian borders. U.S. borders. Borders of time and distance. After dinner we took a silent, groggy walk along the spotlighted Hudson, and when it was time to go, he got on the subway and I hailed a cab, not wanting to take the subway home alone. He was going in the opposite direction. He was not going to see me home. There was a bigger border between us than I thought.

I'd almost adjusted to the fact that he was simply a valuable old friend I'd talk to now and then, when he wrote to me all about his reactions to the circus and our evening, remembering my responses to everything, even to the colors of the tulips we passed on our walk. So there *had* been something going on beneath the sneezing and coughing. . . . The letter was sweet and sensuous and intelligent and educated. When I read it, a circus image came to my mind: A trapeze artist, practicing her routine, missteps and falls into the net. The language of the letter flowed like a great net.

He was glad to chat with me when I called. He was going to spend the summer in London, Ontario, unusual for him, since ordinarily he traveled. But he had a project with a publisher, and now the project was in trouble, so he had to stay home.

He was asking me for help—no, advice. Advice I might be able to give. He had a contract problem, and he didn't have a leg to stand on. But when I started to make some calls for him, I was so resentful at having to do one measly thing for yet another person that I stopped. And when I stopped, I had a brand new idea for me, and it was this:

He would have to work this out himself.

Oh, I realized, he had not asked me to make the round of calls I was making. I had volunteered. *Well, I better unvolunteer,* I said to myself uncharacteristically.

"I'm going to watch him," I said to Ruta. "I'm just going to watch him solve this problem. I'm not going to involve myself." Where had my grandiosity gone?

He called again. We talked. I called him back. We talked. He called again. We talked again, and again, and again, over weeks that stretched past a month. I gave him a few people's names, but didn't—and, in fact, *couldn't*—help him beyond simply listening to him, and watching, fascinated, to see how he would solve his problem.

He did not blow up at anyone. He was stopped at every point by some obstacle. Each time he maneuvered around the obstacle. He talked to colleagues all over the world. He discussed his problem with his therapist. He planned, revised, got stymied. He was pitted against a corporation with whom he had a weak contract and a weak position, and he was going to lose. He was not screaming at how unfair the world was or kicking himself for signing the weak contract. He was saying what a lesson he had learned, he was saying how he would never do *that* again. His schedule was blown. Part of his professional life was blown. He felt shitty, but he had tried everything, and he really had. But he was outwiled. And when he recognized that, he stopped and faced the truth of it. What was he going to do now? He wasn't sure. Take stock, he guessed, then go on, he supposed, but right now he was going to sit around licking his wounds and feeling stymied.

So I became a confidante, not a rescuer. He was a successful man who had survived more than one professional crisis. And he had survived melanoma. Without me. He had lived a whole life without me, and made lots of his own mistakes.

Our calls were closer together, cozier, sexier, always late at night. After the call I'd go to bed and watch the sex channel.

"I have a whole house with a guest room, Mol," he said one night. "You could write here. Why don't you come up for a week?"

"A *week!* Oh God, no, I couldn't come for a whole week." Why, we hadn't spent more than five hours together in person. "How about a weekend?"

"Well, if you came for a weekend, you'd just have to turn around and go home again immediately—the trip's too long for a weekend, Mol."

"Oh."

"Well, think about it."

"OK, I'll think about it. Thanks for asking. Really, thank you, part of me would love to come tomorrow, and another part of me is terrified."

"I can understand *that,*" he said in breathy sympathy. "I feel the same way."

"He feels the same way," I said to Ruta.

"Oh," she said therapeutically.

"But *a week,* my God, what the hell will we do in London, Ontario, for a week?"

She said nothing.

"Ruta?"

"Yes."

"I'm going. I mean, after all, I'm going to have to take my clothes off in front of somebody sooner or later."

"Mmmm."

"Mmmmm," I said in a totally different context. Two nights later he called and I said yes I would go and he said he was glad and I said I was glad and he said again I could have a whole room to myself and that he had two cats and I said I might be allergic to the cats and he said he'd vacuum really well and then there was a silence. It was the first elongated silence we'd had on the phone. It was an expensive, long distance silence. Of course, he outwaited me. I had the patience of a moth.

"Mmmm," I said, "Mike?"

"Mmmm?"

"I don't look like I looked in high school."

"I don't either."

"Yes, but marathon runners don't have to worry about how they look. They always look fantastic."

"Yes, but I have scars."

"Scars?"

"From the cancer surgeries. A big one on my calf, another one on my groin and upper thigh."

"Melanoma?" Ruta repeated from her chair behind me as I lay on the beige couch and looked at the watercolor of the sea on the wall in front of me.

"But he's off the charts. It's been ten years. He's not even a statistic anymore."

"Mmmm," I heard behind me.

We tried to have sex on the telephone. We verbally undressed each other, tried to masturbate together, then felt stupid and hung up. My video porn lessons from Eve's Garden didn't help in the end. It would have to be the real thing. Each of us went to have our AIDS tests and reported to each other our negative results. I'd nearly fainted in the heat on First Avenue outside the lab. ("I always nearly faint when I'm around blood," he said. "And I had a lot of blood tests when I was sick.") After I ignored his reference to his illness, he introduced the subject of birth control.

"We don't need any," I said.

"We *don't?*" he said.

"I've had a tubal ligation. I chose not to have children," I blurted out.

"No condoms? No IUD's?" he said. He didn't ask *why*. He was purely focused on the physical.

"No."

"Hmm."

"Does it bother you? I mean, I really decided. I decided in another context, with another man, but really it was my decision. Having children isn't for me."

"Well, I haven't thought about it a lot. I mean, I've thought about it, but not really *concentrated* on it. I've had plenty of opportunities, and . . .

I've avoided every one. I guess it hasn't been for me, either. I could have had children with my ex-wife. But I didn't. And she has a child now."

"So does my ex-husband." Jonathan, I'd heard, had remarried and had twins.

"Now that I think of it"—his voice changed slightly, a little lower, a little more hesitant—"I avoided dating women who had children for many years. And that's some feat in London, Ontario. Everybody has children here."

"That's one of the reasons I live in New York!" I hadn't thought about it that way, but it was.

"One of the reasons I love New York is those small packages of cereal and laundry soap and toothpaste and bread just portioned for one person lined up on the supermarket shelves. You can't imagine the hugeness of the family-size boxes here."

We had been born one month apart. We had married and divorced in exactly the same years. We had gone out into the wildernesses of our lives. We had not wanted to express ourselves through children, though we expressed ourselves through scholarship and through art—both of us through writing. We had not defined ourselves through parenthood—we were only the parents of texts. Though plenty of writers have both children and texts, producing books for us was a matter of our gifts being exercised against great odds.

I had my tickets and my passport. I wore my purple linen skirt and my coral linen top. I got a new haircut, and I starved myself for a week.

On July 6, 1991, I spied him in the Toronto airport in a yellow T-shirt, running shorts, and flip-flops. *You can't get farther away from the elegance of Tilla Szabo,* I thought, *from silk shirts to T-shirts. . . .* I dragged two huge suitcases full of things I wouldn't wear and wouldn't use up a long ramp, and he couldn't come down to help me because of the customs barrier. Finally I stood in front of him, but he couldn't bear the tension of looking at me directly, so he rolled his eyes toward the ceiling while he grabbed my shoulders. Then I wound my arms around him and we stood there in the midst of a reunion of several grandmothers and their grandchildren. We did not move. It was hot and humid and his back was drenched in sweat. A turbaned guard told the family to move on. Then he tapped our shoulders. I drank in the smell of Mike's sweat and his shirt and his neck, so recognizable. He smelled of his man's odor inside of which was his boy's odor. "Move on, please," the guard said and we walked out into the thick, moist air, and drove two hours to London, city of trees with its own little river Thames, to the yellow brick house of the scholar.

Naked and drenched with the exertion of lovemaking on a humid July afternoon, murmuring to each other. *How glad I am I found you, how glad I am I found YOU,* saying, *Let's not let each other go this time, let's not be so stupid, let's, let's;* the pronoun *we* leapt bloomlike into being from the sandy waste of the past two decades without each other. A loneliness roiled up around us and parted. We made love again, profoundly shy, not like a man and a woman in our forties, but like twenty-year-olds, picking up where we left off weaving our way. How we knew which strands exactly we dropped and recognized their hues was our mystery. But we dropped them when we were shy, and here we were shy again, and passionate. I did not recognize the sounds that came out of me. They must have been the yelps I made twenty years before. Mike said not one word. Tilla, voluble, had narrated nearly every move. Now I had to listen hard for the lightest shifts. . . . His bony kneecaps dug into my kneecaps and I thought, *We can't do it this way for the rest of our lives,* and I knew that rest-of-our-lives meant the other shore. The little boat I felt in open water had sighted land. Or a landsman.

I shifted, he shifted, it took us a long time to reach our orgasms. The pattern resumed under our hands on our own bodies as we moved. I felt clumsy, and he fumbled, but we held the strands in our hands and we wove.

"You look like you did in high school," he said to me, blinkered by love.

"You look *better* than you did in high school." I sighed. He did, too. He wasn't a serious athlete in high school. But there was a big oval chunk taken out of his calf, and a patch on his buttock where the skin was taken to cover the oval on his calf. There was the knotted scar tissue at his groin, so tough and hard he must barely have known I was touching it.

I did stay a whole week. And one afternoon we dressed up for tea on the lawn of a nineteenth-century house on the banks of the Thames. Over our scones he said, "Well, I feel the m-word lingering at the limits of this conversation."

"What are you talking about, Mikey?" I said.

"The m-word," he repeated. He was dressed like a Creamsicle: orange sherbet shirt and white slacks. I wore a sundress the color of a lavender Necco wafer.

"Oh," I said, feeling my face break into tiny cracks all over like the inside of an antique porcelain cup. You can still drink out of those antique cups.

"I'm not ready to say it yet. But I know it's out there," said my Creamsicle.

It was Christmas morning in London, Ontario. Mike and I had been seeing each other for six months, commuting between the two cities. Icicles the size of pitchfork prongs hung off the cold, cold glass of the sunroom, and our feet were bundled in double wool socks. I had my coffee, and Mike had his tea. He had his Cheerios, and I had my muffin. Before us were two piles of gifts. We each had a stack for the other, bought from Santa's lists we exchanged, fearing we didn't know one another well enough, but of course we did. And we had ignored the limit we set. My big find for him was a Classics Illustrated Comic Book for his collection, and his big find for me was not on my list: a box of watercolors and paintbrushes.

"Paints!"

"You used to paint in high school, didn't you?"

"But I haven't painted in twenty-five years!"

Was it like weaving a pattern or restoring a fabric? I mucked about with the paints all afternoon while I cooked, and the cats, Roma and Fellini, begged for food and it snowed and we never got out for our drive to look at the neighbors' lights. Instead, we went to bed early and made love under the down comforter for our first noel.

And then it was January 3 and we were taking the tree down at the time trees should come down, not on Christmas Eve as the tree at La Grange had gone, but at Epiphany, and off to a special recycler for bark mulch, too. I had not sneezed once. My allergy, like my grandiosity, seemed to have disappeared. Drifts outside were the size of sand dunes, and inside, there were drifts of tissue paper for repacking the ornaments. In the midst of elaborately layering the ornaments in the paper, I felt a terrible tension from Mike. He sat on the sunroom couch, ice diamonded on the panes behind him, so I sat down next to him, then realized what was going to happen, just the way it happened in novels. He said, "Molly, will you marry me?"

And I, like the other Molly in his life, said, "Yes."

That afternoon, we called our mothers.

"Not bad, nothing new, really," Polly said at first when I called and asked how she was.

"Am I interrupting the football game?" (Polly was a dedicated Buffalo Bills fan. I pictured her in her bathrobe in her BarcaLounger with a cup of instant coffee and a box of low-salt crackers.)

"It's just that lousy halftime stuff I can't stand anyway."

"Good, I'll give you some halftime entertainment you'll like better."

"Yeah?" she said.

"I'm getting married!" I screamed. "To Mike!"

"Well, well, well, isn't that nice," she said. "After all this time, you finally have each other. Isn't that nice."

"Yes, it really is, it really is nice."

"Well, when are you going to do it?"

"We're not sure. We haven't decided anything. Don't worry, we're not having a big wedding. I'm really not sure what we're going to do."

"Well, I'm glad you're getting married, and I'm really glad you're not having a big wedding. You wouldn't do it here in Buffalo, would you?"

"No, I don't think so, Ma."

"Good, then I won't have to buy a dress because I won't have to go."

I heard this with as much relief as there was in her voice.

"Gee whiz," my mother was saying, "you're both forty-four, that's still . . . that's still young enough. . . ." she trailed off, ". . . that's still young enough for kids," she finally said. She had brought it up. Her sliver of hope pierced the afternoon like a sliver in my palm.

"I don't think so, Ma, I don't think we're planning on that. We're both going to be forty-five." I still hadn't told her I had had a tubal ligation. And I hadn't told her that I'd be marrying a man for whom my choice was OK.

"Plenty of women have kids now at your age," she continued.

"Polly, I don't think we're planning on it."

"Well, I couldn't help thinking . . ."

"Did I hear the game go on again?"

"Yeah, it's on, but nothing's happening," she said.

"Don't you want to watch?"

"I'll watch in a minute. It isn't every day you call up and say you're getting married."

"Isn't it nice? We're thrilled, Pol, it feels just right."

"Mike's a nice boy. I'm glad you're back with Mike." Then she suddenly fired, "Even though he probably isn't very good-looking. He was a dopey-looking teenager."

"Polly! He looks great! What is the matter with you?"

"Nothing's the matter with me."

The subject, dew-like with possibility, was there with Mike's mother, too. "I don't suppose you're planning on any children," she chortled on the phone.

"No," I said neutrally, "I don't guess we are." I didn't offer her any explanations, either. I couldn't really. There wasn't a catch phrase I could use. *Oh no, I don't have the calling for it,* I might have said, using Lily's standard line, but how could I pass my future mother-in-law off so lightly? I was neutral as cardboard, and as stiff.

But our happiness sported a flexible, almost otherworldly personality, equipped with the capacity of keeping us in its protective cloud. And that benign cloud *moved.* It swept us completely across the continent.

The following August Mike bought a glamorous suit, and I made my wedding dress and my hat, too, dolling it up with a band and a rose I made from silks the colors of the dress. Every texture delighted us, and felicitously, all the colors seemed complementary. We were making a play all for ourselves.

As we approached the little town in Washington State where we got married, I remembered I'd forgotten about a bouquet—and there on the mountainside ahead of us were drifts of wild sweet peas, and because I'd brought ribbon (in case my hat fell apart), I tromped in my brand new shoes into the sweet peas with some toenail scissors and harvested a big bouquet, a lucky thing, since the flowers wouldn't last. They had appeared at the only moment they were needed and desired. It was like writing a poem where all the rhymes fell into place, with no reaching, except across a field of peas.

We'd found a married couple in legal practice together who'd marry us. We'd found the state with the fewest license restrictions. We'd found a town and a charming place to stay. We'd even found a photographer. But the best shots came from my own camera, lent to a woman I didn't even know and whose name neither of us can remember, someone in the legal office of the lawyer couple who were marrying us on the steps of County Courthouse, who suddenly volunteered to come take pictures. Our faces are radiant in the breezy light of the Straits of San Juan de Fuca. Happiness presided over our union in a whimsical wholeness, wagging its planetary tail.

34.

When I'm introduced to a stranger and we begin one of those conversations where the getting-to-know-you questions fly—What do you do, Where are you from—I try to sneak in "Do you have children?" and wait to see what happens. If the person says "Yes, I do!" I inquire into the kids' various states of being, and chances are, the parent will be so engrossed in answering that it will take another meeting on another occasion—or perhaps another meeting many occasions hence—for the person to find out I have no children, let alone to discover it was by choice.

Although I do say I am childfree by choice, anticipating their reactions makes me anxious, and I hasten, always, to reassure them that I like children, and in fact devoted years of my life to working with kids. Somehow I feel this will shoehorn us out of their discomfort, for they are likely to be embarrassed. They've misjudged me. I ask myself why I feel a need to comfort them—I haven't hurt them after all—and know it is because I'm determined to be accepted, not controversial. And so I behave like a coward.

I had my Cowardice Alert in the on position as I set out with Arcadia Scott, a near stranger, to share a 100-odd-block-long cab ride in the rain in the dark in slow traffic, but I shut it off immediately when my companion said quietly and comfortably that no, she had no children. A friend of Maggie's, she'd helped organize the Harlem Euro-African Poetry and Visual Art program that I'd just helped introduce, and though we'd spoken on the phone, this was the first time we'd met in person, settling back on the lumpy seats for the ride downtown after the program. I knew I was in treacherous territory: She could have lost a baby, lost many babies, could have tried unsuccessfully, could have waited too long, could have decided no, but be so shut down about it we couldn't have a conversation. . . .

And so I rushed to tell her that I, too, had no children, and for me, in fact, it really was a choice, even though I was married, and that, in fact, it was a happy choice for both of us—I even used the word *liberating*—until, in the rainy streetlights of nighttime Broadway on the Upper West Side, I watched her face open and saw her turn toward me and smile one of those smiles that can take up nearly half of a tiny face. She was a gamine of a woman with alternating jet-black and bleached-red pixie braids, dressed in a bright coat with tiny shoulders and a flared skirt, like an urban columbine. I learned in a jumble from her reedy voice that she'd been married for twenty years—she didn't look as though she could have been married for two decades—and was in business with her husband, and though they'd tried, in a lackadaisical way, to have children, they'd had to admit they didn't really want them.

"We could have," she said, "we could have spent thousands of dollars on fertility measures, but"—she hesitated before she said this, looking me over, maybe trying to decide how much censure she'd provoke—"but, I'd honestly rather take a big trip to Africa collecting!" She and her husband had a business dealing in African art. "Now why, why, well it's very hard to give a single reason why you don't have children," she mused. "What reason do you give?"

I give two categories of reasons, I explained to her: "One's from environment, and the other's from my soul."

"The environment one can't matter," she stated with sudden assurance. "It's what's inside you."

"But I'll give you both, just so you'll have the full picture. First the environment: I had a family I didn't want to replicate, the kind of family that actually said to me when I was a little girl, 'Don't ever have children!'"

"Really?"

"Well, they didn't always say that, but sometimes they did, my father did, and my grandmother, and my mother said, 'Only if you really want to.'" In the cab I realized again the gift, manufactured by frustration and inability to cope, that my parents had given me: They told me that I had a choice about what to do with my womanhood. Drunk as my father was, depressed as my mother was, conventional as Gram acted, they agreed it was terrible to be a mother if you did not want to be. "Of course the problem was," I continued, "that I thought they didn't want *me*. At least they didn't want me *as a child*. They needed me to be a parent. I did a lot of unnaturally early caretaking of my father and little sister."

"Sister! My little sister is *completely consumed* by motherhood. It is *all* she thinks about! She has two kids, one girl and one boy, and a concerned husband and *no life*, I mean no life of her own. Or a thought in her head except if it's about those kids—and they're adorable kids, they really are. But I don't want them, and my husband doesn't want them. We want to be striking bargains with Masai tribeswomen for stuff like this!" She pulled out a small drum-like object made, I guessed from the feel, from skins. Then she removed a leather thong, and pulled the top off. "Smell this!" she said.

"Whew!" I backed myself right into the door handle to avoid the stench.

"Face paint! That's what you're smelling, special-occasion face paint. This is a makeup drum! An actual Masai makeup drum. Hey, the Lancôme counter never smelled like this!"

I took the skin case from her again and opened the lid again, feeling like Pandora: Inside was a pungent smell of mashed herbs and a deep smell of animal grease, and earth and cow and bark and leaf and berry and maybe dung. It was a profound smell, and that container was empty. It had no face paint in it. It was only the empty drum, the place for possibility, and it reeked of the possible.

"This," she said, "is the smell of *my* decision not to have children. The smell of something so deep inside—I mean, this smell is deep inside. It is positively *vaginal!* So who cares about your environmental answer? Everybody has family environments. It's your insides, your gut that matters when you decide what to do with your life. *Here* is the gut!"

"Well, the gut of my decision is that I didn't want to, it wasn't in my nature. Strangely," I said, "even though I'm an energetic person, I didn't have the energy for kids."

"I know what you mean! Here I have the energy to get on and off airplanes and learn Swahili and camp out on the dirt" (it was very hard to imagine this artfully eye-shadowed woman camping on the dirt) "and follow Billy, that's my husband, into the preserves, and sometimes I think, Girl, you don't even have the leftover energy to take your clothes to a dry cleaner, what would you be doing as a mother? I can't do it all."

"What about your mother? Does she mind?"

"My mother has the energy of eight women! All she *is* is energy. She is a full-time painter—and always was—and she raised four of us, two girls and two boys, and she sometimes had an extra job when my father wasn't doing so well, and she is going strong! My mother is my best friend. She understands me." She stopped. "She *mostly* understands me. We all have different energy levels."

"My relationship with my mother is more complicated." And I hadn't been married for twenty years, either. The cab crawled even more slowly because the rain had turned to snow, but finally we were at Union Square.

"I've got to give you a card," she said. We both fished in our bags for our cards, and our money, and we paid the driver and each went to her corner of Union Square. "Remember this smell," she called to me. "Choice from the gut!"

Fourteenth Street was nearly empty of pedestrians, and no one was at the bus stop, but the bus loomed up and I decided to take it because the suddenly squalling snow made the very short walk home seem impossible. The bus itself took three times the normal amount of time to get to my stop. I thought of my mother, whom I loved so hard, even though she did not turn out to be my best friend.

In the November just after we were married, I got into the Pigmobile, Mike's ancient car, and drove from London, Ontario, through the first snowstorm of the season to Buffalo to get to my dying mother. Polly was home from the hospital. She hadn't had to be put in the nursing home as my sister predicted. The horrible papers I had filled out for Medicare hadn't turned out to be necessary since she was stabilized at home. I found a clause in the insurance that said they would pay for a visiting nurse, then took more money from the little cache from the sale of La Grange and paid the nurse extra to come more often. My cousin Howie came. And her two friends for more than fifty years, Flo and Ann Louise, were there all the time. And I did duty for my sister, too, since Gail herself was in no shape to help. She'd been hospitalized, beaten up by the boyfriend who bought her the toaster oven.

I stopped eight times in the blizzard, first at the usual doughnut place, then at a second doughnut place, a tearoom, two gas stations, the toll plaza before the American border, and a highway exit, just to rest for a moment each time before going into the storm again. It squalled and stopped and squalled; the windshield wipers never moved fast enough. Three hours turned into six. The terrible heater miraculously stayed on. I would have thanked my lucky stars for that, if I could have seen any lucky stars. At the highway exit, I wept for the fourth time. I had broken down in sobs eating a peanut doughnut—Polly's favorite—pulled myself together eating a maple doughnut—Polly's other favorite—sniffled through a cup of tea, and squalled again like an irate child, just as the weather was squalling, at the top of my lungs in the Pigmobile with no other passenger cars on the Queen Elizabeth Way, just tractor trailers that passed me throwing road sop on my windshield, but whose guiding red taillights I was grateful for. *Oh little pig eating Mommy's food in your Pigmobile, oh little honeypie, you can do it, you can leave your husband for tonight with his cats by the fire, and you can drive. Honey, you can drive all night.* And I did. And no accidents, either, though two close calls, both with tractor trailers fishtailing on the ice by Lake Ontario.

I arrived trembling.

"Hi, Mom!" I screamed, shaking the snow off my hair.

"My God, Molly," Flo exclaimed, "what happened to you? You look terrible!" I hadn't even bothered with lipstick. Somehow I'd managed to lose my slithery makeup case. It wasn't nearly the size of that Masai face paint drum. I'd been driving and crying for six hours.

"Hey, Mol," my mother said, looking at me with expectation, "didja bring me my milk shake?"

I'd forgotten.

"God, I forgot! I've been on the road six hours!" I had called them twice from the highway to report on my progress.

"It's a snowstorm out there, Polly," Ann Louise said. "Molly, you poor thing, let me get you some coffee. Have you eaten?"

"Well, I ate two doughnuts."

"Oh, what kind?" my mother asked. "Peanut? Maple? Oh, I wish I could eat 'em now!"

Don't worry, I ate them for you. The doughnut communion. This is my body. Do this in remembrance of me.

My mother could eat very little. She had decided against chemotherapy. The radiation treatments her doctor had scheduled were over: She had diabetes, lung cancer, hypertension, and the onset of senile dementia. Like tearing off the pages of a calendar backwards, Polly was getting younger and younger as her body diminished.

"OOOh, I've been waiting for you, Molly!" she said, raising her arms from the BarcaLounger like a child from the crib. "I wouldn't let no one cook me dinner, but you!"

Her two friends, both much better cooks than I, looked at me helplessly. She wouldn't allow them to feed her. Only me. I took a step into the room and twisted my ankle in my oversized boot.

"Molly, you better sit down," Flo said. "You look terrible. We tried to tell her you'd be late and we should feed her, but she wouldn't let us. She only wants you. All she said was, 'Molly is coming.' " Flo talked about her friend in the third person, though Polly was only three feet away.

"Oh your mother's been waiting for you!" Ann Louise said. "She wouldn't let us do anything. She wants you to do it all! The nurse was here and she's had all her pills and her doctor called in, and she's fine for the night, but she needs her dinner."

"You mean," Polly said in a weak voice, "you didn't remember my milk shake?"

"Oh God, Ma, it's a snowstorm out there! I forgot it. I'll get you one tomorrow. Two. From the good place. Not just McDonald's, OK?"

"Oh, I was looking forward to one. . . ." She looked desolate, and a guilt and an anger rose up in me with stems thick as rhubarb. "Scramble me some eggs!" my mother was saying. "And toast, too, make me toast, Mol."

I went in my boots and my coat to the stove.

"Take your coat off, Molly," Flo said.

"Hey, you've still got your boots on!" Ann Louise said.

For that matter, I still had my bag in my hand.

I took off my wet boots, having messed up the rug. I went into the bedroom and put my coat away. I would sleep in my mother's bed. She slept in her chair, which, to her, was more comfortable. She said she hoped she would die in her chair.

I went to the stove and got out the frying pan and the eggs. The eggs smelled disgusting to me. The butter smelled metallic from being too long in the refrigerator. I hadn't had dinner myself, but I knew I was not going to be able to eat what I had cooked. Scramble, scramble. Baby food. I cut the toast in strips the way my mother had cut toast in strips for me when I was sick with chicken pox, so long ago. I loved her and drove through snowstorms for her. And I hated her, loathing that she had not let her friends cook dinner. Hysterical, hungry, and exhausted, I could have smashed her head open with the frying pan I instead made her meal in. Flo and Ann Louise had gotten her chair turned around toward the kitchen area of her apartment, so Polly could watch me make the food.

"Now, Mol, I wantcha to open that cupboard over your head."

I opened the cupboard over my head.

"See those cans of soup?"

I saw those cans of soup.

"Now, bring those cans of tomato soup forward on the shelf, and put those cans of chicken noodle behind them."

"Ma, for Christ's sake these eggs are gonna burn," I said.

"Come on, Polly, Molly's making you a nice dinner," Ann Louise coaxed. "Here, your dinner is ready." I was putting the eggs on the plate and buttering and cutting up the toast.

"Oh, this tastes nice!" Polly exclaimed. "Just what I wanted." Thank God. The stench of the eggs gagged me. I went to the bathroom and brushed my teeth.

She'd made very good progress eating.

"I'm not much of an eater, except when you're here!" she crowed. "Now let's get back to those cans up there, Mols, those cans have got to get moved."

Now I was supposed to climb up on the footstool and move the cans. I blew my nose. I set my lips.

"Polly, I'm too tired to move cans, tonight," I said.

"Just a few."

"OK, just a few," I said, climbing on the footstool. I moved the tomato soup cans to the front of the cabinet. I moved the chicken noodle to the back.

"Make those labels show to the front," she said.

"You ate all your toast, Polly!" Ann Louise said. "Look, Flo, she ate all her toast. She hasn't done that since last week."

I made all the labels show. I got down from the footstool. "I can't do any more cans tonight, Pol. This is it in the can department. We can do more cans tomorrow." Like a teenager I rolled my eyes at Flo.

"Come on, Ann Louise," she said, "let's let Molly get some sleep." The two indefatigable sisters left, and my mother dozed off.

"I had a wonderful childhood," Polly began when I got out the tape recorder the next day. This was how the story always began. "I hated the garage where my parents lived. So every Friday night after school I went to Grandma's and Grandpa's farm up the road. I rode Paint out through the fields to where Grandma Molly worked right there alongside Grandpa and the hired men. She hated the work in the house! She had muscles like a man and she liked to work with the men. She did the cooking, though, but a hired boy did the dishes and another hired man did the cleaning up! I had Paint all weekend. He was blind, but he knew where to go! He took me to the schoolhouse on Monday morning, and he turned right around and went home all by himself. He was a darn smart horse. After school I walked home to the garage to stay the week with my folks, but I couldn't wait to get to the farm on Fridays. I loved the farm!"

What made the dark-haired, round-faced girl with the Buster Brown haircut and the sailor blouse prefer her grandparents to her parents? I, too, often preferred my grandparents to my own parents. They were calmer, and nicer, and they listened to me, and they didn't try to push each other down the cellar stairs. The face of the little girl in the photos of Polly as a child is a storm cloud, then wicked with delight, then placid, then squinched up with the sun in her eyes. The photos of the ebullient little tank of a body tell nothing except that the child looks vigorous, not frightened or sad.

"I loved my father. Thought the world of him." How I, her daughter who feared my dad, hated to hear her stories about her beloved father, my grandfather, who'd paid me no attention whatsoever. "But my mother, she and I weren't on the same wavelength. Nope. She loved me. Yes, she did, but I'd rather be with Grandma. Grandma's name was Molly, Mols, and that's who I named you after, Molly McMann."

Who was the little one who'd crouched inside Pauline until the months before her death and arose, fully her little girl self, with confidence and demands? I didn't know. But I saw in her dying her final exercise of that child. In love of her, I was that child's servant. The clarity of my mother's childishness made me know for sure I had taken care of this little girl all my life. I was born as her grandmother. I had her name, Molly. And I, too, would have paid a hired man to do my woman's work. I admired the Molly McMann in my mother's stories, though I knew she was as made up as Paul Bunyan.

Polly had no legend about my adored Grandma Ruth, with whom I'd felt so companionable, learning from her the skills that Polly eschewed: embroidery and charity clubs. But what kind of a mother had Ruth been to my mother that Polly would go to her death revealed as the child she had remained? I didn't know the answer. There were so many questions I didn't know the answers to. But my care of my mother reinforced what I'd come to think of as my golden refusal to be a mother. Instead of having one, I was escorting the child I'd so reluctantly taken care of into the next world.

My husband, a cancer survivor, picked up the burden my mother's cancer put on me as his own. I cried, and he held me; I screamed, and he held me; I yelled at an unsuspecting airline attendant who really had done nothing wrong and he smoothed it over; I put all the wrong checks in the wrong envelopes for my bills and he sorted it out; he backed up my computer; he did my laundry; he made love to me; and most of all, he helped me make plans. He knew how to do it. He knew how to maintain control when circumstances were out of control. *We go ahead and make our plans,* he said, *you have to make your plans and then cancel them later if something happens, but you make your plans anyway,* he said, *because otherwise you're suspended in nothingness and afraid and unhappy and insecure and anxious and depressed.*

I was surprised at what he already knew: We actually canceled very few of our plans. We figured out what we had to schedule and, always to my surprise, it usually happened. When I felt I could slip out of my handmade skin and merge with my mother again, inside her dying, there was my husband, a man who knew about dying, giving me a guide, and using a simple analogy that made sense to me: a syllabus. Something where you tried to keep to your deadlines, but if you couldn't were guided in the changes. The pun of deadline was not lost on us. We had deadlines for Mike's courses, deadlines for airline tickets, deadlines for my schedule of private students, deadlines for my mailings for the workshops I'd designed, deadlines for registration, and above all, deadlines for the process of my becoming a permanent resident of Canada. Now we lived in two countries with two currencies, two tax structures, border crossings, declarations, bag searches.

When I was not checking Polly on the phone, I was calling a doctor, and when I was not calling a doctor, I was calling Aviva, the kind nurse who liked my mother, and when I was not calling Aviva, I was calling the social worker. And then my mother again. Then the doctor, Howie, Flo, Ann Louise, the doctor, Gail, the nurse, Mike, Ruta, my mother, my uncle, the funeral home, the funeral director, the minister. Callcallcallcallcall.

"Are we living our lives," Mike asked one day, "or administering them?"

We were putting one foot in front of the other. We were using the stepping-stones of our syllabus to cross the death flow. And when Polly's death flow was the strongest, our deadlines were the most urgent. Together, almost as friends, we'd picked out her coffin clothes and perused the insurance policies she misled herself into thinking would pay for everything. They paid for about a quarter of everything. La Grange paid some. And I paid the rest, carrying out the mystique that my mother had really arranged it all. I hear about insurance you can get that covers the plane fare, the loss of work, the wear and tear on your car, the hotel bills. But I didn't have that insurance. I had a lot of credit cards, and I used them.

In December Polly was hospitalized for the last time.

"She's really fading," said Aviva, in her confident competence, telling me long distance that the end was really here. I dialed USAir.

At the end of the week was my immigration appointment with the Canadian consul in New York. This appointment was harder won than tea with the Queen. It had required letters and forms and Xeroxes and X rays and medical certificates and divorce papers and marriage certificates and tax documents and mortgage statements and all of it mailed by separate deadlines. No form had a phone number on it; there was never

any way to communicate with a person one to one. It was small me dealing with Government, and this Goliath did not make me feel like David
because I was too spoiled. Americans don't usually experience themselves as outsiders in this way, and I was shocked that I couldn't just find
a number and call and explain my situation to someone. If the appointment was canceled, I would have to wait months and months for another,
and the convoluted process not only would be delayed, but would have
to start all over again, since the X rays and medical documents were
good only for a short period.

But Polly wasn't dying on the schedule of the Canadian government.
All right, I would miss the immigration appointment. Not the worst
thing in the world.

"For someone supposed to be at the very end," Howie said as I approached her room, "she's pretty energetic." She was still talking to people, weak, but recognizing them, even greeting Howie's wife, the one he
had left the farm to marry. Now he lived and worked in Buffalo.

Polly had livened up the minute she'd heard I was on my way, Aviva
told me. By my third day there, she was sitting up in bed demanding a
chocolate milk shake. Mike had driven down from Canada. We went out
to get the milk shake, and when we returned Polly was perched like a
baby owl on its branch, mouth open in expectation. She grabbed the
milk shake with a force I didn't think she had left and slurped it down to
the last gurgle in the straw. I didn't have enough experience with dying
people to recognize the tenacity of the life force that reemerges in waves.

"I have an appointment with the Canadian Consulate in New York,
Pol," I said, "and I'm going to go back to make the appointment, and then
I'm coming back on Saturday morning." My husband's face brightened.

Polly had sunk back into bed, uncomprehending. "That's nice," she
whispered. "Comb my hair."

I began combing her sparse gray hair with a baby comb I'd brought.
No daughter of mine would ever do this for me. Nor would I ever feel

the mixture of love and loathing that Polly had to feel from me at that moment. Yet she herself had not combed her own mother's hair. The attendants in the nursing home had given Little Ruthie her hairdo, as part of their jobs. Would a matter-of-factly neutral touch be better than the cloaked contradictory emotion my hand held in check?

"So I'll be back in two days," I said at the door an hour later. "Aviva and Howie and Flo and Ann Louise will be here. Do you want the light on?"

Silence. Then, weakly, "Off."

"OK, good-bye, Mom." I turned off the light, and said again by the door, "Good-bye, Mom." It was just before 5, and already dark. Though Polly was facing the darkened window in her darkened room, her body positioned away from the door, she swiveled her head on its arthritic neck back toward me, and opened her eyes wide, wider, so that the whites glowed in the hall light. The pretense of her own nightgowns was long gone. Her glasses, her teeth, had been abandoned. Then she opened her mouth wide, wider. She seemed about to speak, but did not, and stayed with the look of an oracle, while I waited for her. Mike, in his parka, stood waiting in the hall. "What's the matter?" he whispered.

"Good-bye, Mom," I said again, and as she stared past me I realized she wasn't going to speak, though her mouth and eyes gaped. And I closed the door. Then I flew to New York and had my interview, becoming a Permanent Resident of Canada, and Polly died a few hours before my plane was scheduled to return. The planning had gone awry at the end.

Night after night for weeks after the funeral I had the same vision of her: I woke at 4:30 A.M. exactly and felt smoke in the room, I looked up and saw a wing-backed chair with its back to me. Slowly the chair turned, as if on an oiled pedestal, and there was my mother with her newspaper under a dim lightbulb, saying, "Molly, don't bother me, I'm reading now." Don't bother me. But bother *with* me. The image was our story. I had the stunned feeling I always had when I closed a big long book I had been reading over hours and hours. Where was I and who was I without that author's voice? Slowly I'd feel my legs cramped beneath me, and the sunlight outside, and want to stretch, and go out, even though I was still in the cloud of the book, thinking about the ending and the main character and wanting to talk about it and deciding to look for someone else who'd read it. But the only other reader was my sister, and she had disappeared, refusing to come while Polly was dying and not showing up for Polly's funeral, where I used all the muscles in my arms to close the book of our mother.

35.

How do you grow up if you don't have children? How do you remake the original love—mother love—into a mature love? Becoming a parent provokes this conversion, but the transformation into adulthood without the bearing of children means metamorphosis. The change is not instant and permanent like parenthood. It is a surfacing into adulthood and a diving down into childhood, and a poking into sharp air again, then a plunge into watery warmth, gradually converting your gills to lungs. After a time, you breathe in air exclusively, just as all adults do.

But birth is not the only event that propels us into adulthood. Death does, too. Any sharp change that brings us face-to-face with what we thought life was but now must revise instigates the entree into maturity. So the childfree grow up, either by evolution or by the swift witchcraft of event—or both. Gradually the childhood world vanishes into its own reflection and we look back from the other side of the mirror. To consciously refuse to be a parent and yet consciously to grow, to determine both to love and to understand love, is a project big as any in life. It is not necessary to originate a child to discover your origins—though it takes longer if you do it on your own.

As a little girl, just as soon as I could manage to fall in love with an idea, I did. The idea I picked was consciousness itself: awareness, the attendance on the minutiae of change. A person changing violently, like my father, requires vigilance. But a *concept* evolving requires awareness, calmly satisfying and deep. I valued this understanding because events drove me inward so far that I often lost touch with them, living instead through a book. While fantasies saved my mental life, they still made a wall between me and my own felt experience. A clinical word for this is *denial*. An aesthetic phrase is *preparing for art*. Yet for richly lived experience—and that includes pain—denial must give way to awareness. And for poetry awareness must operate keenly because it is the source of precise language. And so you must perceive sharply, whether that is the stab of a crimson dahlia against a wet wrought-iron fence, or the stab of realization as it spreads across your tearstained face.

But being with children, for me, always meant being in a blurred state. Focused on them, hyperaware of their safety and progress, my own inner life receded to a pinprick, and as a self I was lost. To attend my little sister—so frenzied and so needing of an anchor—meant a kind of giving over that even a fully formed adult can have difficulty doing, let alone a girl struggling to grow. My father, of course, required attention of a different kind: a parapet of watchfulness formed from fear. And Polly herself was often as lost to me as if she'd gone to live where she felt most at home—between pages.

Thus I clung to awareness, confident that it would guide and save me. I knew awareness worked: It had gotten me good grades, gotten me published, kept me alive. Being taken over by bodily forces—being pregnant, then focusing first on the helpless infant and then on the burgeoning child—seemed to shroud awareness in fog.

Yet love, too, is a kind of fog, and certainly requires surrender. One day I wrote a poem called "Waking Up," and ended it with these lines:

> *How childish I feel when I remake*
> *childhood's dream: all things delivered in a stream*

of consistency—no crack, no fissure, no mistake,
all done when planned. But swans arrive at their lake
each year, called home by the angle of sunbeams.
Surrender to nature's perfection means

to know one's nature, no mistake. Sometimes it seems
a life's asleep beneath my frenzy, and I wake
from a promise of youth I no longer make.

I had come to accept—and enjoy—my perceptions after the ceasing of my vigils. I no longer had to keep guard.

Then one day some months after my mother died I noticed how much I loved making a domestic fuss—over dinner, over the color of a wall, even over the shade of a lipstick as it vibrated against a blouse. It amused me that I had the mental time to make these commotions—and that the energy they required almost always involved mistakes: the purple potato for the recipe can't be found; or the paint swatch, when enlarged, overwhelms the wall; or the lipstick, meant to go on flesh, will never match a woven fabric. Perfection of that sort never happens. Fuss is the play, not the applause.

The way a radiator hiss/ makes a perfect indoor snowy silence hush, I found myself writing, *the flicker of a bother trues the world in which we kiss.* When the rattle of a radiator made silence more silent, and when kissing my husband "trued" a world, I realized that my childhood romance had become an adult love, that there was no turning back, and no reason to, since the love *now* contained the love *then.* Wrapped in this consciousness, I sat down to title my next book of poems. I called it *Original Love.*

36.

Good garden loam: the smell of possibility. Leo, my Ontario gardening friend who runs a local taxi company, is outraged by the responsibilities he feels unable to bear. On occasion we can share a shocking confessional intimacy, about one stage up from strangers on a plane. I come to the odd meeting of his Iris Society. I have an interest in irises, but Leo has a passion for them. He has a miniature woodland iris garden, which I go to look at in wonder and envy, and on occasion he comes to my little garden. On one of his visits Leo asked what I was working on, and, on an impulse, I told him I was writing about my choice not to be a parent. "It was all in my wife's hands," he said, shoving some iris roots into my basket.

"My wife worried endlessly about whether she was ready," he poured out. "When she decided she was, first came the thermometers, then the sex calendar, and we did it and did it and did it and finally she got pregnant with Jillian, thank God. You have no idea how hard it is to perform and perform. Then came all the problems with Jillian's hearing, and just when she started healing from the last operation, my wife starts in about whether we were ready for another one. Well, I wasn't ready. That I was able to say. Just give me a rest. So she rested for about six months, and out came the thermometers and the sex calendar again. I'm telling you, I didn't know what hit me. These children seemed to be her prerogative.

After Hugh was born she said, 'Now we have our family.' We! If I'd have ever, ever been half conscious of how much responsibility I would take on with my wife and my kids, I know this is a terrible thing to say, because I love my kids, I really do, and I love my wife, but I'm not fit for this. I'm a goddamn nervous wreck all the time." He stopped briefly to scratch his lip, then rushed on. "It's almost impossible to stay centered. I've got the fleet of cabs on my shoulders with all the maintenance and the new car buying—if we can afford new cars this year—and Jillian's ears still have problems. Just making sure the kid isn't in pain, or that she heard the teacher's homework assignments, takes loads and loads of attention. I'm not an absentee father. I'm an involved dad. And I'm a committed husband. But I'll tell you the truth, I can regret it. I have noise till ten P.M. and then I have exhaustion. Complete exhaustion. I thought in my twenties, well, first marriage, then kids. I didn't give it any more juice than that, and I can't give it more than a passing thought now, because the decisions are made. But I'd be more conscious next time. This really doesn't suit my personality." He panted as if he'd been doing laps.

Since Leo is one of the few men, other than Mike, I ever have a soul-to-soul talk with, I seized the opportunity. "So, Leo," I inappropriately queried, "if you hadn't had children, would your marriage have a purpose?"

Leo got a nosebleed.

"Companionship!" he said as I ran inside for the tissues. "Simple companionship, thanks," he whispered as he mopped up his nose. "I don't usually get nosebleeds, but it's the emotional way you talk."

"*Me?* The emotion *I* have when we talk? Oh look, Leo, I'm sorry. Thank you for these irises." I handed him more tissues. "Is it stopping?"

"Yeah. Yeah, I think so." He held his head back. "All this whether to have children stuff is very emotional. It's emotional for men. It really is. The guys I know, they would never say this, but really, it's their lives. What we're talking about when we talk about marriage is the pattern of your life."

"Yes, it really can be an important, or, an overwhelming part of life. Though not everyone is married, Leo."

"God, everyone I know is. I think it's stopping. Hey look!" He was very pleased, and so was I, to see the next Kleenex almost white. I went inside to get a paper bag for him to dispose of the tissues. "And they all have kids," he shouted after me. "Everyone who works for me full-time. Plus the two women who drive. Most of the student part-timers are married and have kids. Even the gay couple who drive on the weekends have adopted a kid together." I returned with the bag.

Leo shook his sizeable head of gray and red hair, looking stricken and overwhelmed. "Of course there's a purpose to marriage without children!" he said. "It's about simple companionship. Partners on life's path." He thought a moment, then said quite formally, as if he were testifying, and I suppose he picked a good place to do it, since we were standing on the half-constructed brick path in my garden: "I would like to go along life's path sharing it with someone—and not running wildly down the path either. Just going along it. A nosebleed for God's sake," he said. "I can't talk about this shit."

"We've got to stick to gardening. Really, I'm sorry. I never meant to cause you to bleed, Leo."

He got up to leave. "The next conversation we have is strictly about beetles," he called over his beefy shoulder, then lumbered over the lawn toward his cab.

Simple companionship. My parents rarely had it, though both sets of my grandparents seemed to. It occurred to me, not for the first time, that I skipped the married with children part of my life and proceeded right into the atmosphere of grandparenthood, the companionship two people feel after their kids have left home. But for Mike and me, it's after we've separated from our youthful miseries. Nothing holds us but a We we have constructed.

When I wake up in the middle of the night, as I typically do, I love his back on the other side of the bed. In the circle of the tiny book light attached to whatever novel I've kept to read at those times, I think how thankful I am for that furry spine, and how I can barely have enough of it. I don't actually read so much as watch the print of my book, and feel my nightgown slip against the sheets as I turn around to see him happily sleeping (for nothing wakes him up) through his routine eight hours. When I put my novel down and shut the light and lightly tap him, he turns and throws one arm over me and then I sleep again.

Having only had the routine of art in my life, and the external routines of classes and school, the internal life of domestic routine was very new for me. The beginnings of our marriage were fraught with my mother's death and complicated with our adjustment to our Canada–New York commute. But we were determined to preserve the best of our former lives and merge it with the new life we were creating. It really was like bringing a garden back to life, hauling soil, carting stones, nailing up trellises, pruning trees. And I had other adjustment problems, coming not only as a galumphing American into Canada's quieter society, but as a New Yorker, a woman who learned by hard experience to act boldly to get what she wanted. It was as if I were a thick-stemmed sunflower crashing into a shade garden of ferns and feathery pink astilbe. In New York I was used to demanding, in Canada all I had to do was ask.

And yet the sense of completeness I have, the wholeness and fulfillment, did not come from insisting that the world fill my internal prescription. It came because all I had to do was ask. I asked myself who I was, and eventually I knew what I needed. My old life, like deadheads on rangy petunias, completely fell away.

If I could have told that girl, who waited to hear her father's car crawl up in the driveway, that things would never be as bad as they were at that moment, I think she would not have believed me. I imagine whispering into her ear, a skinny little shrimp with lank hair wearing a soiled blouse, her face at once both horrified and grim, that her life will be an adventure and that she will become a poet and live in two countries with a boy she would meet very soon. I see her turn her head a little bit on her neck, straightening her slump just a bit, and watch a slow, noncommittal sort of astonishment begin in her spine, delight moving up her vertebrae till it hits the top of her head and moves her shoulders back. I tell her—she is fourteen years old—that if she holds on for thirty years she's going to love her life. This girl does not say, "Thirty years! How will I hold on?" She does not dare complain or hope; instead, she walks. She walks across the empty plain, requiring that emptiness completely. Paradoxically, for her it will become full of creativity.

When I said No to having children, I felt as if I went to some viscerally interior place, the place of recognition. I'd always thought that the positive, the embracing, the Yes that is so characteristic of women's assumed responses, would let me affirm who I am. But it was a refusal that led me to understand my own nature. It was the saving no. The saving no seemed to emerge from the ready emptiness that is required for all creativity, not just for the making of art. That No can't be confused with loss, or the painful emptiness of not having what you need. Like a well-proportioned, unfurnished room with open windows, the affirming refusal invites life. It's a room, not a womb. Like a womb, it harbors life, but unlike a womb, it *leaves room* to create the rest of life.

Mike Groden in a James Joyce T-shirt and a pair of ratty running shorts is making his lunch. He is methodical. He has the same lunch every day: one vegetarian sandwich, whole grain bread, one turkey sandwich, one Granny Smith apple. He makes the sandwiches on a paper towel and uses it to flip the crumbs into the sink. Then he uses the paper towel for a plate and goes to our former dining room, now a music room, and plays an Elvis Costello CD while he eats and feeds minute bits of turkey to the cats. He talks to them, gently teasing them and scratching their ears. I can see and hear him because I'm in the sunroom with a pile of manuscripts, still in my bathrobe looking up from my schedule having realized, not for the first time, that I made two commitments at the same hour. I ask him what he thinks I should do and he has a sensible answer. Roma, the calico, leaves for her postprandial nap upstairs and Fellini, the orange tabby, flops next to him on the couch. When a student calls, Mike is patient and kind. When a colleague calls, he is serious and witty and makes a good suggestion. His editor faxes him a query. He decides to call the producer of a project he's working on. But before he calls her, he comes in to tell me what was in the paper that morning. Clearly, I am so busy reading the manuscripts I am not going to get to the paper.

I see a kind, consistent, intelligent, sensible, sensitive, stable man with an easy sense of humor—he has just made a wicked arcane joke about textual criticism that only a player in the James Joyce wars (or the player's wife) would understand. We make an appointment to have sex. We love doing this. We love knowing that we'll put our minds down at a certain time and get into bed, make love, have a tiny nap, and then make dinner.

Another student calls and my husband is clear about his directions, and fair in his deal. It occurs to me, not for the first time, what a terrific father he would have made. He is even-minded, even-handed, and understanding, all my dad was not.

One day on a train ride from New York to a poetry reading I was giving in Providence, looking out at the marshes, counting the snowy egrets that have come back to the New England coast, I found myself reading a book about women who have chosen to be childfree. The book was *Will You Be Mother?* by Jill Bartlett, a British journalist. She had compiled lots of interviews with women, and one group of those interviews was about sterilization, and how relieved and happy those women interviewed were to put the childbearing issue to rest. One of the interviewers mentioned reversing the procedure. *Reversing the procedure?* I thought in a panic. What if I could reverse the procedure I'd had? *Then Mike could be a father!* I fantasized wildly, but deeply, as longing dislodged regret inside me. Like a tide pool stirred by the stick of the possibility, I suddenly thought of myself as able to bear children again—*If it were possible,* I thought, *would I, would I try for a reversal and suddenly take it all on?* After all, life had become so different! My mother didn't live to see my child! Mike and I had spent five decades becoming who we were and could be excellent parents. (Or, at least, he could be . . . Would I have made such a lovely mother?) Another snowy egret in the greeny marsh. They had come back, they had repopulated . . .

It was as if the heavy stone moved by the stick of this idea had been flipped up to lodge with a thud on my heart. What if my so-called choice was a sham? Aware of how fast I was breathing, how fast the train was flying—it was my life, that train, flying through five decades—I saw suddenly how empty the car was. No one in the seat beside me, only a few tops of heads in the other rows. Literally and figuratively I was in a relatively empty car, having made a minority decision. The marshes stretched on. Patches of white, like crumpled sheets of paper, materialized as water birds when we flew past. Why was I breathing so shallowly? I was panicking.

Come on, think it through. What if you could reverse it, would you? Now that you have your beautiful life? Mike is perfectly happy the way he is. He wants you, he doesn't want a family. There was nothing in the idea of a family that thrilled him. *Besides, the two of you are a family.* I knew we both seemed larger and more encompassing together than the two individuals we were when alone. *Don't you value this relationship beyond anything?* Now was I going to change it? For what? To supply Mike Groden with an opportunity he himself didn't think he'd missed? Wasn't I acting just like all the people who think life's only fulfillment is having children? Was I going to over-fill the magnificent emptiness I'd just managed to achieve?

I couldn't answer at first, busy imagining myself pregnant with enor-mous medical complications, even if it were possible. *An infant in my arms and Mike in the hospital . . . Dishes, laundry, spit up, measles, aunts, uncles, cousins, mother-in-law, schools . . . A little girl walks with Mike—how kind he is to her. . . . Baby shit, schedules, car pools, telephones, insomnia, chiropractors, frantic calls to Ruta, now I am yelling at Mike in the hospital, now my child howls from the back seat of a car broken down in a snowstorm, we're lost, I take off my coat to cover the child, who is cold, and my skin comes off in the coat. Hitchhiking in a snowstorm to rescue my child in the car, I stand at the side of the road without a skin, a mass of pulsing mus-cles over a skeleton, but pushing on, living somehow, doing what has to be done, has to be done. . . .*

As the train came into Providence, I stepped into a beautifully re-stored station, like my own restoration to my senses. No, even if I could have reversed the tubal ligation, I would not have reversed my decision. Yet no woman can decide against having children without questioning it again and again, I thought, as I shook the hand of the man who had come to pick me up. Every piece of this complex issue has a place: after all, who has a real life that goes on a purposeful glowing arc from A to Z? The issue of children is never dead. It raises its head like an errant red tulip popping up in a hedge. Inside the next opportunity lies the very re-fusal of the option that created it, and sometimes that refusal reemerges, then resettles.

Who would I be if I couldn't reconsider? All of importance contains its opposite.

37.

"Ya can't send the stuff till I'm moved, Molly!" Gail yelped into the phone. "They're kickin' me outta here! Outta my little house where I been for ten whole years!"

"What's going to happen?" I asked neutrally.

"I gotta go in an apartment, Mols, a dump. I gotta get Hannah Banana my dog and pack everything up and go up the mountain to the apartments up there. I'm movin'."

She was losing her little house.

Mike and I had gone to Buffalo and cleaned out the storage unit where I'd shucked all the things from La Grange after Polly died. I had all I wanted: the dining room table and sideboard, the dishes and the washstand. No matter what you stored in it, the smell of La Grange roared from the drawers. Ruth was everywhere, and solid. The rest was going to the other grandchildren, and to Gail, too, though she'd probably sell it.

"Now you've got the card, Gail," I said, "so all you have to do is just dial when you get moved in." I'd gotten her the kind of phone card people get their teenage kids, the one where they can call home collect, but nowhere else.

She'd broken her hip from falling drunk out of a second-floor window, she walked with a cane from a beating a boyfriend had given her, and she had arthritis. She was forty-five years old. "I got a nice little honey of an old man with me, now, a Vietnam vet and we draw pictures together!" In the mail I got a line drawing cartoon of Gail in a clawfoot bathtub with a Woodstock poster behind her on the wall. She was bare-breasted and wore sunglasses. Smoke from her cigarette curled toward the top of the picture. It was like the kewpie doll my Dad had sent me, but I didn't destroy it.

Finally she moved in, and I shipped her the bed and the kitchen table and the piano stool and the dishes with the gold rims from Polly. Earlier I had sent what Polly had insisted Gail have: her wedding ring. *I always earmarked the diamond ring for Gail. That, and my fur coat,* Polly said.

"I got 'em, Mol, I got 'em, oh I love you! I haven't slept on a real bed in years! I got drawers for my clothes and everything! And I'm wearin' the jewels, the family jewels! Oh thank you, thank you! Here, I'm puttin' Hannah Banana on the phone to thank you. Come on, Hannah, ya gotta bark up for Molly and thank her!"

"I'm glad you got everything, honey," I said. Hannah was barking in the background.

"So whatcha doin' today, Mol?"

"Well, I have a couple of conference calls about a project this afternoon, but right now I'm a filthy mess. Mike and I are cleaning the basement."

"My God!" she said in wonder. "You have a basement?"

"Yep, a real basement."

"Shit, I wish I had a basement."

And so went our calls. All I could do for her was listen, and so I did. I dug in the garden and worked with my students by fax. I got on airplanes and lectured at universities and returned to Mike and went swimming and gossiped with my friends and I wrote the beginning of this book, which I sent to my sister.

"I'm really sick, Mol," she said when she called. "I got this throat thing and my vocal cords are shot." Now whispery as seed pods, her gravelly voice had lost all its volume.

"I'm running this fever, Mol, and we can't get it down. My honey's got me sitting in a cold tub. This place is a mess. It's an apefuck. I ain't got no doorknob, Mol! Anybody can walk right in here! But Hannah Banana, she'll bite 'em." Hannah was squealing in the background. Gail whisper-yelled, "Lay off the friggin' dog, you asshole!" to the person stepping on the dog.

Getting a sore throat, starting to feel the glands under my ears swell, I walked the phone into the kitchen and put the kettle on.

"But I read what you sent me, Mol!" Gail burbled, her whisper now conspiratorial. "And could I tell you stuff! Ya know, I always hated kids, Mols. They don't go with the sex, drugs, and rock'n'roll lifestyle. And that's my lifestyle. I could puke around kids, I really could."

"You never wanted any? What about when you wanted to marry that hairdresser who died?"

"Who the hell wants to copy our childhood, Molly!" she whispered.

I laughed. She laughed her rickety laugh.

"I miss that hairdresser guy, Mol. He died in my bed, ya know. I got up to make some coffee and came back with a mug for him and the guy had bit the dust. OD'ed on methadone. I just sat there and stared at him. I stared at him almost a whole day before I got myself to the phone. I miss my little house, Mol." She brightened. "Why, during Woodstock Two I had the Hell's Angels staying there! I left the door right open and said, 'Move on in, boys, my casa is the party casa!' And those Hell's Angels, Molly, were the cleanest guests I ever had. They even scoured out the shower!"

"Clean house, clean mind," I said, quoting Gram. We laughed again.

"But, Mols, I'm so goddamn sick."

"Have you been to the doctor, Gailie?"

"Yeah, yeah, but I gotta see a specialist, a specialist in Kingston, and I ain't got no car. And the bus, Mol, I'm too sick to take the bus."

I arranged for the local taxi to have an account where my sister would only be taken to and from medical offices or hospitals.

"We're going to get you going to the right place, Gailie," I said.

"I love you!" she said. Then she put the dog on the phone.

"Now, Mrs. Peacock," said the woman's voice, calling me my mother's name. "This is the taxi service. I know you said the account was only for medical offices, so I called to say, we refused a fare from a friend of your sister's." Already, Gail was handing out the taxi service.

"Gail, for crying out loud, I can't afford for all your friends to take cabs around Woodstock!" I yelled into the telephone that night.

"Lighten up, Mols," she wheezed. "It's only a goddamn cab."

"Did you go? Did you see the specialist?"

"She thinks its throat cancer, Mol, but I gotta go to another guy and make sure."

"Oh, honey."

"I'm not thinking about nuthin'. Not till I see the next one."

"So let's talk about something else."

"Yeah, wanna talk to the dog?"

"Honey, I'll talk to the dog next time."

"Hey, wanna talk about Ted? What a fuck he was. I could tell you stories about him when you were in college, Molly. It would curl your hair."

"So, tell me."

"Nah. Ya know your tubal ligation?"

"Yes."

"Well, I had one too! I said none of this shit, I'm not havin' no kids. I hate the smell of 'em and I'm not having no abortions, neither, so I went and had my tubal and Medicare paid for it. I'm one of the truly needy, Mol!"

"You did! You had a tubal ligation? We did the same thing?"

"Yup. Sisters to the end."

I could barely assimilate the information. Gail was so wasted with years of alcohol and drugs, and I had just swum a self-righteous half hour in the university pool. But we were sisters. We loved the same domestic treats: gardening and food and animals and friends. And we had made the same choice not to have children.

During the next call her raspy whisper quavered with alarm. I was standing up at a file cabinet as we talked, but her panic made me sit and force air into my lungs. "It hurts so bad, Mol, I can't stand it!" she whispered. "My honey says Woodstock's weather's hot as Phnom Penh, but I'm cold, Mols, I can't stop shakin'. I've got throat cancer, Mols, I'm gonna die, I'm gonna die, Mommy, oh Mommy, I'm gonna die."

"Oh, honey, I'm so sorry, so sorry." I rocked back and forth with sorries.

"Oh, Molly, I called you Mommy! I'm so fucked up!"

"I know you did, hon. Have you got your bathrobe on? You need to keep warm."

"I love my bathrobe! Thanks for sending it! It's the best thing in the house! I got my nice bed and my bathrobe. Mols?"

"Yes?"

"Can I call you Mommy?"

There it was, as it always had been. The bud of motherhood caught in the bulb. Part of me said, *You can't, you can't do this!* and the larger part that was stable as a house said, "Sure, you can call me Mommy." After all, it would only be for a little while.

"Mommy, I'm not going there."

"Where, honey?"

"Down the cancer road. I'm not going down it. I'm not going through the hospitals and all the shit. I'm not doin' it."

"I don't blame you, Gail. You don't have to. You can do it the way you want."

"They're gonna bury me in potter's field, Mol, I'm gonna have an unmarked grave! Welfare don't give nothing to bury you!"

"I won't let you be buried in potter's field, sweetheart, you'll get a nice little plot, and I'll make sure you do."

"That's what I want, Mol, a nice little plot!" She was sobbing and suddenly her voice was clear. "I'm so scared," she said.

"I know you're scared, Gailie, you have every right to be scared."

"Oh, Mommy! I'm so scared I'm gonna die and go to potter's field!"

"You might die, honey, but you're getting a nice grave like everybody else and a nice marker with flowers on it."

"I'm not going to the hospital, Mol." She was whispering again.

"There's no reason why you should."

"I'm not doin' that shit!" Her voice was stronger.

"You can die just the way you want, Gail, just like you live the way you want."

"Yeah!" She was sobbing again. "I lived the sex and drugs and rock-'n'roll lifestyle, Mol."

I pictured La Grange just after it was sold and before the neighbors tore it down. The roof was leaking, it had no basement. Raccoons had gotten in from the top and woodchucks from the bottom. The road that cozily ran past it had been widened till the semis grazed the oval island where the Esso pumps once stood. The big maples had gone from road salt poisoning. Where had I put those pictures I took when they demolished it? Shoved into a box of Polly's tax statements I couldn't throw away.

My mother's cancer, and my sister's cancer, and Mike's history of melanoma made the illness always present. On the skin cancer checkup schedule, it was time for Mike to endure a visit to a specialist. After such appointments we would feel homeless. We would leave the blank walls and metal chairs of the office and sit like two skeletons in a coffee shop, crumbling over our teacups. But the cups, like Miss Muffet, sat on their saucers, and the thick saucers sat on their Formica tables, the tables framed by booths. And these solid facts we knew and understood and the flesh would grow back on our bones and the lips would grow over our teeth and our eyes would reappear, and our hair, and a softness would grow into the world, and after a time daylight would pool in the spoons we held.

But this time the cancer specialist was absolutely sure the lump in my husband's leg was metastasized melanoma. However, Mike's own surgeon was distrustful. In a little examining room in our hospital in Canada, the surgeon planned to take the surface lump out, and I had asked to watch. He made a nice neat incision and popped up a glob of fat like the marble of a sirloin. It was yellow as a buttercup, and as benign.

When we came home I planted lavender. Leo came by with a load of ferns I plopped in the shade garden. The university year was over. The chives bloomed. I planted chamomile. The phone rang late at night, a boozy voice from long ago. It was Ed, Gail's boyfriend at the Christmas when Fergus Buxton came for his drink. Was I sitting down? he was asking me. "Oh, Ed!" I coughed, and after catching my breath coughed again and again and finally stopped when I was able to hear him say why he called. The police had found Gail dead in her apartment, with six drained bottles of vodka and every pill bottle in the house empty.

She had done it, made her exit, and there'd been an autopsy. I had to call the hospital to instruct them about the body. By the time I saw her she was a plastic bag of ashes. Maggie, Lily, and my cousin Howie met Mike and me at the funeral home in Woodstock to pick out an urn. It was to be her last house, so we picked out a tiny mansion: pale green onyx you could see the light through, though it would be dark down there underneath the hand-carved stone we also chose, full of morning glories and her name, Gail Peacock, and her dates, 1950–1996.

Rain poured down on the graveside funeral, where the Episcopal priest spoke and I spoke and her old boyfriend Jules showed up and her other old boyfriend Ed read the Twenty-third Psalm. From under umbrellas her friends stepped up to throw garden flowers numbly on the little square of earth, like the basement dug for a dollhouse, that was prepared for her urn. At the graveside, I remembered the getups she had worn all her life—her cheerleading outfit, her buckskin jacket with fringe, Polly's fur coat, the Egyptian cotton robe she died in—and at last her wooden wheel toy, riding round and round the kitchen floor, driving us all crazy, before she finally slumped over her handlebars, exhausted, a ragamuffin.

Mike held my left elbow and Maggie held my right elbow and Howie stood next to Lily as Gail's friends came up to mumble at me. A few took off their sunglasses in the rain. I took the box of snapshots from Gail's vet friend and I asked about the dishes with the gold rims.

"I don't remember them," he said.

I asked about the bed.

"She was sleeping on the couch," he said.

I asked a woman whether Gail had been wearing a diamond ring. "She didn't have no diamond ring!" the woman said. "I woulda known that!"

"You wouldn't have recognized her, Molly," said Jules, humble and sober, curls clipped, wearing a baseball hat. He threw his arms around me. *I remember that goddamned Maalox bottle*, I thought as I patted his back.

At the end of the service, our feet sunk in the grass, soaked from the downpour, we waited for the piper Ed had found. Up she stepped, in full regalia, to pipe Gail's last song. Gail would have squealed at the purple delphiniums we brought, and loved that all the flowers were garden blooms, no corny funeral glads, and she would have loved her stone and her urn and the fact that we all turned out in the pouring rain as if we were in an art film. The bagpiper piped and I wept. Lily held the tissues and Maggie held my purse. The piper played, moving farther and farther from the grave, then down to the road to the gate.

38.

It had been a long time since I cried so hard lying down on Ruta Arbeiter's beige couch with its woven square of royal blue mat for her patients' feet. Early summer sun illuminated nearly each thread of the rug on the gleaming bare floor, high above New York. I tucked the paisley pillow under my neck and continued to mumble.

"I should have been able to do something, but I can't think of a goddamn thing I could have done."

"Maybe that's because you couldn't have done anything else." Her voice flowed out from the rocking chair behind my head which was turned so her good ear was at an advantage. In the twenty-one years we had known each other, I had reached the conclusion that a so-called cure with a beginning, middle, and end, progressing linearly over time, was not what I was after, nor was it in the nature of what transpired between Ruta and me. What we have with one another is Conversation. The Old French root of converse, *converser*, means to pass one's life, to dwell with habitually, familiarly.

The sun almost gilded each thread in the antique carpet when it streamed through the room. Conversing makes a life into threads, which curiously glow through repetition. Weaving is the repetitive movement that creates the textile, and inside that word *textile* is another word, *text*. Ancient personal history, like an antique carpet, almost burnishes in this process. I had come to love Polly and Ted and Gail as golden characters in the story of how I made my paradise, piece by piece. And now they were all dead.

"I could feel everybody at the funeral thinking, *Why didn't the sister DO something!*"

"I thought you said they all wore sunglasses and could barely speak."

"There were different groups of them, from different parts of her life, people from her childhood like Howie, looking suburban and clean, and then Ed in a Sunday suit, and Jules, scrubbed and sober, and then the vacant-eyed characters behind the sunglasses who could hardly put one foot in front of the other, the drugged-out ones." By this time I knew that no one was blaming me, so I wept in the sunlight and blew my nose, then howled again.

"She asked to call me Mommy!"

"What did you say?"

"I let her. Why not? She really needed one."

Ruta and I hadn't scheduled a regular appointment for years. I called when I needed to talk, either from Canada by phone or in New York in person. Our interactions had transformed over the years into a gossipy shorthand.

"Jules called. Even after she died the boyfriends don't stop calling me!"

"And what did he say?"

"That Gail would tell him over and over how Ted would make her dance for him, saying he'd beat the shit out of her if she stopped. That was when I was in college, after I'd abandoned them."

"Abandoned them?"

"Oh, Ruta, you know what I mean." I sighed. "After I went off to have my so-called selfish life." I continued with what Jules had said at the funeral: " 'Your father, Molly, your father wrecked your sister. All the things he did.' "

"What things?" I'd asked him.

"You know, she'd go off in a bar sometimes and start slugging me, calling me Teddy, and once I even hit her back. God, I wish I hadn't hit her back," he said. Gail had left him after he slugged her, crawling out a bathroom window and running shoeless through the snow to a neighbor.

On Ruta's wall was an old Dutch painting of a gray sea and a long horizon: the long horizon of the sea, beyond which we see nothing.

"I looked straight ahead, Ruta, I walked out of that house and went to college and refused, refused to be her mother." *Oh Daddy's girl who rode on his boot,* I thought, *little Gailie.* "Whenever I considered reaching out toward her . . . I should have . . . I'm cold-hearted," I said numbly.

"Molly, there are some people you know you can't reach out toward. If you do, you'll be dragged under," Ruta said, and I knew she was right. It was a little girl I wanted to reach, not an alcoholic, or a drug user. I thought of Lily at the funeral saying, *I hope she finds more peace in death than she did alive.*

"You have five minutes," Ruta said into my silence.

"The whole story is so sad I can't even think of whose fault it was."

I went to the bathroom and peed interminably—I'd held it all this time—then washed my hands and looked in the mirror: forty-nine years old and sole survivor. *Shouldn't my head be bandaged? Shouldn't I be walking with a cane?* I combed my hair. I wielded a hypoallergenic lipstick, then walked of my own muscular volition into Ruta's living room to see her standing there in a yellow vest, reaching up her arms—she's shorter than I am—to hug me good-bye.

At home the cats, by now as accustomed to two houses as we were, greeted me at the door. They wanted their dinner. I know what people mutter about the animals of the childfree, that the animals are shadow-children, that the affection lavished on them is misplaced. But ours teach me how to live, as my parrot did. Feline Buddhists, who live in the moment, they insist on their needs with nonchalant purpose, as Hannah Banana must have done. Gail called Hannah *my baby.* When she referred to herself as she talked to the dog, she called herself *Mommy.* Why is it that I am who I am and she was who she was? Hap. The root that means fate or fortune. What *hap*pened? Old Norse *happ* is chance. Old English *gehaep* is orderly, fitting. Happiness comes from *hap,* but what happened to Gail? I became whole while she stayed in pieces, and the reasons are as tangled as the necklace chains at the bottom of a child's jewelry box.

39.

Now I am an orphan, no parents or sister—and no children to pass on to, no nieces or nephews, either, only a few cousins. Let go from the family tether, like a balloon let go from a child's sticky hand, I wander through the countryside. And how do I feel? I am relieved it's over. I'm done with it all, and a landscape unfolds before me, the landscape I looked at through a window all my life.

There are some people who might describe my marriage with tragic overtones: Ah, just when Mike and Molly found happiness, it was too late for a family! But we are happy through and through with the *hap* that has nothing to do with when things are going right or when things are going wrong. Things always go wrong and right. Happiness is the underpinning, the *gehaep*, the fitting orderliness that became *happy*, the underlying pleasure of living.

I wanted to have a journey, not a family. And I wanted to live through time and not be bitter. A journey for a woman of my generation and income and artistic ambition—inchoate as it was when I started out—did not include children. I never did think I could have it all, and now I am sure of it. Long ago in that kitchen in Buffalo, I saw what I would not replicate and my tiny fury ballooned, and long ago at La Grange I had an idea of what I loved and meant to claim, and now I sail that idea through its vistas. Back then, in a world of overalls and housedresses, no one I met outside school or church had a college education. What I aspired to, having read about other lives, was a way of being that aimed at wholeness, not motherhood.

Trying to make sense of what has happened, and what I've done, has led me to try to break down the process into logical steps. But so often what happens in life makes a circle rather than a line. Realizing I was motivated by conscious survival, I hoped I could make a wise connection between the flowering of my needs and the progress of my circumstances. In the growing security of that link, my chances became my choices.

The mechanism of chance that is choice is like a carousel. The carved horses go up and down like the people in a life, and the central pole revolves like the decision to be childfree. In turn, the decision propels the platform where the horses rise and fall. Life moves both up and down *and* in circles. Perhaps you cannot decide to be whole any more than you can decide to be happy—though you *can* carve and paint your horses. And aren't those shapings decidings? That carousel, out in all weather, needing to be repainted, regreased, attended to. How human a machine it really is.

40.

Flopping out of my ratty bathing suit, I padded toward the medium lane at the Fourteenth Street Y during Women's Only swim. It was a joy to sport a worn-out suit—it meant I was a swimmer for real. The members complained so loudly when the pool was cold that I expected it to be warm as a bath, and it was. The caps of the other swimmers glided up and down the lanes of our turquoise nirvana. Oh white tiles and echoes! The pool was a temple with its own high priestess, our lifeguard. Deep in the rectangle of chlorinated water I cast off conscious thought and swam, counting, till my laps were done. Beached like a seal among other seals at the rim of the shallow end, I breathed damp air and found my flip-flops. We swimmers probably all passed each other on the street without saying hello. We'd never recognize ourselves in street clothes, without our caps and goggles. At Women's Only swim we showered without pulling the curtains, hung our suits up to dry and lolled naked in the sauna, where, to my surprise, a sleek young woman spoke to me: "Miss Peacock?"

I opened my eyes, but the lights were kept low in the sauna.

"Huh?"

"It's me, Hazel Roth!"

I grabbed my breasts. "My God, Hazel," I said, "is that you?"

"Am I interrupting you?"

"No, Hazel, it's just that teachers are supposed to meet their former students for tea in lace collars, not nude in the sauna, honey."

The red halo of hair was still there on top, and I noticed, on the bottom. I realized I'd seen this stunning woman before, but never thought to connect her with the child I knew, hair hidden under a swim cap.

"It's great to see you!" she chirped.

"It's wonderful to see you, too, Hazel," I said. She threw eucalyptus oil on the sauna rocks and they steamed as I clambered to pull my towel around me. "It's a bit weird to meet you like this, though."

"Yeah?" Clearly she didn't think so.

"How long have you been swimming here? I heard you came back to New York after college. I heard from Fionula. She's finishing her Ph.D. dissertation in philosophy," I said. "She told me Niles is a Resident now, specializing in psychiatry, like his dad."

"I know, I'm his roommate!"

"What kind of roommate?" I exclaimed.

"The together kind," she murmured.

"Hazel, I'm going to drop dead from the heat. Let's move."

Our clothes were in different rows of the locker room, and I dressed in peace, shouting occasionally over the metal barrier, finding out that she worked for the Environmental Protection Agency, that Philip Wu ran a theater company. Friends Seminary grads didn't turn out to be CEO's. When we were dressed we made a date to have tea, and I left it up to Hazel whether to bring Niles. Thus we wrapped ourselves in the light, silvery scarf of talk that many students share with many teachers, and at our tea I will gossip with her and be glad to hear all she says, and she will tell me her scandals and ask me cautiously about my life, and I will freely tell her in the way of ex-teachers who become like great-aunts. I love this ersatz aunthood. And we may fall out of touch, in the way of students

and teachers, and then be in touch again. After all, when I taught her—
when I learned something about how to be from her—I knew she was
not flesh of my flesh. The intimacy in the sauna shocked me so much I
considered switching to Early Bird swim. But I told myself to relax. We're
only bodies.

41.

New York Cake has no sense of chic display. The store consists of tray after tray of decorations, and expensive items like sugar-coated violets. The whole store is so sugary it is almost dusty. Maybe that *is* dust on the plastic packages of Halloween spiders and Santa faces and birthday candle holder rosebuds. People wander the cramped aisles with the look of horror and wonder that belongs to the overwhelmed. Of course, I like this place because it reminds me of the store at La Grange, the jumbles of Necco wafers and Welsh's Fudge Bars next to newspapers, flour, and 3-in-1 oil. It's a sanctuary of sorts, a collection of poems.

On this day I am making a love poem for my husband to eat. The Belgian chocolate is home in the fridge. Now all I need are the silver hearts. La! Ten bucks for more than I will ever need. There is nothing, not one thing in all the world less necessary than what the ten dollars I spend now buys. And there is no effort less essential than beating and pouring a batter into the brownie pan and blocking off where the cut marks will be when the ultra-brownies are done, then placing, so gingerly, the edible silver hearts.

"Hey! They're ready!" I call from the kitchen of our little apartment, whisking them out of the oven. Here . . . they . . . are. The hearts apparently dove into the batter, seeking shelter. Or the batter grew up around the hearts, urging them to dive inside. But they didn't dive quickly enough.

"So what are those silver measles all over them?" my tactful husband asks. "They look like little pancreases!"

"This is not a pancreas! *This*," I stoutly inform him, "is a silver heart."

"Well, it looks like a pan—" He stops when he looks at my face. Bowing to the maxim that effort counts more than product, he grins and shuts up.

The brownies are delicious, and the melted hearts are edible, after all. I think, of course, that they were *supposed to melt*. You can't hold on to their original shape forever, only their original love.

ACKNOWLEDGMENTS

My deepest thanks to

My indefatigable agent, Kathleen Anderson, for faith and steely judgment.

My Riverhead editor, Julie Grau, for her firm grip as catcher on the other side of the trapeze; and publisher, Susan Petersen, for netting a firefly at first flash.

My McClelland & Stewart editor, Ellen Seligman, for her graciousness and insight, and my Canadian agents, Bruce Westwood and Hilary Stanley, for their guidance and panache.

My American friends, the steadfast Nita Buchanan, the sparkling Barbara Feldon, the dreamer Katie Kinsky, the complexity expert Phillis Levin, the crusty William Louis-Dreyfus, the sure-footed social historian Georgianna Orsini, the hopeful Peggy Penn, and the wild encourager Anne West, for years of cheerleading and love.

My Canadian friends in The Sisters of Perpetual Motion Book Club, the savvy Susan Downe, the zesty Ann McColl Lindsay, and the lyrical Thelma Rosner, for their loving tolerance.

My poetry editor, Carol Houck Smith, for understanding, and Joan Stein, for her compassion.

Condé Nast House & Garden editor in chief Dominique Browning, for giving me the chance to write prose; and editors Cathleen Medwick and Katrine Ames, for showing me how to do it.

And to Mike, for his fortitude, his advice, and love.

Molly Peacock, author of four books of poetry, received her Master's degree from the writing seminars of The Johns Hopkins University. President of the Poetry Society of America from 1989 to 1995, she continues to advise its *Poetry in Motion* program on the nation's buses and subways. Among her honors are fellowships from the Danforth, Ingram Merrill, and Woodrow Wilson foundations as well as the National Endowment for the Arts. A former learning specialist at Friends Seminary, she has been poet-in-residence at Bucknell University, University of Western Ontario, and University of California, Riverside. Her poetry and essays have appeared in *The New Yorker,* the *Paris Review, The Nation,* the *New Republic, Elle,* and *Mirabella.* Currently she is a contributing editor at *Condé Nast House & Garden.* She lives in both New York City and London, Ontario, with her husband, Joyce scholar Michael Groden. *Paradise, Piece by Piece* is her first nonfiction book.